Exploring
England's
Heritage

OXFORDSHIRE TO BUCKINGHAMSHIRE

Catherine Murray

Published in association with

ENGLISH ❖ HERITAGE

London: HMSO

Catherine Murray is an architectural historian who worked for English Heritage on the recent Resurvey of Listed Historic Buildings. Most of her fieldwork has been in Buckinghamshire, but she also knows Oxford particularly well from student days. Now she lives in south Oxfordshire, caring for a young family and a listed home, and attempting to pursue a special interest in domestic architecture.

© Catherine Murray 1994
Applications for reproduction should be made to HMSO
ISBN 0 11 300030 8

British Library Cataloguing in Publication Data

A CIP catalogue record for this book is available from the British Library

Front cover: Oxford from Hinksey Hill, detail from painting by William Turner of Oxford. Agnew & Sons, London / The Bridgeman Art Library, London

Back cover: Grand Union Canal at Soulbury, Buckinghamshire. John Bethell

Frontispiece: Windsor Castle, Berkshire, and the River Thames. British Tourist Authority

Exploring England's Heritage
Other volumes already published in the series:

CUMBRIA TO NORTHUMBERLAND
John Weaver
ISBN 0 11 300029 4

DEVON AND CORNWALL
Andrew Saunders
ISBN 0 11 300025 1

DORSET TO GLOUCESTERSHIRE
Martin Robertson
ISBN 0 11 300028 6

HERTFORDSHIRE TO NORFOLK
Judith Cligman and Nigel Crowe
ISBN 0 11 300045 6

LONDON
Elain Harwood and Andrew Saint
ISBN 0 11 300032 4

YORKSHIRE TO HUMBERSIDE
Jane Hatcher
ISBN 0 11 300026 X

Contents

Foreword *by Barry Cunliffe*   *vii*

Acknowledgements   *viii*

Notes for the Reader   *ix*

Introduction   *1*

1 **Prehistoric and Roman Sites**   *7*

2 **Towns and Villages**   *15*

3 **Small Houses**   *33*

4 **Country Houses and Castles**   *41*

5 **Churches and Chapels**   *57*

6 **Educational and Charitable Institutions**   *73*

7 **Living off the Land**   *89*

8 **Travel and Transport**   *101*

9 **Monuments**   *109*

Select Bibliography   *116*

Index   *118*

Maps   *124*

Foreword

Today as midsummer approaches, Oxford is crammed with tourists. The roads near my office are choked with open-topped buses, their multilingual commentaries extolling the virtues of the city, while the pavements are impassable with crocodiles of visitors, eyes glued on the coloured umbrellas of determined guides. Dons wearing full academic dress attempt to make their way to and from the Examination Schools, to the delight of foreign photographers, and might as well be extras employed by the Tourist Board.

Oxford, Stratford-on-Avon and London together make up the golden triangle – golden, that is, to the tour operators – and millions of tourists are led through their crowded streets each year. The great majority of those who visit Oxford come for only a few hours, then move on to Stratford to stay overnight before returning to familiar London. It is London that takes the brunt. Westminster Abbey will be host to over 3 million, more than 2 million will visit the Tower of London, and then of course there are the museums and art galleries welcoming their annual tidal wave. Tourism, as governments are pleased to remind us, is one of Britain's biggest industries.

Looking at the tired, bewildered faces of the tourists off-loaded and scooped up again outside Oxford's St Giles, I long to grab them and say, 'It's all right – this is *not* what it's about. England is a beautiful, gentle country full of fascinating corners, breathtaking sights – an eclectic mix of unsurpassable quality. All you need is someone with vision to show you how to start looking.'

Well, people with vision, as well as the knowledge of our cultural heritage and the ability to communicate, are not in ample supply, but the members of the team assembled to write the eleven volumes of *Exploring England's Heritage* share these qualities in abundance. Each author has a detailed and expert involvement, not only with the region they are writing about, but also with the buildings, the earthworks, the streets and the landscapes they have chosen to introduce us to. These guides are no mere compilations of well-worn facts, but original accounts coloured by the enthusiasm of people who know what makes a particular site so special.

Each volume introduces approximately 100 places. Some are well known (who would dare to omit Stonehenge or Hadrian's Wall?); others are small-scale and obscure but no less interesting for that. We are led down alley-ways to admire hidden gems of architecture, into churchyards to search for inscribed stones and along canals to wonder at the skills of our early engineers. And of course there are the castles, the great houses and their gardens and the churches and cathedrals that give England its very particular character.

Exploring England's Heritage does not swamp you in facts. What each author does is to say, 'Let me show you something you might not have seen and tell you why I find it so particularly interesting.' What more could the discerning traveller want?

Barry Cunliffe

Acknowledgements

Sensible women recognise that book-writing and young children do not go together. I was blinded by enthusiasm and owe an enormous thank-you to my family – especially to Emma for her early interest in windmills and white horses, to Michael for placidly visiting so many buildings before he was even born and to Philip, my husband, for his 'layman's' view, his linguistic expertise and his unfailing support. I would also like to thank Vanessa Brand at English Heritage and the staff at HMSO for their patience and editorial advice, and Brian Anthony for daring to consider me a fit contributor when he first negotiated this series into being.

Buckinghamshire I know through my fieldwork for the recent Resurvey of Listed Historic Buildings, where my task was made more enjoyable by the guidance of Roger Evans and Martin Andrew at Buckinghamshire County Council, and by that of friends in the Inspectorate at English Heritage. My research into the other three counties has been more of a personal venture, dependent on the generosity of owners and curators in giving me such ready access to their buildings. I am particularly grateful to those householders and pub landlords who allowed me to clamber through their lofts, to the bursars of the Oxford Colleges, to Paul Quarrie at Eton, and to the management of Hook Norton Brewery. Diane Chablo kindly gave me a preview of her research into St Catherine's College, Oxford, and the Oxford Archaeological Unit provided vital clarification of the recent findings at Uffington. Other pitfalls on the archaeological front have been avoided, I hope, with the aid of specialist staff serving the county councils of Berkshire and Northamptonshire.

For their kind permission to reproduce photographs, author and publisher are indebted to the following (gazetteer-entry numbers are given in bold): Aerofilms Ltd; Ashmolean Museum, University of Oxford; John Bethell; The Bodleian Library, University of Oxford (**42**, illustration from the *Builder*, vol. XVIII (1 December 1860), p 769, N 1863 c.1; **68**, engraving from David Loggan, *Oxonia Illustrata*, 1675, Douce L subt.27 plate XIX); the Bridgeman Art Library, London; British Tourist Authority; Buckinghamshire County Museum; J Allan Cash Photo Library; Olive Cook; *Country Life*; Ebenezer Pictures; English Heritage; The Provost and Fellows of Eton College; Anthony Kersting; His Grace The Duke of Marlborough; National Trust; Mrs John Nutting; the Royal Commission on the Historical Monuments of England (National Buildings Record and National Library of Air Photography); and Skyscan Balloon Photography.

The maps and diagrams have been redrawn by Nick Cannan of English Heritage, all except **24**, which was drawn by Judith Dobie. I am most grateful to both of them and to those who gave permission to adapt original work: English Heritage (**1** and **6**); British Geological Survey (map in introduction based on BGS 1:625 000 geological map, south sheet, NERC copyright reserved); Milton Keynes Development Corporation (**77**); and the Ordnance Survey (**7, 9, 12, 16, 19, 70, 81, 83** and **85**). John Chenevix Trench generously allowed me to use his survey plans for preparing the perspective of Amersham Museum (**22**), and the drawing of Leadenporch House, Deddington (**24**) was derived from the survey published by R B Wood-Jones in *Traditional Domestic Architecture of the Banbury Region*, Manchester University Press, 1963. The plan of All Saints, Brixworth (**43**) has been adapted from those published by M Audouy in the *Journal of the British Archaeological Association* CXXXVII, 1984, but also draws on other work by E D C Jackson and E G M Fletcher, and by H M Taylor.

Notes for the Reader

Each site entry in *Exploring England's Heritage* is numbered and may be located easily on the end-map, but it is recommended especially for the more remote sites that the visitor makes use of the relevant Ordnance Survey map in the Landranger series. The location details of the site entries include a six-figure National Grid reference, e.g., SX 888609. Ordnance Survey maps show the National Grid and the following 1:50,000 maps will be found useful: 140, 141, 142, 151, 152, 153, 163, 164, 165, 166, 174, 175, 176.

Readers should be aware that while the great majority of properties and sites referred to in this handbook are normally open to the public regularly, others are open only on a limited basis. A few are not open at all, and may only be viewed from the public thoroughfare. In these circumstances readers are reminded to respect the owners' privacy. The *access codes* in the heading to each gazetteer entry are designed to indicate the level of public accessibility, and are explained below.

Access Codes

[A] site open for at least part of the year
[B] site open by appointment only
[C] site open by virtue of its use, e.g., a road, public house, church or bridge
[D] site not open but may be seen from the public highway or footpath

Abbreviations

AFK	A F Kersting	ES	Edwin Smith
AL	Aerofilms Ltd	JAC	J Allan Cash
BE	Berkshire	JB	John Bethell
BL	Bodleian Library	N	Northamptonshire
BTA	British Tourist Authority	NT	National Trust
BU	Buckinghamshire	O	Oxfordshire
CL	*Country Life*	PM	Philip Murray
CM	Catherine Murray	RCHME	Royal Commission on the
EH	English Heritage		Historical Monuments of
			England

The county names and boundaries used in this guide were correct at time of going to press, and are those used prior to the Local Government Commission review of 1993/4.

Further Information

Further details on English Heritage, the Landmark Trust and the National Trust may be obtained from the following addresses:

English Heritage (Membership Dept), PO Box 1BB, London W1A 1BB
Landmark Trust, 21 Dean's Yard, Westminster, London SW1P 3PA
National Trust, PO Box 39, Bromley, Kent BR1 1NH

Introduction

To the Romantic traveller of the 19th century, this area would have had few attractions. There are no rugged heights or gloomy ravines, no bandits, and no Gothick horror. Instead, the four counties of Berkshire, Buckinghamshire, Oxfordshire and Northamptonshire share a pleasantly gentle landscape of low hills and broad vales. The only acknowledged beauty spots are the beechwoods and hidden valleys of the Chilterns. The history of the four counties is likewise a gentle one, in sympathy, perhaps, with modern taste. In a generation less obsessed with '1066 and all that', and more concerned to understand everyday history, the modest farms and villages, parish churches and country houses of this area have much to offer.

The history of these buildings is inseparable from that of the landscape. Made from the stone, clay and timber that the land provided, they were built to serve the needs of people who depended on the land for their living. If we are to enjoy these buildings as a key to the area's heritage, we shall first have to spare a little time for the landscape.

Running across the north-west of the area, across north Oxfordshire and Northamptonshire, are the Jurassic limestone hills that begin in Gloucestershire as the Cotswolds. On top of these hills grazed the sheep whose fleeces brought so much wealth in the Middle Ages, while underneath them lies the stone that gives local buildings so much dignity. The stone outcrops along the line of the hills in layers of varying quality and colour, each layer representing a newer formation within the Jurassic period. In the humpier hills of the far north-west are the oldest stones – those of the Middle Lias (also known as marlstone) and the Upper Lias. These stones are stained by iron to warm dark browns and tawny oranges, and look particularly lovely at **Great Tew** (13, O). Some can be finely worked to provide ashlar walls and window mullions, but most are porous and suffer badly from the weather. For this reason they were often used in conjunction with the slightly younger oolitic limestones, harder-wearing and creamy in colour, that outcrop immediately to the south. At **Blisworth** (10, N) and at **Rushton Triangular Lodge** (97, N) the combination results in dashing stripes! The best oolite, quarried around Burford (O) and at Weldon and King's Cliffe in Northamptonshire, lends itself to detailed carving, and was snapped up by the aristocracy for country houses like **Kirby Hall** (36, N) and **Deene Park** (34, N). Limestone roofing slates, quarried principally at Collyweston (N) and Stonesfield (O), complement the stone walls superbly.

Further south, fine stone becomes a rare luxury, and buildings take on a meaner appearance. All along the north edges of the Oxford Plain and the Vale of Aylesbury you see houses of rubbly Cornbrash limestone, with straw thatch roofs and wooden details. In the Vale itself even this poor-quality stone can be hard to find, for it is often overlain by thick beds of clay (Oxford, Kimmeridge, Greensand and Gault) and gravel. This may well explain why medieval traditions of timber framing linger on here, giving a false impression of comparative poverty. False because there was plenty of wealth in this area too, derived from fertile arable fields and rich meadow grazing. Grand brick buildings, some dating back to the 15th century, help set the record straight.

Impressive views north-east across the Vale can be gained from Ivinghoe Beacon, Coombe Hill, Watlington Hill and other high points along the sudden chalk scarp of the Chilterns and Berkshire Downs. Along this ridge survive the most spectacular of the prehistoric sites, exposed by nature and shunned by a medieval population that preferred the more hospitable terrain of the valleys. Parts of the Chilterns still retain the medieval pattern of remote

Chiltern beechwoods, West Wycombe. ES

1

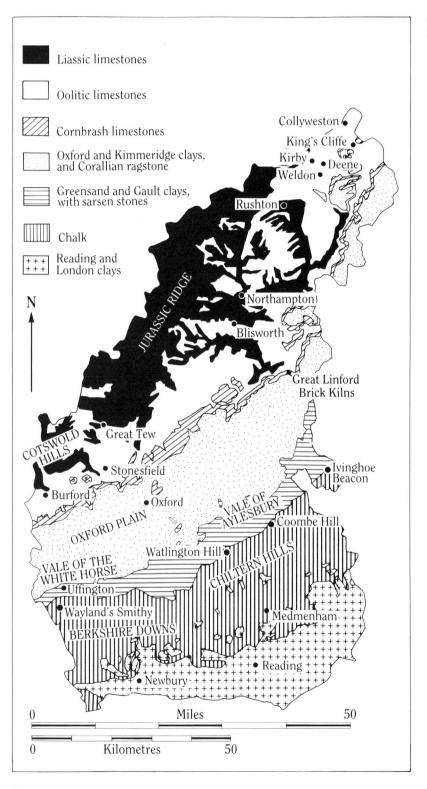

The land and its building materials (after British Geological Survey). EH

Ewelme church and almshouses, Oxfordshire. JAC

valley settlement with woodland surviving in between, but the Downs are now laid bare by vast open-field systems. They were cleared for sheep, to supply the cloth industries of Reading and Newbury. Throughout this chalky hill country, the buildings are suitably humble structures. They are rarely, except around **Uffington** (21, O) and **Medmenham** (15, BU), made of the soft chalk itself, but exhibit picturesque combinations of timber, flint and brick.

The different landscape types outlined above were not perhaps always as clear as they are today, for they were once shrouded in primeval forest. Only

fragments of the great medieval forests of Salcey and Rockingham (in Northamptonshire), Wychwood (in Oxfordshire) and Bernwood (on the Oxfordshire/Buckinghamshire border) remain today, but the work of clearing them away was begun by Neolithic man. He settled first in the river valleys, but there are signs of activity even on the high chalky ground below **Wayland's Smithy** (6, O). Clearing continued, and by Domesday the area had become a land of farms. To a large extent, it remains a land of farms today, and has a rich heritage of farmhouses and farm buildings, mills and market towns.

The predominance of these building types, and the continuing strength of the agricultural economy, can be explained in two ways. On the positive side, the land is not only eminently suited to farming, but also capable of adapting to market forces – the hills are not so bleak that sheep could not be replaced by dairy herds or limited cultivation, and the arable valleys could support both grain and livestock. On the negative side, it has to be admitted that until recently there was little real alternative to farming. The land provided no natural fuel apart from wood, and few mineral resources apart

3

Fingest, in the Buckinghamshire Chilterns. CM

from building materials and a little iron. The only industry of any significance, that producing woollen cloth, continued to run as a cottage industry until the very late 18th century. It was then that wool manufacturers such as the blanket makers of **Witney** (83, O), began to make tentative changes, importing first ideas, then coal, from the north.

Improved communications were a key factor in effecting this change. As the network of turnpike roads slowly spread across the area during the 18th century, travel became easier, and Witney mill owners could contemplate fact-finding trips to Lancashire. By the early 1800s canals had linked the Thames Valley to the Midlands and the west, improving trade and bringing in their wake an alien heritage of Welsh slate roofs. The railway revolution of the late 1830s and 40s brought coal, and, with it, the soaring ostentation of the **Bliss Tweed Mill, Chipping Norton** (74, O). In the 20th century roads have dramatically increased the rate of

change, with new motorways spawning industrial estates, new towns and the commuter society. Thankfully, however, much of the area still feels remote, with secluded villages quietly tucked away down minor roads.

This remoteness lingers perhaps because the area is one of through-routes rather than destinations. It lies strung between the Midlands and London, never belonging completely to one or the other, but serving as a melting pot for the ideas of both. The capacity to absorb and digest different traditions dates as far back as the 4th millennium BC, when the Ridgeway linked Wayland's Smithy with similar long barrows in Wiltshire, but the Jurassic Way led to a Welsh/Irish form of portal dolmen being built at the **Rollright Stones** (2, O). The conversion of the area to Christianity in the 7th century provides another example: **All Saints, Brixworth** (43, N) shows the driving force of northern monasticism housed in a basilica with southern-style

'porticus'. By the later Middle Ages we can see a general north-west–south-east split at vernacular level, with cruck and box-frame traditions of construction competing for social superiority.

By the 16th century, London was exerting the dominant pull. There had been earlier examples of royal sophistication at **Windsor Castle** (40, BE), **Eton College** (60, BE), Higham Ferrers (N) and **St Mary and All Saints, Fotheringhay** (53, N), but it was not until *c.*1550 that high-society fashion took such a grip on the architecture of country houses and churches. Deene Park and Kirkby Hall echo the early Renaissance classicism of the Somerset Protectorate, while **Blenheim Palace** (29, O) and the **St Peter, Gayhurst** (57, BU) take us into the Baroque. During the 18th century the vagaries of fashion became even more marked, especially as the Thames Valley gradually became a play park, with riverside villas, for the London aristocracy. Hunting Victorians (e.g., the Rothschilds of **Mentmore**

Radcliffe Square, Oxford, with the Camera and Bodleian Library. AFK

Towers (37, BU)) and boating Edwardians continued the process of colonisation, and by the 1930s, commuter trains had brought upper-class suburbia out as far as **Amersham** (8, BU) and Beaconsfield. Nowadays Londoners arrive to settle in the area without their previous missionary zeal. Instead of bringing London to the countryside, they come to search out peace and their rural heritage.

There is one remarkable exception to this natural pattern dictated by geology and geography, and that is the area's supreme tourist attraction – **Oxford** (19, O). Oxford is a magnificent accidental quirk: small seeds of learning grew there more on account of royal and monastic patronage than because of any special qualities in the site, and these were nurtured by a college system that arose as much out of chantry provision as out of concern for education. It remains a peculiar world, romantic in its detachment from real life, precious for the idealism of its academic quest. Individual students escape, or move on to face the rigours of graduate unemployment, but the buildings, timelessly beautiful, remain to welcome the next generation. If you stand in Radcliffe Square, looking up at the majestic drum of the Radcliffe Camera, the lavishly decorated spire of St Mary's, the exotic pinnacles of All Souls, even the comfortably solid bulk of the Bodleian, you can hardly believe that Oxford is not an earthly Elysium.

5

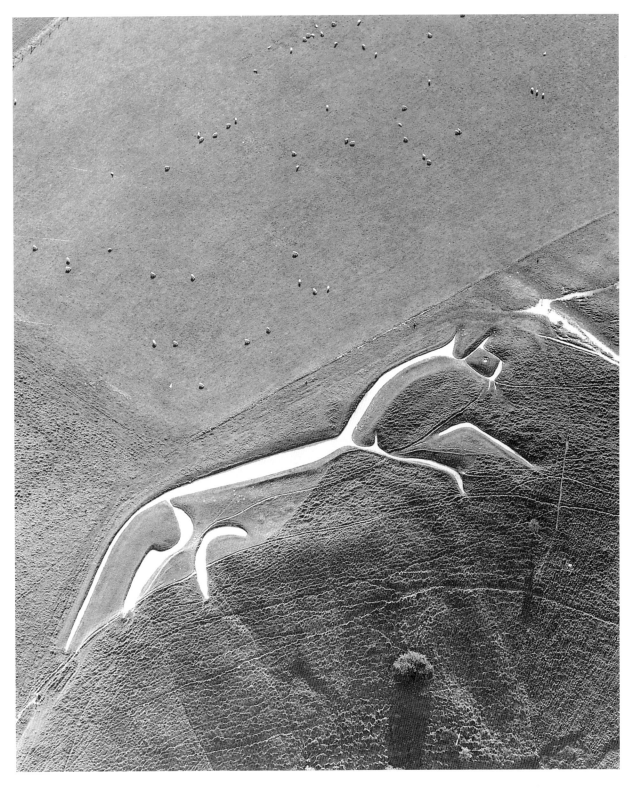

1

Prehistoric and Roman Sites

As this book is concerned only with visible heritage, it is bound to give a rather warped picture of antiquity. Most of the prehistoric sites in the area are set bleakly astride the hilltops of the Berkshire Downs/Chilterns, or the Jurassic ridge of north Oxfordshire/Northamptonshire. They are all rather specialised and might well lead you to conclude that Neolithic man was constantly burying the dead and going for walks along the Ridgeway; that Iron Age man never left his hillfort; and that the Romans spent all their time lolling about in villas and having baths.

These distortions arise from the uneven manner in which time has treated antiquity. Hypocausts are now easier to find than post holes, while hilltop banks and burial mounds stand out more than riverside settlements covered by silt and later occupation. Archaeological excavation of hidden sites such as the Neolithic causewayed camp at Abingdon (D), or the round Iron Age houses at Pennyland, Milton Keynes (BU), prove that there was also life down in the valleys, and that much of it was concerned with day-to-day survival. Even the seemingly unrepresentative sites included here can, when scrutinised with modern technology, tell us more of everyday life than first appearances might suggest.

The earliest major monuments in the area are from the Neolithic period (c. 4000–2000 BC), and are mostly concerned with burial. Typical long barrows, like those near **Walbury Camp** (5, BE) or Lambourn (BE), are often reduced to indistinct low mounds, and are hard to appreciate if you have not seen a reconstruction such as the one displayed at the Oxfordshire County Museum, Woodstock. This features a tomb chamber from the long barrow at Ascott-under-Wychwood (O), gratifyingly complete with its jumble of fragmented skeletons. The long barrow at **Wayland's Smithy** (6, O) is much more evocative (you can go inside!) and

informative. It was built on land cleared for settlement or perhaps even farming, and its chambers housed a succession of burials. These factors suggest a much more stable society than dependence on hunting had hitherto allowed.

Wayland's Smithy bears strong resemblance to the long barrow at West Kennet, near Avebury in Wiltshire. This is perhaps hardly surprising, for the two are connected by the ancient Ridgeway/Icknield Way that led along the scarp of the chalk Downs and on to the Norfolk flint mines. By contrast, the **Rollright Stones** (2, O), on the Jurassic ridge, belong to a different cultural tradition. They include an Irish form of portal dolmen and the only stone circle in the area. Unlike the Wessex examples at Avebury or Stone Henge, this circle has close-set stones forming a continuous wall, and probably dates from the end of the Neolithic period or the early Bronze Age.

Bronze Age round barrows, the earlier ones containing single burials, the later ones containing cremated remains in urns, are often found in conjunction with the older Neolithic sites. Great Rollright and Lambourn, for instance, obviously retained their ritual significance into this era and beyond. Lambourn boasts a group of over forty round barrows just off the road to Kingston Lisle. They vary in form, and include the bell, bowl and disc types known from 'Wessex Culture'. At nearby Rams Hill, there were further barrows, arranged in lines, and also a Bronze Age settlement with early rectangular buildings and later round ones. Around the settlement there was first a ditch, then a rampart, and finally palisades.

Such defences became a common feature during the Iron Age. Strung along the Ridgeway are a whole series of hillforts – Ivinghoe Beacon (BU), Blewburton Hill (O), Segsbury (O), **Uffington Castle** (3, O) – that date from the 6th century BC onwards. There are many more – e.g., at Walbury Camp and

Wayland's Smithy, Oxfordshire. AFK

Bracknell in Berkshire, at Gerrards Cross in Buckinghamshire, and at Rainsborough (near Aynho), Daventry and Hunsbury in Northamptonshire. A good lowland example can be found at Dorchester (O), where two parallel dykes defended a settlement otherwise surrounded by river.

There is much speculation about the purpose of these forts. Were they frontier posts, towns, centres for trade or ritual, grain stores, or merely enclosures for livestock? Obvious clues suggest a combination of answers. Many of the forts are associated with former places of burial and ritual, and most are sited along trade routes, either hilltop ridges or river valleys. They are also associated with field systems, even on steep slopes such as the Manger at Uffington. Limited excavation has revealed that some forts (e.g., Ivinghoe Beacon and Blewburton) contain traces of huts and storage pits, but evidence points to only sporadic occupation. Early defences, usually in the form of box-ramparts, were built, abandoned, and later re-fortified with cruder banks and ditches, as at Uffington.

Also uncertain is the purpose, let alone the date, of the long, broken ditches and banks that snake across the Oxfordshire and south Buckinghamshire countryside. A southern ditch is loosely aligned with the Ridgeway, while a northern ditch roughly encircles the area between Blenheim, North Leigh, Charlbury and Kiddington. Current work on the latter disputes its value as a defence (the intriguing gaps, or breaks, between ditches supposedly used for chariot sorties!), and suggests that it was a boundary line of late Iron Age and early Roman date. The ditches are together known as 'Grim's Ditch' or 'Devil's Ditch'.

The supernatural has often been used to explain the inexplicable. Wayland's Smithy and the Rollright Stones have given rise to a richly imaginative folklore, but their function is now at least partially understood. The **Uffington White Horse** (4, O) happily still defies explanation and remains as mysterious and exciting as ever. It is not the only chalk figure in the area – there are undated crosses at Bledlow and Whiteleaf in Buckinghamshire – but it is certainly the most exotic.

We know too much about the Romans for them to retain much mystique, and there are few major Roman sites in the area. The capitals of the main subjugated tribes were situated just beyond its borders at St Albans, Cirencester and Silchester, but were linked by the great roads of Watling Street (A5), Akeman Street and a north–south route from Towcester (Lactodorum). Of the smaller service towns like Dorchester, Alchester (near Bicester) and Irchester (N), little remains above ground. Villas, however, do show that the land was widely colonised and farmed. The villa at **North Leigh** (1, O) is an especially opulent example, close to Akeman Street, with mosaics in the Cirencester (Corinium) manner.

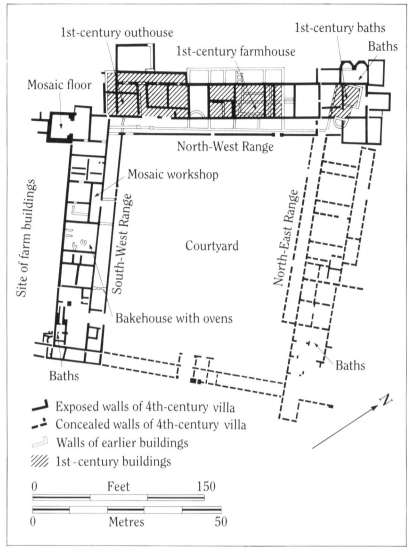

North Leigh Roman Villa. EH

Mosaic floor at North Leigh Roman Villa. EH

1

North Leigh Roman Villa, Oxfordshire
1st–4th century

SP 397154. 2 miles (3 km) N of North Leigh village. Off A4095 between Witney and Woodstock
[A] EH

This villa is set down in the fertile valley of the River Evenlode, close to the course of Akeman Street. It is no bleak structure from prehistory, with crude banks and massive chunks of stone, but a civilised country house, a Roman equivalent to Kirby Hall (36, N). The floors and foundations of the two wings now exposed tell of a secure and settled life with wealth to spare for comfort and show. This was a well-appointed house with sturdy stone walls, beautiful mosaic pavements and luxurious heating systems.

The villa grew in phases, in this respect more like Deene Park (34, N) than Kirby. A modest farmhouse was built, probably late in the 1st century, on the site of a former Iron Age settlement. It stood in the centre of the later north-west range, with a detached hall or barn to one side and a set of baths to the other. These three elements were gradually linked into a single range which sprouted side wings. By the early 4th century, the wings had been extended so as to enclose a courtyard, and the initial range had been rebuilt to include hypocaust heating.

The residents lived in style in the north-west and north-east ranges, where there were two sets of baths and a multiplicity of rooms with colourful mosaic floors. Sadly, these mosaics suffered at the hands of early 19th-century souvenir hunters, and only one of them can be seen today. It is a handsome example, with elaborate geometric patterns similar to those found on pavements at Cirencester (Roman Corinium). A damaged section reveals the hypocaust system below. Hot air escaped from the underfloor channels and pillared cavities via flues in the wall tiles, and so gave further heat to the room. The room itself was formerly very fine, with painted walls, vaulted ceiling and an arched screen.

The south-west range was more basic, and housed service rooms such as a bakehouse and a mosaic workshop. Aerial photography shows that there were further buildings behind this range, and also to the east. These were probably the farm buildings that served what must have been a substantial estate.

2

Rollright Stones, Oxfordshire
Neolithic and early Bronze Age, 4th and 3rd millennia BC

SP 296308 and 299308. 2½ miles (4 km) NW of Chipping Norton, on minor road to W of A3400

[A]

The mythical story of the Rollright Stones is that of a proud king and his army. A witch challenges the king to

Rollright Stone Circle. JB

take seven long strides forwards, promising:

> If Long Compton thou canst see
> King of England thou shalt be.

The king duly takes seven very long strides, only to find Long Compton hidden from view by a low mound. The witch then turns him and his retinue into 'hoar stones' and herself into an elder tree. The 'King Stone' still stands alone to the north of the road, while the 'King's Men' are transfixed in a circle, and his 'Whispering Knights' hide away down a path to the south-east.

Even without this romance, the lichen-covered stones are fascinatingly ancient. Shaped only by wind, rain and the chipping of souvenir hunters, they originated as local surface boulders, but their arrangement was carefully calculated. Their purpose was most recently investigated in 1982–6, and the excavation and survey work was published by George Lambrick.

The oldest group, that of the 'Whispering Knights', is a portal dolmen used probably as a burial chamber for a chief family. It consists of two tall portal stones with a blocking slab between, one remaining wall slab, and a fallen capstone which rested on the others to provide a roof. The base of a possible stone cairn covering was discovered in the course of the excavations, along with fragments of middle Neolithic pottery. The considerable labour required to haul the capstone into place implies that this was a construction of great tribal importance.

The 'King's Men' form an almost perfect circle *c*. 36 yds (33 m) in

diameter and are slightly later in date, belonging to the late Neolithic or early Bronze Age (i.e. *c*.2500 BC). The circle was restored in 1882, and only a third of the stones are in their original positions. These stones, and the recent survey work, show that the circle was built as a continuous wall of stone slabs buttressed by a very slight bank dug from the circle floor. To the south-east is an entrance to the circle, with portal stones at right-angles, while taller slabs opposite mark a through-axis. The wall-like form and absence of outer ditch are unusual for the area and may, like the early form of portal dolmen, point to Welsh/Irish influence via the nearby Jurassic Way.

The circle doubtless served a ceremonial function, but attempts to find an axis of astronomical significance have proved indecisive. The role of the outlying 'King Stone' is therefore a puzzle. It is not truly aligned with the circle and may well be of different date. It is not associated with a long barrow, as previously supposed, but there are remains of Bronze Age round barrows and earlier burials nearby. One barrow had a wooden marker post, and it is possible that the 'King Stone' served a similar purpose.

3

Uffington Castle, Oxfordshire
Iron Age, c.500 BC and later

SU 298862. 6 miles (10 km) W of Wantage, signposted to S of B4507

[A] NT EH

This is no castle, but a large hillfort set on a high plateau above the White Horse, next to the Ridgeway. Its shape is irregular because it follows the natural contour lines, and it is defined by a bank, a ditch and then a smaller outer bank or 'counterscarp'. Their present mounded form disguises two building phases. The site was first fortified with a walled rampart and ditch, and then strengthened by deepening the ditch to create large banks.

The earlier phase was first discovered in *c*.1850, when excavations by Martin

Atkins revealed two parallel rows of holes that had once contained wooden posts. Chalk rubble had been packed in between so as to form a thick wall. This 'box-rampart' construction was confirmed during recent work by the Oxford Archaeological Unit, who also discovered a supporting chalk ramp on the inside and a small ditch outside. Pottery found below the rampart dated it to c.500 BC or shortly afterwards. Similar ramparts have also been found at Blewburton Hill and Ivinghoe Beacon further along the Ridgeway. Another feature of construction was the lining of the inner wall of the ditch with sarsen stones, as described at Segsbury by Thomas Hearne in 1725. He tells of 'vast red stones . . . in the form of a Wall' being raided for building work.

The later Iron Age strengthening of the fort was comparatively unsophisticated. The ditch was much enlarged and the contents 'dumped' over the ramparts to create a taller bank. This was held in place by a low retaining wall inside the enclosure. The counterscarp

was thrown up over a rough wall of chalk rubble.

The main entrance to the fort is on the west side, where the bank is bent round to join the counterscarp. There was possibly another entrance opposite, on the east side, but if so, it was soon blocked. Smaller entrances were made to the north and the south in the late Iron Age or early Roman period, when the banks were breached and the sarsen stones thrown into the ditch. Roman coins have been found on top of the newly formed causeways. This new north–south route through the fort is mentioned in Saxon charters and persisted for centuries as a parish boundary.

The interior of the fort is so far unexcavated and its function remains open to conjecture. It may have contained a town, or served as a trading or meeting place along the Ridgeway. The distinct phases of construction, however, imply only intermittent occupation, and suggest that it was primarily for defence.

4

Uffington White Horse, Oxfordshire
Iron Age

SU 301866. 6 miles (10 km) W of Wantage, signposted to S of B4507
[A] NT EH

To many the White Horse is the most fascinating of the Uffington monuments, partly because of its strange sinuous shape and partly because of its rich mythology. 18th- and 19th-century commentators saw Saxon links with Hengist and Horsa or with King Alfred, who defeated the Danes at the nearby Battle of Ashdown in AD 871. 12th-century crusaders' stories promoted the belief that it was the horse or dragon of St George, and that the dragon was slain on the small hill below. From the more distant past comes a legacy of fertility rites and summer revels. Only an assessment of the likely date of the horse can determine which of these associations is most relevant.

We know that the horse existed by the late 12th century, as the hill was named after it in a charter of Abingdon Abbey in 1170. It was also mentioned, along with a foal, in a contemporary list of wonders of the world. However, the only definitive clue to its earlier history is its shape. The thin, stylised form with beak, ears and curving legs has been compared to figures on coins of the 1st centuries AD and BC. But if the horse had originally been more naturalistic in shape, as suggested by aerial photography and 18th-century accounts, an early Saxon date might be more probable.

There has certainly been much opportunity for the horse to 'slim'. The present shape is a restoration of the 1950s, after the horse was concealed during the war. Before this it suffered from the natural processes of hillwash and erosion, and was intermittently scoured clean by the local population. The great scouring of 1857 was the subject of a book by Thomas Hughes (better known for *Tom Brown's Schooldays*), who gives a vivid account of the traditional festivities which followed. The various races included a

Uffington Castle, with the White Horse and Manger to the left, and the Ridgeway path beyond.
ASHMOLEAN MUSEUM

11

precipitous chase down the steep slopes of the Manger after a cart-wheel, and a frenzied free-for-all to catch a pig.

Nowadays the matter is more serious, and the exact shape of the horse, stylised or natural, is being researched by the Oxford Archaeological Unit. A trench cut in 1990 showed that the belly line at least had always been a narrow one – never more than a metre wider than at present. Resistivity surveys, checking for disturbed soil over the whole area of the horse, have also shown up a skinny figure, with much the same stylised lines but slightly different legs. The inner back leg seems to have been less curved and the outer back leg more detached. Another trench confirmed the beak as an ancient feature, but longer than at present. Unlike the belly, it was formed by digging through the topsoil and infilling with compacted chalk rather than by exposing the natural bedrock.

These findings support the theory of an early rather than Saxon date, and make it more likely that the horse was cut in connection with the Iron Age hillfort above. They also show that the original horse lay at a steeper angle than at present, and was more visible from below. The purpose of the horse, however, remains unknown. It may have been a tribal emblem of the Atrebates or Dobunni, but was most probably of religious or ritual significance, perhaps associated with the horse goddess Epona. This might account for the fertility myths and its discreet omission from Christian charters of the 10th century. Small nearby mounds containing Bronze Age, Roman and Saxon burials also serve to confirm a continuous ritual use of the site.

5

Walbury Camp, Berkshire
Iron Age

SU 371619. 7 miles (11 km) SW of Newbury, near Inkpen. Car-park at E end approached from West Woodhay

[D]

Walbury Camp is impressive for its vast size, 82 acres (33 ha), and its spectacular

site high on the chalk Downs. From here there are splendid views, especially across the Kennet Valley to the north. It is difficult to appreciate the camp from inside, as the enclosure is cultivated and the banks become invisible from the trackway that crosses it. However, the trackway leads on to an imposing north-west entrance, and then continues along the ridge to the nearby long barrow on Inkpen Hill. This is the best vantage point for a view of the whole.

From here a bank can be seen running round Walbury Hill, enclosing the gently domed hilltop, but with steep slopes falling away below. The bank roughly follows the contour line, with a slight dip to the south, and so gives a natural, irregular shape to the camp. The most substantial part of the bank is at the north-west entrance, where the ends turn slightly inwards and there is an obvious outer ditch. Here there are also traces of two outer banks (now somewhat eroded by thoughtless car parking), which formerly defended the entrance from the easy approach along the ridge. The south-east entrance has no such defences and, although possibly original, may have been cut through at a later date.

The camp is unexcavated, so we have no precise information about its date or function. There is, however, evidence for long-term interest in the site. Flint scrapers and axe heads of the Neolithic period have been found, and pit depressions inside the camp mark hut circles or possibly even Neolithic flint mines. Also Neolithic is the long barrow on Inkpen Hill. Bronze Age barrows lie

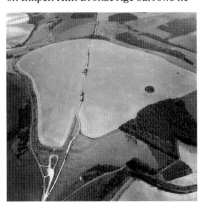

Walbury Camp, with north-west entrance in foreground. RCHME

beyond this, on the Wiltshire border, and a Bronze Age urn was discovered close to the camp itself. Even after its Iron Age heyday, the hilltop continued in use. Saxon sceattas (coins) have been found, and a later gibbet, recently vandalised, made a prominent landmark on top of the long barrow.

6

Wayland's Smithy, Oxfordshire
Neolithic, c.3500–3300 BC

SU 281854. 3 miles (5 km) SW of Uffington, signposted off B4507 and B4000

[A] EH

This Neolithic long barrow or burial mound is set on a slight rise just off the Ridgeway, enchantingly hidden by an oval ring of beech trees. Its satisfying completeness is due to restoration work by the Department of the Environment, undertaken after painstaking excavation by Professors Piggott and Atkinson in 1962–3 had revealed at least two phases of construction. The stone burial chambers you see today belong to the later phase, and resemble those at West Kennet, near Avebury. They have been radio-carbon dated to c.3300–3400 BC, and belong to a long barrow (Barrow 2) that tapers away behind. This was found to conceal a smaller barrow (Barrow 1), built some 50–200 years before, around a mortuary chamber of perhaps even earlier date.

The later, visible barrow is an impressive mound 57 yds (52 m) long. It was built of chalk dug from flanking ditches, and has a kerb of local sarsen stones. At the taller (south) end is an imposing facade of large sarsen slabs with the stump of a blocking stone in the central entrance. If you step over this, you find yourself in a small antechamber, which gives into a central passage with a further chamber off to each side. These chambers are walled and roofed with large stone slabs and, like the facade, have restored drystone walling in the gaps. Fragments of eight skeletons were found in the left chamber in 1919.

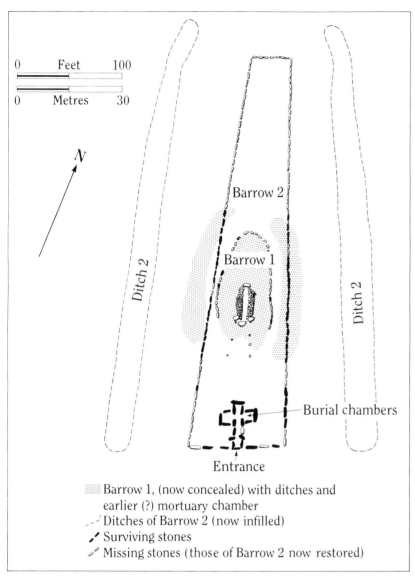

0 Feet 100

0 Metres 30

N

Barrow 2

Ditch 2

Barrow 1

Ditch 2

Burial chambers

Entrance

▒ Barrow 1, (now concealed) with ditches and
earlier (?) mortuary chamber
Ditches of Barrow 2 (now infilled)
Surviving stones
Missing stones (those of Barrow 2 now restored)

Wayland's Smithy, as excavated in 1962–3. EH

The earlier barrow (Barrow 1) consisted of a smaller mound, again with sarsen kerb and flanking ditches. Buried in its south end were traces of another mortuary chamber, long and narrow with low rubble side walls and an enormous post hole at each end. These holes were capable of taking half tree-trunks, over 4 ft (120 cm) in diameter, which may well have stuck up above the mound as markers. The excavators believed that the posts supported a tent-like wooden structure, but it is also possible that the chamber was more like a box, perhaps with a wooden lid. Inside, on a floor of sarsen slabs, were found the bones of at least fourteen bodies, including one child, all in various states of articulation. The bodies may have been exposed to the elements and birds of prey before final burial, or may have been rearranged *in situ*, perhaps as the number of occupants grew.

The use and re-use of the site for important burials probably reflects some deep ceremonial significance, but it also shows how settled the Neolithic people had become. They had probably camped on the site beforehand, clearing it perhaps for agriculture, and were then happy to devote much time and labour to constructing the monument and tending the dead.

Magical explanation persists, however. For the Saxons, the barrow became the forge of Wayland, maker of the gods' armour, and charters of AD 955 refer to it as 'Welandes Smidthan'. Even 18th-century travellers were told that the mythical smith would shoe their horse for a small fee, as long as they looked the other way.

Towns and Villages

Until the later 19th century, settlement in this area reflected the rural hierarchy of agricultural villages served by market towns, which were in turn served by major administrative centres. This theme governs the choice of entries here, and holds good despite the dramatic differences that result from the geography and geology of the area. **Olney** (18, BU) and **Amersham** (8, BU) may seem poles apart in terms of visual appearance, but met very similar social needs, as did **Blisworth** (10, N) and **Blewbury** (9, O) lower down the scale. From the late 19th century, however, the pattern began to change, first with the growth of the Northamptonshire shoe towns (Kettering, Wellingborough, Rushden, etc.), then with the outflow of light industry from London.

This outflow has distorted the modern map with large new areas of grey. In Berkshire, John Betjeman's 'friendly bombs' failed to stem the spread of Slough; Bracknell was reborn as a new town in 1948; and Reading grew bloated with high technology injected by the M4. Further north, in the late 1960s, development corporations planted Milton Keynes (BU) by the M1 and caused Northampton to rupture across the Nene Valley. The M40 sprouted trading estates around Banbury (O) long before its carriageway was ever begun. These growths owe more to the car than the landscape. Only at Corby (N), designated a new town in 1950, do the ironworks provide truly local justification.

The deeper roots of the county towns show through in steadier, healthier growth. **Oxford** (19, O) is the only genuine city – it became the centre of a diocese in 1542 – and is a uniquely taut combination of town and university. **Northampton** (16, N) comes a close second. Both were important medieval trading centres, formerly defended by walls and castles, and both had Saxon origins. Saxon Northampton, centred around St Peter's, faded as Market Square became more dominant, but Oxford still has an obvious Saxon grid of streets. Another major Saxon centre was Wallingford (O), which has retained not only its grid pattern of streets, but also its defensive banks. Just within these banks, the open areas known as 'Kinecroft' and 'Bullcroft' hark back to former stock enclosures.

The identities of the county towns of Buckinghamshire and Berkshire are less distinct. Aylesbury has a handsome County Hall and courtrooms dating from 1723–40, but Buckingham, not to be outdone, has a gaol – a mini-castle built by Viscount Cobham of Stowe in 1748. Reading was a major cloth town in the Middle Ages, but only became the administrative centre of Berkshire in 1867. Before that the honour went to **Abingdon** (7, O) (now, confusingly, in Oxfordshire), as witnessed by its magnificent county hall-cum-market house, which Celia Fiennes dubbed 'the finest in England'.

Many smaller towns also have fine market halls, less imposing than Abingdon's, but with the same arcaded ground floor and community room above. The one at Amersham dates to 1682, and has a lock-up built into one corner. Other special examples are those at Rothwell (95, N) and Watlington (O, built in 1664–5 with an upper schoolroom). The recurrence of such splendid buildings is significant, for most of these towns depended on their markets. Some had small-scale manufacturing; others, like Newbury (BE) and **Burford** (12, O), thrived on the woollen cloth trade; but most sold local farm produce. Witney (83, O) still has its 17th-century butter cross, Higham Ferrers (N) the tall stone shaft of its medieval market cross. Squares at Northampton, Abingdon and Olney, and wide high streets at Burford and Amersham all served a market function.

The rural population that supplied these markets lived, for the most part, in villages. Until the late 18th and 19th

Sheep Street, Burford, with 'Calendars' in the foreground. CM

Amersham Market Hall. JAC

limestone at Blisworth, chalk at Uffington, timber, brick and cob at Blewbury. Sadly there is no space here for Haddenham (BU), where many houses are built of a chalky cob known locally as 'wichert'.

A final category of settlement is that engineered by a lordly patron. The functional estate village of **Nuneham Courtenay** (17, O) shows the high-handed approach of a landowner keen to rid his park of its native peasantry. Parks at Stowe (38, BU) and Wotton (41, BU) were purified in the same way, and a delightfully basic row of thatched cottages built at Leverton, near Hungerford (BE), for labourers on the Chilton Park estate. **Great Tew** (13, O), by contrast, was seen as a picturesque asset, and cultured into prettiness.

Paternalistic landowners of the later 19th century were more concerned to provide for better living standards, but kept a style that was suitable to their tenants' class and situation. Hence the hierarchical terraces of railway housing such as **Spencer Street, New Bradwell** (20, BU) and the pseudo-vernacular quaintness of the labourers' cottages at **Medmenham** (15, BU). The latter, like the picturesque Rothschild cottages at Ashton (near Oundle, (N)) and across the Vale of Aylesbury (at Mentmore (37,

Charity cottage at Blewbury. CM

centuries, when farmers moved out to live on newly enclosed farms, there were only a small number of isolated farmsteads. Most clustered together, with farm buildings around the houses, in villages of varying plan. Some are set out along a main street, perhaps with back lanes or branches along cross-routes. The village of Steventon, with its grand line of houses facing the medieval causeway (see Chapter 3), comes to mind. Often, as at Blewbury and **Uffington** (21, O), houses wind round lanes that enclose greens and paddocks. **Marsh Gibbon** (14, BU) has a series of straggling hamlets of the kind

commonly known throughout Buckinghamshire and Oxfordshire as 'ends'. It also contains a clear example of the type of 'squatter settlement' to which the labouring classes were reduced in the 18th and 19th centuries.

The villages included here are not necessarily the most charming ones. Lovers of chocolate-box picturesque should go to Turville or Hambleden in the Buckinghamshire Chilterns. Instead, they have been chosen to illustrate building types and the fascinatingly varied character of the area. This arises from the use of local materials: brick in **Brill** (11, BU), banded

River front at Abingdon. JAC

BU), Wingrave, Hulcot and Waddesdon), show that few cared more for the rural ideal than the new country squire, fresh from industry or City banking. Lutyens's cottage row at Ashby St Ledgers (N), was built in 1908–9 in much the same spirit. The unusually handsome set of council houses at Filkins (O), subsidised by Sir Stafford Cripps, were a novel departure. Built in 1929 of Cotswold stone and slate, they recognise a new order but attempt to integrate it with the old.

7
Abingdon, Oxfordshire

SU 4997. 5½ miles (9 km) S of Oxford, via A34

Abingdon was the county town of Berkshire until eclipsed by Reading in 1867, but has probably benefited from the change. Apart from a rather insensitive shopping parade, its core is relatively untouched and boasts a number of dignified public buildings, most notably the County Hall. Many 18th- and 19th-century rendered facades disguise earlier gables and jetties, and several early 18th-century buildings display brickwork of rare virtuosity.

Medieval Abingdon grew wealthy as a market town, and the Market Place still provides its heart today. Trade benefited both from water transport provided by the Thames, and from the patronage of the wealthy Abbey of St Mary. Of this abbey, first founded in the late 7th century, little remains except for the 15th-century gateway and a range of service buildings in Thames Street. These are worth visiting for the chimney of the 13th-century Chequer, with rare gables and side vents, and the fine 15th-century roof of what is now the Long Gallery. The Thames is no longer navigable for freight, but a picturesque frontage of former warehouses can be seen from the far bank.

With both these advantages came drawbacks. The abbey exacted heavy dues, and the Thames was a barrier as well as a trade route. A local guild, the Fraternity of the Holy Cross, was formed to counter both problems. It fostered a spirit of civic independence, reflected in the increasing grandeur of the parish church of St Helen, which grew to be five aisles wide. The fourth aisle was probably built by the fraternity itself, which also financed the earliest of the splendid almshouses around the churchyard (see St Helen's Churchyard (72, O)). The fraternity's greatest achievement was the building, in 1416–17, of a new stone bridge across the river, with a causeway leading to a further bridge at Culham. The town

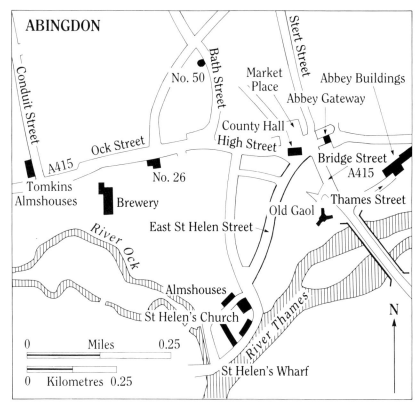

Abingdon. EH

bridge still has original ribbed arches at the near end, and Culham Bridge is almost unaltered. The improved crossing boosted trade so much that Abingdon soon overshadowed its rival, Wallingford (O), and gradually acquired administrative supremacy.

This is splendidly manifest in the County Hall of 1678–82, built by Christopher Kempster of Upton, near Burford. Kempster worked under Wren at St Paul's, and Wren's influence is very obvious. The design is compact and classical, with giant Corinthian pilasters soaring up between the arches of the ground-floor market and the round-arched windows of the courtroom above. The hipped roof is adorned with pedimented dormers and a central lantern, and has balustraded lead flats, from which buns are thrown on occasions of celebration. A less magnificent but equally forceful civic building is the Old Gaol, built in 1805–11 by Daniel Harris of Oxford. Its

three radiating wings and central octagon now serve as a leisure centre.

There is much early housing in the centre of Abingdon, albeit disguised by 18th- and 19th-century render and sashes, but the most enjoyable concentration is in East St Helen Street. No. 26 is obviously 15th century, with jetties and gables. The right gable has cusped wooden side lights, the left 17th-century ovolo mullions. No. 30 also has two gables, but was beautifully refaced in the early to mid-18th century, in chequer brick with a moulded band, gauged window heads and a pedimented doorcase. The plaster refronting of the King's Head and Bell is more Baroque, with stately pilasters and swagged escutcheon.

Also in East St Helen Street is Twickenham House, a classy mansion of pure red brick with white-painted dressings, fine railings and a superb doorcase. It was built c. 1740 for Joseph Tomkins, who belonged to a prominent

local family of maltsters. The buildings of Benjamin Tomkins are more endearing. No. 50 Bath Street, dated 1722, and 26 Ock Street revel in the very best of Thames Valley brickwork, with moulded dressings and rubbed red brick details. Most exquisite of all are the fancy window heads with scalloped edges, fluted keyblocks and carved flower vases. The Tomkins Almshouses of 1731–3 are scarcely less magnificent.

8

Amersham (Old Town), Buckinghamshire

SU 9597. 14 miles (23 km) SE of Aylesbury, off A413

Amersham's wide market place of a High Street, tapering gracefully in towards the end, is a little like that at Burford (12, O), but it lies in the Chilterns, not the Cotswolds. The only local building stone, flint, was used for the church, but nearly everything else is either timber-framed or built of beautifully mellow brick. The different colours and styles not only make for picturesque variety, but reflect a whole range of social needs. Besides the coaching inns, almshouses and handsome Market Hall of 1682, there are big houses, little houses and plenty of houses in between.

The oldest buildings are timber-framed, and include several 15th-century hall houses from the upper end of the social scale. No.49 High Street is described elsewhere (see Amersham Museum (22, BU)), but The King's Arms opposite comprises two hall houses joined together, both with tension braces and splendidly jettied cross-wings. Upper floors and chimneys were inserted in the later 16th century, and some of the detail belongs to a restoration of 1936, but the interesting pair of arches in the right-hand wing are original. They suggest that this part of the building served as a shop.

Some of the later framed buildings were also fairly prestigious. The strangely tall block that is now nos. 56–60 (private houses), has wall paintings of the Nine Worthies dating from c.1600, and was once a single house. Division

Amersham High Street, with the King's Arms. CM

into smaller units, or a facelift of a smart brick front was a common fate for this type of building. Framing often appears only in gable ends, down side alleys, or round the back. Other framed houses were modest from the start. Turpin's Row (dated 1678), at the far end of High Street, was a purpose-built range of cottages, narrow and mean, with flimsy wavy timbers.

Brick buildings and refronts reflect the hierarchy even more clearly. There are grand 18th-century villas (e.g., Hinton House, Piers Place and Elmodesham House), middle-class houses with sashes and classical doorcases, and simpler cottages with vernacular casements. The brickwork itself was more subject to fashion. Chequer brick was popular in the 18th century, while in the early 19th century a more uniform red was preferred, with glazed or yellow dressings. Nearly all types have a sense of style, and few cannot rise to a finely worked window arch or band course. My personal favourite is Town Mill, at the very far end on the right. It has a lovely chequer brick facade of *c*.1700, with coved eaves and symmetrical cross-windows, arranged with narrow end lights as at the Old Red Lion, Marsh Gibbon (14, BU).

These richly varied buildings line the High Street without modern intrusion.

Betjeman's 'Metroland' engulfed the hill above but left the old town almost intact. The new town is worth penetrating, at least as far as the second right-hand turning off the road to the station. It leads to the concrete villa of High and Over, and its neighbouring Sun Houses, built in the International Modern style by Connell and Ward between 1929 and 1934. Now surrounded by suburbia, these square-

cut blocks of architectural purity have all the melancholy of an unrealised dream.

9

Blewbury, Oxfordshire

SU 5385. On A417 between Reading and Wantage, 2½ miles (4 km) S of Didcot

Blewbury is a village of delightful surprises. It meanders within and around a great loop, the centre criss-crossed by winding lanes and paths that reveal unexpected greens and paddocks. Several paths are still bounded by the thatched cob walls of former farms and small-holdings. Others run along small brooks and lead past the neglected watercress beds of The Cleve. All is leafy and rural.

The ancient origins of the settlement lie with the Icknield Way, now the A417, and the multi-terraced hillfort on Blewburton Hill, first built in the 6th or 5th century BC. A village on the present site is mentioned in a Saxon charter of AD 944, but the earliest surviving structure is the church, grandly rebuilt on a cruciform plan in the later 12th century. Its crossing and chancel have

Cob walls at Blewbury. CM

19

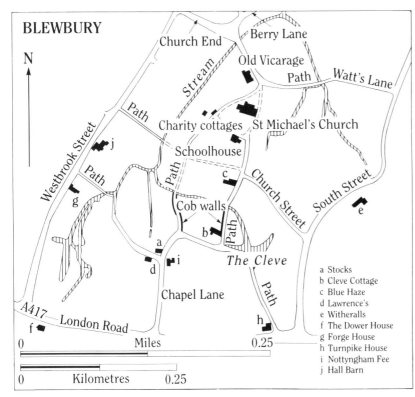

BLEWBURY

N

Church End
Berry Lane
Old Vicarage
Path
Watt's Lane
Stream
Path
Charity cottages
St Michael's Church
Westbrook Street
j
Schoolhouse
Path
Path
c
Church Street
South Street
g
Cob walls
e
b
Path
a
i
The Cleve
d
Chapel Lane
Path
A417
London Road
h
f
0   Miles   0.25
0   Kilometres   0.25

a Stocks
b Cleve Cottage
c Blue Haze
d Lawrence's
e Witheralls
f The Dower House
g Forge House
h Turnpike House
i Nottyngham Fee
j Hall Barn

Blewbury. EH

heavy vaults with rounded ribs, and
nook-shafts with waterleaf capitals.
There is more waterleaf in the slightly
later south aisle.

Around the churchyard are the more
communal village buildings: a bulky
vicarage of 1872, built in white brick
Gothic; two tiny charity cottages of 1738
and 1858, the first once tinier still; and a
handsome schoolhouse of 1709. This
housed a charity school founded by
William Malthus, with separate
classrooms for girls and boys, and
accommodation for master, mistress
and weaver. The weaver taught 'work'.
The building is of beautifully soft red
brick with a wooden cornice, cross-
windows, and winged putti on the door
hood.

Other buildings, many of them
thatched, illustrate the varied use of
local materials. Farm buildings are
usually timber-framed and
weatherboarded, but walls and other
humble structures are often built of cob.
This mixture of chalk, chalky mud and

straw was protected from rising damp by
setting it on a flint and rubble base, but
it needs frequent limewashing and a
thatch roof to prevent it from dissolving.
Ordinary houses illustrate a clear
change from timber framing to ever
more solid brick, with 19th-century tile-
hanging helping to disguise earlier
flimsiness. The collection of late
medieval and 17th-century houses is
particularly good.

The oldest houses have 15th- and
16th-century timber frames. There is a
cruck truss (see introduction to chapter
3) in the gable end of Stocks, but Cleve
Cottage and Blue Haze have the more
usual box frames, with upright posts and
upper floors jettied at one end. Typical of
the early date are their large plaster wall
panels and large curved braces. By
contrast, the later 16th- and 17th-
century houses, such as Lawrence's and
Witheralls, have smaller panels with
short diagonal braces, simpler roof
trusses with vertical queen struts, and
central chimneys of narrow brick.

Special features include the fine
bracketed oriels and ovolo-mullioned
side lights of The Dower House, and the
continuing fashion for gable-end jetties.
That at Forge House has brackets
decorated with scallops and zigzag, and
patterned brick infill above.

Brick infill became common during
the 17th century. At Turnpike House,
old plaster panels were ripped out to
match a new brick-filled wing with
smart gables. At Nottyngham Fee,
panels run riot with herringbone and
diagonal bands of glazed brick. Superior
houses soon dispensed with timber
framing altogether and made the most
of chequer patterns and brick
mouldings. Perhaps the most ambitious
was the all-brick wing of c. 1670–80 at
Hall Barn, splendid with giant pilasters,
moulded bands and scalloped window
arches.

10

Blisworth, Northamptonshire

SP 7253. 5 miles (8 km) S of
Northampton, off A43

Blisworth is not a pretty village. It has
only recently been by-passed and is still
recovering from the grime of the A43.
But it is eye-catching for its eccentric
use of local building stone. The village
sits on a geological border, where the
iron-stained Lias stones outcrop to the
north but are covered by paler oolitic
limestones to the south. All the older
houses use both types of stone, dark
brown and creamy grey, engagingly laid
in horizontal stripes. Yet another
variant, a superior orangy-brown
freestone, is used for window and gable
dressings. Similar patterns are found
elsewhere, e.g. at Rushton Triangular
Lodge (97, N), but rarely are they so
comprehensive as at Blisworth.

Most of these stripy houses are 17th
century. Some are very much altered,
but there are several excellent examples
of the local vernacular style. Illustrated
here is 3 High Street, a substantial
former farmhouse of two full storeys
with attics and cellar. The two original
bays have handsome windows with
ovolo-moulded stone mullions and

3 High Street, Blisworth. CM

cornices, and a splendidly tall end wall with steep coped gable. The small stair lights are in the centre, but the chimneys are placed at either end, probably indicating a late 17th-century date. The thatched roof now extends over a later bay with rather more imperfect stripes.

Other fine houses include 21 Stoke Road, with window cornices raised over tall central lights, and 11 Courteenhall Road. This has peculiarly zebra-like stripes, with wide bands of dark brown and narrow bands of pale stone, the lower courses precariously following the slope of the hill. Painted texts and carving hidden inside suggest that it was a well-to-do home of some status, but, like many of the smaller houses in the village, its eaves were raised and a new slate roof built in the 19th century.

Blisworth served a rural community

of farmers, and still has farm buildings at the north end of the village, behind the Royal Oak and at Cliff Hill Farm. A barn here is dated 1633. More cottages were built for farmworkers in the 19th century (e.g., 13–17 Courteenhall Road), again with stripes, but prettified with fancy gables and patterned roofs. By then, however, the Grand Junction Canal had brought alternative employment. A large warehouse at the west end of the village, and Blisworth Stone Works, on the Stoke Road, serve as reminders of the canal boom. A tramway used to carry stone from quarries on the hill down to wharves near the entrance to the great tunnel (see **Grand Union Canal: Stoke Bruerne Wharf and Blisworth Tunnel (87, N)**.

11

Brill, Buckinghamshire

SP 6513. 10 miles (16 km) W of Aylesbury, off B4011

Brill has a peculiarly exposed situation on top of a hill overlooking the Oxford Plain, and its best-known landmark is the 17th-century windmill, a post-mill of the same type as the one at Pitstone (82, BU). Cold winds can make for a bracing visit but are well worth braving, for the village makes an excellent guide to the history of brickwork. All around the windmill the hillsides are pock-marked with old clay pits and traces of brick kilns, and the village houses are built of bricks of every different size, colour and moulding.

Brick building was common in Brill at an unusually early date. The Manor House, grandly built on an E-plan, set a lead early in the 17th century with walls of long, narrow bricks, pale in colour and laid in English bond, with alternate rows of headers and stretchers. Lesser houses at first kept to cheaper timber framing, and used the narrow brick only for fireproof chimneys. Square chimney shafts set on the diagonal, or decorated with 'V' nibs, reveal that many such early buildings lurk behind the later fronts of High Street and Temple Street. Quite soon, however, prosperity and readily available clay made brick walling

The Square at Brill, with The Old Vicarage. CM

more affordable generally. Narrow bricks of the later 17th century can be spotted throughout the village, for instance in the lower walls of 2 Temple Street, the house with the delightfully wonky wooden porch.

During the 18th century the use of bluish vitrified brick became fashionable, and builders began to pattern and arrange their facades with greater care. Neighbouring houses in the triangular 'Square' illustrate the possible variety. A simple chequer pattern could be achieved by laying alternate blue headers and red stretchers in Flemish bond, as at no. 1. At nos 33–34, dated 1740, quoins and window surrounds are picked out in red, and the wall surface dignified by a plinth, a band course and a moulded brick cornice at the eaves. The Old Vicarage, built in 1773, is even more sophisticated. Here, as at Bernwode House in the High Street, the main wall surface is laid in vitreous header brick and divided up by vertical strips of red. The effect is most elegant.

Individual examples apart, there are two particularly attractive groups of houses in the village. One jumbles along the south side of The Square, and shows taller hipped houses intermixing with low gabled cottages, the brickwork patterned and patched at will. The other is a matching pair facing on to The Green, near the east end of the church. Rose Cottage may have modest casements, but its vitreous headers and red strips rival those of The Old Vicarage, and its window heads are beautifully worked in gauged red brick, finely cut and rubbed so that the joints are minutely narrow. Its neighbour, The Old School House, looks like an early 19th-century shadow, chequered and pale.

12
Burford, Oxfordshire

SP 2512. 18 miles (29 km) W of Oxford, off A40

The character of Burford is determined by its position on the edge of the Cotswold Hills. Its houses are built of

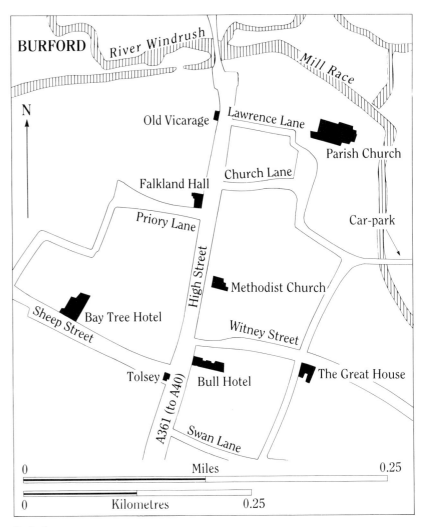

Burford. EH

pale Cotswold limestone, and its broad High Street served, from at least the early 12th century, as a market place for Cotswold woollen cloth. What makes it so attractive, apart from the natural homogeneity of the building materials, is the gentle descent of the High Street, down the hill to the bridge over the Windrush. Medieval timber frames, 17th-century stone gables and polite Georgian facades are packed higgledy piggledy either side.

Several buildings in the High Street immediately testify to Burford's early dependence on trade. Halfway down is the mid-16th-century Tolsey, a market

toll house with open ground floor, while a few doors further down is the former George Inn. This has the arches of a medieval screens passage in the carriageway, and a 15th-century lodgings range in the rear courtyard. The rear gallery can just be seen through an adjacent doorway. The Bear and the Bull also served visiting traders, the Bull with an 18th-century brick front unique amidst all the stone. Other buildings, such as Castle's butcher's shop, have lean-to shopfronts that hark back to the 15th century.

Trade brought wealth, manifest in the magnificence of the parish church.

By the mid-12th century, it was already a fine building, rich with chevron and beakhead ornament. Subsequent enlargements included the splendid 15th-century spire and fan-vaulted porch, and a large chapel, added in the early 13th century, for the merchant guild. Guild control probably accounts for the town's independent spirit and the surprisingly even distribution of wealth reflected in its merchant houses. Although these were later subdivided, in the Middle Ages they were large, impressively finished, and great in number.

Moulded stone archways reveal the existence of several grand 14th-century houses in High Street. One, no. 94, even has ballflower ornament on a rear arch. These houses would have had a full-height hall, with upper storeys only in end cross-wings. The beam ends that are visible, e.g., at Classica House, show that such upper floors were jettied and timber framed. There is more obvious evidence for this in 15th- and 16th-century buildings. No. 109 High Street has two jettied upper storeys with traces of the original cusped lights, and Castle's, next door, has timber-framed gables with 15th-century traceried bargeboards and c.1600 oriel windows. Calendars, in Sheep Street, has close-studding jettied out over an ashlar ground floor with a late 15th-century arched doorway and window surround.

By the late 16th century, fashionable houses were no longer jettied, but were being built completely in stone. This was readily available from local quarries, those at Upton and Taynton producing particularly fine freestone for ashlar facings, mouldings and carvings. (See chapter 7 and Abingdon (7, O).) Falkland Hall, built in 1558 for Edmund Silvester, clothier, is the most imposing example, with three stone storeys and a stone oriel window. Smaller houses include those improved by Simon Wisdom, whose initials appear over Tudor doorways in the High Street at The House of Simon and no. 96. He also rebuilt Wysdom Cottage, by the bridge, in 1576, with stone mullion windows and gables.

Gables remained in vogue throughout the 17th century. The Bay Tree Hotel in Sheep Street, dated 1649, has three of them, above a sophisticated facade with string courses raised as dripmoulds over the windows. At the Old Vicarage (1672) there are pedimented Dutch gables, a final fling before the classical cornices of the early 18th century. These are not as tame as they might sound. The Great House in Witney Street has a pediment floating delightfully in the middle of a castellated parapet. It was built for John Castle, and had castellated chimneys as well. A more conventional house, with splendid Corinthian pilasters, became the Methodist Church in 1849.

Other fine ashlar fronts belong to the later 18th and early 19th centuries, but the town as a whole declined with the wool trade and the re-routing of the Oxford–Gloucester turnpike. This has preserved it from development but heightened its attractions for antique dealers and craft shops. May it not suffocate as a result.

13

Great Tew, Oxfordshire

17th–early 19th century

SP 3929. Between Banbury and Chipping Norton, off B4022 to Enstone

Great Tew is a charmingly pretty village. Clustered round the green and straggling down narrow lanes are thatched cottages of warm brown ironstone, set in old-style gardens with roses, clematis and box hedges. The effect is quite intentional, for Great Tew was, and in part still is, an estate village. From 1819 onwards its cottages were built or embellished in supposedly traditional style for Matthew Robinson Boulton, son of the steam engine manufacturer. His aim was not merely to improve housing for estate workers, but to secure a picturesque asset for his country park.

As consultant architects, Boulton chose Thomas Rickman, and later his pupil, Thomas Fulljames. Rickman's brief was to follow the lead of the existing vernacular style, but make it more distinguished. Two cottages on the west side of the green illustrate the process. 'Old Thatch' is a little-altered 17th-century cottage, low, with rubble walls and wooden door-frame. Its windows have ovolo-moulded stone mullions, square leaded panes and simple hoodmoulds. No. 31, next door, is an early 19th-century version, but taller and built in ashlar. The similar steeply pitched thatch roof is emphasised by adding an extra gable to the front. The window style is also slightly different, with chamfered mullions and diamond lattice glazing.

Many old cottages were beautified

'Old Thatch' and no. 31, Great Tew. JB

simply by adding supra-vernacular features, such as Tudor archways or window hoods with carved diamond stops. The Post Office received a bay window, and no. 27 a handsome gabled porch with wooden tracery and cusped bargeboards. No. 12, down the lane beyond the Falkland Arms, acquired a heraldic shield, bogus datestone and Gothick buttresses!

Some features, however, are perfectly genuine. 17th-century buildings have lobby entries or through passages, and a large number have stair turrets jutting out at the rear. The Falkland Arms also has a rear outshot and later 17th-century cross-windows. The lane beside it leads to The Square, sufficiently out of sight for Boulton to alter little. The medieval church, restored by Rickman 1827–8, occupies an isolated position beyond Tew Park, next to the 17th-century walled gardens.

Great Tew is also known for the experimental model farming of J C Loudon, an agricultural theorist employed from 1808 to 1811 by Boulton's predecessor, G F Stratton. The experiments were not a success and have left little trace except perhaps for some tree planting. Loudon's own house, Tew Lodge, has also gone, but he immortalised its novel paper roofs in a pamphlet of 1825.

14

Marsh Gibbon, Buckinghamshire

SP 6423. 12 miles (19 km) NW of Aylesbury, off A41

Marsh Gibbon is a modest village, unspectacular but packed with social interest. Like many others in rural Buckinghamshire and Oxfordshire, it is not so much a single village as a straggling series of small hamlets or 'ends'. This entry looks at the central part, which is only superior to Town's End and Little Marsh in that it contains the manor house and the church. Otherwise it was built to house the farming community. Its buildings reveal prosperity, decline and an enlightened attempt at rescue.

Housing reform c. 1870, Marsh Gibbon. HENRY TAUNT

17th-century prosperity provided for a major rebuilding of the village. There is some timber framing of c. 1600, but most houses were rebuilt in local rubble limestone, with window dressings perforce in wood. Cromwell House (illustrated in chapter 3), at the west end of Church Street, is typical of the style, and still has its thatched roof, swept over the small gables of the upper windows. Chimneys, with proud diagonal shafts of narrow brick, show that the house was much better heated than any medieval hall. They also dictate the compact plan. Squeezed in front of the main chimney is a small lobby, with original panelled door, and a cramped staircase, lit by a small window. The rooms are more generous, and one of them has fragments of wall paintings.

Similarly aligned chimneys and doorways show that many other village houses had the same lobby plan, but the Old Red Lion, dated 1684, has much higher aspirations. Its symmetrical cross-windows and acanthus scrolls are fashionably 'polite', and it even has narrow 'closet' lights in front of the end chimneys. The central door leads through to the rear outshot, which has a whole turret for the stairs.

Such grandeur has few rivals, and other village buildings show obvious signs of decline in the later 18th and 19th centuries. Added doorways show how farmhouses were divided up for labourers, while new cottages were built of the humblest materials. The College, immediately north of the churchyard, is an extraordinary group of squatters' cottages, huddled together on a scrap of common land. Some are built of poor-quality rubble, but several are of mud or cob. The Cottage, near the north end, is a particularly good example: cramped, low and thatched, with curved sloping walls, and two small windows lighting the tiniest of outshots.

Living conditions within The College were described in 1884 by Sir Henry Acland, Regius Professor of Medicine and promoter of the Oxford University Museum (71, O). In a pamphlet for the International Health Exhibition, he told how he visited 'Lowmarsh' in 1858, and had been shown tiny hovels with damp mossy roofs and gaping floors, built on land reeking with slush from pigs and privies. The only water supply was an unsavoury pool of peat-coloured water, used as much by animals as by men. By the time of the exhibition, however, things had changed. Water ran in pipes to the several hand pumps still standing in the village, and 'a long row of pleasant and well-built cottages' had been built in present-day Church Street. Each cottage had three bedrooms, an allotment garden in front, a bakehouse and earth closet to the rear, and a pigsty beyond.

Today these sturdy stone buildings are known as 'Acland Terrace', for Acland himself was the landlord who had recognised the village's desperate need for improvement.

15

Medmenham, Buckinghamshire
1900

SU 8084. Between Marlow and Henley-on-Thames, off A4155

In 1900 *Country Life* ran two fascinating articles in praise of Robert Hudson's new estate buildings at Medmenham. Hudson was cast as a patriotic hero, rescuing his neighbourhood from rural decay by building houses 'as comfortable as they are handsome'. His remarkable chalk cottages have now begun to disappear behind private hedges and fencing, but are well worth seeking out for their delightful details and period flavour. There are some in Ferry Lane, others up in the hills at Bockmer End, and there is a lovely group of school and laundry buildings in a lane just north of the main crossroads.

Hudson had made his fortune from soap and could afford to be a gentleman in the grand manner. For his own residence, he first 'restored' Medmenham Abbey (a former home of Sir Francis Dashwood and the notorious Hell-Fire Club), and then built Danesfield. This Tudor fantasy of gleaming white chalk, high above the Thames to the east of the village, is now a luxury hotel. Hudson's architect, Romaine Walker, was employed to improve and beautify the estate in matching style.

Like the big houses, the estate cottages were built of local chalk. They supposedly follow the vernacular tradition but are infinitely more glamorous. Windows have stone mullions and leaded lights, doorways have carved Tudor arches, and gables have fancy bargeboards. Jetties, oriels and ornate chimneys all help to create the prettiest picture of a rural ideal. Hudson saw the cottages as an attractive asset, and bore the immense cost (£2,500 for the six Abbey Cottages illustrated) himself. The tenants lived rent free.

Country Life was most impressed, both by the aesthetics of the architecture and by Hudson's philanthropic intentions, and described the superior living conditions in great detail. Each cottage was described as having a 'large' family kitchen with fitted cupboards, sink and water tap, as well as a back scullery and three separate bedrooms. Outside there was an earth closet, yard, shed and vegetable garden. Compared to 'the dilapidated hovels' of the rest of the village, this was real luxury. The magazine's other commendations might now sound a little forced. The front parlour was 'one of the smallest conceivable', so that it could be easily cleaned and required 'but a tiny carpet and very little furniture'! Nor did the cottages have 'over-much space', as this lead to 'the nuisance of lodgers'.

The picturesque group of laundry, school, and schoolmistress's house was planned with similar practicality. Little schoolgirls could easily pop next door to assist the laundress and so acquire 'a kind of practical knowledge that no woman should be without'.

16

Northampton, Northamptonshire

SP 7560

When Celia Fiennes visited Northampton in 1697, she described it as 'a large town well built', beautified by 'an abundance of new building'. Northampton was then in the throes of recovery after a disastrous fire in 1675. The abundance of new building in the late 1960s and 70s might not be so highly commended. Celia's 'noble prospect' of the town was obscured by vast residential suburbs and industrial estates, and the centre was invaded by malls, car-parks and ring roads. Fortunately this redevelopment was not quite so sweeping as the fire, and the town's surviving 'heritage' is now better valued.

Market Square, enlarged after the fire to grand proportions, makes an impressive centre-piece, even if the buildings around it are pleasingly down to earth. A pair in the south-west corner are particularly cheerful, with colourful stucco and bold pilasters. The one with chunky swags and scrolls is late 17th century. Others are of more dignified ironstone ashlar, and include Welsh House of 1595, beautifully rebuilt in

Abbey Cottages, Medmenham, as they appeared when they were newly built in 1900, without the recent garden fences. CL

Northampton Market Square. AFK

1975 but sadly only as a facade. Its fine 18th-century neighbour has a delightful Gothick oriel.

Opening off Market Square are alleys that lead into Drapery and Mercers Row, two of many streets still named after their specialised medieval functions. The fire swept away the vast majority of medieval buildings, but good 18th-century houses survive in Sheep Street. Changes in style mark the spread of the town eastwards, with Regency terraces in Albion Place, off Derngate, and c. 1840 stucco (classical, gothic and Jacobean)

in Spencer Parade. Beyond, to the north and the east, sprawl the red-brick terraces of the shoe industry (81, N).

Back in the centre of the town are two outstanding buildings that belong to the post-1675 reconstruction, and are therefore associated with the supposed directorship of Henry Bell. The exciting church of All Saints is an ingenious example of Wren's influence, rare outside London, and is planned as a Greek cross with central dome. It has quirky windows with ovals and classicised tracery, gorgeous plasterwork inside, and remarkable 1680s fittings that include a throne for the mayor. The diminutive facade of the Sessions House is a more graceful piece of Baroque, with delicate central bays contained between imposing Corinthian doorcases.

The Guildhall is not late 17th century but gutsily Victorian. The right-hand part was built in 1861–4 by Edward Godwin. Like Oxford University Museum (71, O) it has the gothic flavour of a Flemish cloth hall, with a steep roof and central tower, but has an even denser array of arches, plate tracery and carving. Bands of pale limestone and brown ironstone provide Ruskinian pattern. The extension by Matthew Holding, a local architect, is equally exotic.

Away from the immediate centre lie two fascinating churches that survived the devastation of 1675. They both date to the mid-12th century, but show a surprising contrast in style. St Peter's, down Marefair, is a long, aisled church, richly decorated with carving, chevrons and coloured banding. Holy Sepulchre is much more severe, partly because of 14th-century alterations, and has a rare round nave. Like the other round churches at Cambridge and the Temple, London, it may have been influenced by crusaders' tales of the Holy Sepulchre at Jerusalem.

It is also worth making a pilgrimage to St Matthew's in Kettering Road, not so much for the architecture as for the contents. Opposite the agonised *Crucifixion* by Graham Sutherland sits Henry Moore's *Madonna and Child*, slightly melancholy but forever calm, reassuring and solid.

CENTRAL NORTHAMPTON

N

A508 — Shoe industry

Holy Sepulchre Church — St Matthew's Church

The Mounts — Kettering Road (A43)

Sheep Street

A4500

Site of Castle

Railway Station

Horsemarket

Market Square

Abington Street

Drapery — Spencer Parade

Marefair

Mercers Row — Guildhall

Billing Road

(A45)

All Saints Church

Sessions House — Central Museum

St Peter's Church

Albion Place

A428

(A43)

Museum of Leathercraft

0 Miles 0.5

to Eleanor Cross, Hardingstone

A508

0 Kilometres 1.0

Central Northampton. EH

17

Nuneham Courtenay, Oxfordshire
1760s

SU 5599. 5 miles (8 km) S of Oxford, on A4074 (formerly A423)

'Two rows of low, neat houses, built close to each other, and as regular and as uniform as a London street' – so a German traveller, C P Moritz, described the village in 1782. Nuneham Courtenay is little different today, and still arouses the curiosity of the motorist speeding through to Oxford or Henley-on-Thames.

Its striking regularity is the result of high-handedness on the part of an aristocratic landlord. Simon, 1st Earl Harcourt, decided that the old village of Newnham cluttered the views from his new villa (begun in 1756). To improve the landscape, he turned the duckpond into a lake, rebuilt the church as a domed Ionic temple, and transported the population to live out of sight along the Oxford turnpike. The new 'street' was functional rather than beautiful, but has attractively mellowed with age.

The plan is extremely simple. Welcoming the traveller at the north end of the village are the Harcourt Arms, (formerly the New Inn) and a garage converted from the original smithy. Then, leading down the hill, come evenly matched pairs of labourers' cottages, with taller houses for the better-off at the south end. Half-way down the hill another house doubled as school until a new school was built behind in 1835. Tucked away just inside the park is the modest church of 1880, a much closer and more respectable place of worship than the distant Ionic temple.

Apart from the church, the village is built of softly coloured chequer brick. Roofs are tiled and there are remnants of timber framing in the gable walls. Of the cottage pairs, nos. 34 and 35 are the least altered and best represent the standard type. They consist of one storey and an attic and share a central chimney, originally with only one flue per cottage. Each cottage has a central door of old wide boards, and two old

Nos. 34 and 35, Nuneham Courtenay. CM

metal casements with single shutters.

According to William Whitehead, poet and friend of the 2nd Earl, villagers were well pleased with the move to 'happier mansions warm and dry'. Not everyone agreed. The old village of Newnham was probably the 'Sweet Auburn' of Goldsmith's poem, *The Deserted Village*. This laments the lost charms of rustic life, so wantonly destroyed, and prophesies the decline of rural society:

> Ill fares the land, to hastening ills a prey
> Where wealth accumulates, and men decay.

18

Olney, Buckinghamshire

SP 8951. 10 miles (16 km) SE of Northampton, on A509 between Milton Keynes and Wellingborough

Olney is almost in Northamptonshire, and shows it. A typical broach spire greets you across the River Ouse, and the limestone buildings are tinted with the honey-brown of the Upper Lias. The graceful ease of this small town still belongs to Buckinghamshire, however, and happily lacks the brusque realism that can be found further north.

The heart of the town is the triangular Market Place, enclosed by pleasing ranges of ashlar, brick and render. The Bull Hotel, formerly a coaching inn, dominates the west side with an early 19th-century rendered

frontage, but the most imposing building is the Cowper and Newton Museum in the south-east corner. This proudly demonstrates the mid-18th century prestige of brick. Strips of blue-grey brick 'wall' are squeezed between grand red-brick window surrounds with gauged heads and stone keyblocks. Below each sash is a panelled apron. The poet William Cowper lived here from 1767 to 1786, and the house now contains memorabilia and a collection of lace.

An ample High Street, wide enough to accommodate a former stream as well as the road, leads north. It is lined with a handsome procession of well-to-do stone houses. One (no. 25) is dated 1694, and has distinctive thick and thin courses of rubble. Elsewhere only steep roofs, gables and chimneys indicate a 17th-century phase. Most of the fronts were rebuilt in ashlar in the later 18th and early 19th centuries, and make a fine display of assorted sashes, doorcases and cornices. Olney House, on the west side, is particularly grand, with rusticated ground floor, Venetian windows and mansard roof.

There are more of these quality houses, notably Bridge House and

High Street, Olney. CM

Courtney House, in High Street South (which leads down towards the river), and another in Church Street. This last house was the vicarage remodelled for Cowper's friend, the Revd John Newton, slave-trader turned hymn-writer, and author of *Amazing Grace*. Between 1764 and 1780 Newton was Curate of Olney, and preached his powerful sermons in the 14th-century church of St Peter and St Paul on the edge of the water meadows. It is a gaunt building with tall windows of flowing tracery, and the broach spire mentioned above.

The northern end of the town was not so well-off, and became a satellite for the Northampton boot and shoe industry. Here, east of High Street and Wellingborough Road, are late 19th-century red-brick terraces with rear workshops reached by mews-style back lanes. A shoe factory, still with gables and domed lantern, was built for the firm of Hinde and Mann in the 1890s. Olney's other industry, handmade lace, was by then in decline, unable to compete with machine equivalents. The unusual Lace Factory in High Street, beautifully built in 1928 as a central warehouse, was a last-ditch attempt to save the trade. Carved on the gable is a lacemaker, working away at her bobbins.

19
Oxford, Oxfordshire

SP 5106

Oxford may be famous for its dreaming spires, but its foundations are firmly embedded in the real world. As a commercial city it has been alive since the 10th century, and kicking against its university since the 12th. This entry briefly introduces the 'Town'. For 'Gown' see chapter 6.

A relic of Saxon Oxford is the regular grid of streets. Its main axes still cross at

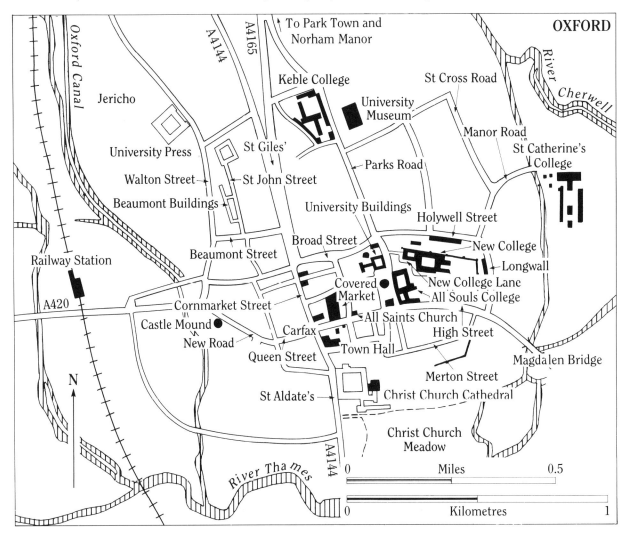

Central Oxford. EH

(*Opposite*) High Street, Oxford. BTA

Carfax, even if Fish Street is more politely known as St Aldate's, and Butcher Row as Queen Street. Cornmarket Street leads north past the church tower of St Michael, with Saxon balusters in its belfry, and formerly passed under the adjacent North Gate, demolished in 1771. The city walls, rebuilt in the 13th century with semicircular bastions, survive best in New College gardens (68, O) and alongside Merton Field.

Visible from New Road is the artificial mound constructed for Robert D'Oilly's castle in 1071. The rest of the castle site has long served as a prison, and is fronted by a toytown 'fort' of 1840, built as a County Hall. Of the other major medieval buildings, Henry I's palace of Beaumont and the great abbeys and friaries are all gone. Only the priory church of St Frideswide survives, engulfed by Christ Church and elevated to cathedral status in 1546. The choir has a glorious combination of massive late 12th-century arcading and delicate c.1500 vaulting, with fans, pendants and star-patterned ribs. Like the Divinity School (70, O), this vault is probably by William Orchard.

Several fine commercial buildings have survived from the later Middle Ages. Cornmarket Street boasts two splendid inns, the Golden Cross, with 16th-century wall paintings, and the New Inn, now part-occupied by Laura Ashley Ltd. The latter is late 14th century, and inside you can see the stone archway into the former courtyard, and the jettied upper floor with traceried wooden windows. The shops in front have been interestingly restored, the left bay with considerable flair in 1952, the right bays more cautiously in 1985–7.

The problems facing the would-be restorer are immediately evident from a glance down High Street. Here there are many timber-framed medieval buildings, built as shops with dwellings behind, but all have been stuccoed over and fitted with gracious 18th-century sashes, canted bays and wooden cornices. These frontages are painted in a gorgeous variety of colours – pink, blue, green, apricot and cream – and are of great value in their own right, but

only the odd jetty, gable or timber hints at an earlier origin. An exception is no. 126, but even here the 17th-century oriel and pediments mask a simpler 15th-century facade. Side alleys leading into the narrow plots behind reveal hidden treasures, such as the restaurant at no. 130A, a fine gabled house of 1637 with excellent original detail.

From 1771 the city was transformed by the Paving Commissioners, who built Magdalen Bridge, tidied up the street frontages and shooed the traders' stalls into the Covered Market. This is still immensely characterful, with its glazed alleys and pedimented ashlar facade. Along with the robustly classical church of All Saints (by Henry Aldrich, 1708), it contrasts with the colourful stucco and provides a civic foil to the ashlar dignity of the college buildings. Ashlar was also adopted for the late 19th-century banks on the corners of Carfax. Lloyds has a riotous design by Stephen Salter, while the sterner Midland bank is by H T Hare. Hare was also responsible for the luxurious Renaissance detail of the Town Hall in St Aldate's.

With Thames and Cherwell around three sides, the city naturally overflowed

Spencer Street, New Bradwell. CM

to the north, its progress marked by dramatic changes in style. There are stone and stuccoed houses of the 16th and 17th centuries in Holywell Street, Broad Street and St Giles', and splendid ashlar terraces of the 1820s in Beaumont Street and St John Street. The modest brick of Beaumont Buildings foreshadows the terraced cottages of Jericho, begun when the University Press moved to Walton Street in 1830. Further north are Victorian middle-class developments such as the classical Park Town (1850s) and gothic Norham Manor (1860s and 70s). The vast 20th-century splurge southwards owes much to the Morris car plant at Cowley.

20

Spencer Street, New Bradwell, Buckinghamshire
1850s

SP 829413. 2 miles (3 km) NW of Central Milton Keynes, beyond Bradwell, the A422 and Bradville, on S side of New Bradwell High Street

When Stephenson's London to Birmingham Railway opened in 1838, it needed trains as well as tracks. Carriage works were established at Wolverton (to the west of later New Bradwell), and terraced housing for railway workers began to spread across the rural face of north Buckinghamshire. Wolverton is still a grid of red-brick terraces, but its original core has been swamped, both by the works themselves and by 1960s demands for a new shopping centre. New Bradwell, first built by the railway company in 1854–61, has fared a little better. One of its original streets has been saved and restored by Milton Keynes Development Corporation. Spencer Street may be functional and unfrilly, but it has a great sense of community and social order.

The London and North Western Railway Company cared for its workers, and built solid houses of yellow stock brick with sash windows and slate roofs. The simple regularity of the design is emphasised by window surrounds and quoins picked out in red, and by a first-floor band that ties each terrace together. All is uniform and equal, except that a taller, three-storey house, with basement, stands guard at either end of each terrace. These superior dwellings were built for the foremen. They make fine architectural full stops, but were in no doubt intended as a domestic reminder of work-place authority.

All the houses used to open directly on to the street. The present front gardens are a softening touch, added when the street was pedestrianised and the houses restored in 1978. At the back there are still the original small yards, with gates into the back alley that used to separate one terrace from the next. But the next terraces are now gone, swept away as slums in 1973, and 'superior' modern flats stand in their place. The only other survivors from the New Bradwell of c.1860 are the church and former school, both designed by G E Street.

21
Uffington, Oxfordshire

SU 3089. 5 miles (9 km) W of Wantage, to N of B4507

The thatched chalk houses of Uffington are very much part of the land. Set down comfortably in the farmland of the Vale of White Horse, they make a leisurely circuit, enclosing a central area of paddock. Only footpaths cross this open space, and, until recently, only a few cottages encroached upon it. Cottages also crept out around the green and the

Uffington chalk: Garrard's Farmhouse (left) and Pear Tree Cottage (right). CM

common to the north-east. To the south, the parish reaches out to the Berkshire Downs, raiding the hills for building stone under the watchful eye of the chalky White Horse itself (4, O).

Chalk is often not regarded as a good building material because it is so soft and porous that it weathers badly. But at Uffington it is unusually hard, and has been used with great care. Everywhere in the village you see chalk walls set safe above the damp on plinths of brown sarsen stone, and sheltered from the rain by overhanging thatch. Cottages of poor-quality rubble are protected by coat upon coat of limewash, but others flaunt ashlar masonry with finely cut chalk mullions (e.g., at Manor Cottage) or window arches (e.g., The Laurels). From the 18th century onwards, brick dressings were often preferred, for their greater durability, and a wider variety of styles became possible.

Two houses on the south-east side of the village beautifully illustrate different extremes. Pear Tree Cottage is a substantial farmhouse of the later 17th century, with typical lobby entry. It was

built of dressed chalk blocks, at the time when chalk was first becoming an affordable alternative to timber framing, but still relied on timber for the window lintels and on narrow brick for the chimneys. These were local materials, like the roof thatch, and they give the building a natural softness. Neighbouring Garrard's Farmhouse is much smarter, and probably belongs to the early 19th century. It has a crisp facade of white chalk ashlar with emphatic red brick quoins and window surrounds. The alien slate roof adds a disconcerting trimness.

Also of chalk is the diminutive school-room (now a museum) that stands at the crossroads south of the churchyard. It is variously dated 1617, 1634 and 1637, and has chalk mullion windows and ashlar walls, patched but still remarkably fine. The church behind was built in the early to mid-13th century, and has an amazingly grand cruciform plan with curious transept chapels. It has lost its spire and is now a little bleak with restoration, but the Early English lancets and roll mouldings are superb.

3

Small Houses

Small houses are built for and by local people, out of local materials. They can tell you more about an area than any other type of building, but are likely to pose two problems for anyone interested in their past: firstly, they are mostly private, and in all but a few cases we have to be content with an outside view; secondly, they are difficult to trace in written historical records, and we have to sharpen our awareness for structural clues. This chapter therefore looks at only a small number of readily visible buildings, but describes them in some detail. It concentrates on the rare medieval houses that seem so very different from our own, and leaves mention of later houses, which are both more numerous and more familiar, to the descriptions of towns and villages in the previous chapter. This introduction makes reference to prime examples of these later houses and hopes to tie a few threads together.

Medieval houses in this area all share a basic plan inherited from upper-class manor houses. The main living room, or 'hall', was heated by a fire on an open hearth, and had of necessity to be single-storey, as smoke dispersed through the roof. A passage (the cross-passage) usually led across one end of the hall, with doorways to front and rear. In the wealthier houses, highlighted here because they have survived best, service or storage rooms might lie beyond the passage, perhaps with a family room above, as at **Leadenporch House, Deddington** (24, O). At **Amersham Museum** (22, BU) the family rooms were in a cross-wing, grandly jettied over the hall to make a dais canopy.

This medieval plan form varied only with class and wealth, but methods of construction show up an intriguingly deep national divide between building traditions north and south of the Jurassic ridge. Leadenporch House, up on the marlstone humps of the ridge, belongs to the 'northern', or Midland, tradition, for it has stone walls and

cruck trusses. A cruck truss is one in which two major timbers, often the two halves of a slightly curved tree trunk, are joined at the top, so as to make a roughly triangular support for the roof. Here at Leadenporch House the crucks are raised, and set into the stone walls, but in timber-framed houses crucks usually rise from ground level and make an A-frame that holds up the whole house, walls as well as roof. This type of construction can clearly be seen in the gable end of the hall at **39 The Causeway, Steventon** (26, O).

During the 15th and 16th centuries, crucks became common throughout the area covered by this book, except in the extreme south-east. Some, like those at Stocks in Blewbury (9, O), remain easily recognisable, but many more have been concealed by later rebuilding – an extraordinarily large number of them are hidden away in the Buckinghamshire village of Long Crendon. Their disappearance was possibly because crucks seem to have been associated, especially in the south, with lower-class rural houses, and were definitely out of fashion by the 17th century.

The 'southern' alternative to the cruck was the box-frame. Here, where there was little stone, a tradition of elaborate timber framing spread from the south-east of England, where upright corner posts and horizontal tiebeams were used to make a basic box shape. The roof supports were then set on top of this box, rather than rising from within the walls. The system could be varied, as at Amersham Museum or the White Hart Inn, Fyfield (73, O), by swapping a tiebeam for an arch-braced collar, so as give more dignity and height over the hall. It also allowed for distinctive features such as jettied upper floors.

One of the most fascinating things about this area is the way in which these two traditions, 'southern' and 'northern', are mixed and gradually re-arranged

Leadenporch House, Deddington. CM

Cromwell House, Marsh Gibbon. CM

along lines of social class. At first they meet on equal terms: at the **Queen's Head, Crowmarsh Gifford** (25, O) you can see a timber-framed aisled hall typical of the south-east, but improved with 'northern' base crucks in the central truss. (Great Coxwell Barn (76, O) shows a similar combination.) However, by the time the hall at 39 The Causeway, Steventon, was built, crucks had moved 'down-market', and fine details were reserved for the superior box-framed cross-wing. The final victory of the 'southern' tradition, among the fashionable upper classes, is evident from such houses as the **Bell Inn, Waltham St Lawrence** (23, BE) and Church Farm, Haddenham (BU), which both affect an extraordinary 'Wealden' style, more often seen in Kent.

By the late 16th and 17th centuries, living standards had improved, and people wanted more space and comfort than the medieval hall afforded.

Chimneys provided both. They cleared the hall of smoke and allowed for an upper storey. Whether inserted into an old house or built into a new one, chimneys became a status symbol and were designed for show. Particularly fine in this area are the brick chimney-stacks of houses in the Vales – those at Brill (11, BU), have clustered diamond shafts or narrow nibs proclaiming the number of flues. At first these stacks were placed so as to leave the cross-passage intact (as at Leadenporch House and Amersham Museum), but increasingly they were built in place of the passage, in line with the doorway. This left only a small entrance lobby in front of the chimney, but saved on living space. At Cromwell House, Marsh Gibbon (14, BU), small window panels next to the doorway show how a narrow stair was often squeezed in as well.

People who could afford chimneys could usually afford solid walls, provided

stone was available locally. In the north-west of the area, they quarried the outcrops of oolitic limestone and iron-stained Lias; in the south (e.g., at Uffington (21, O) they made the most of the local chalk. In the clay vales, timber framing continued a little longer, but with box frames and queen-strut roofs instead of crucks. In villages like Blewbury you can see the gradual invasion of brick, first infilling the panels of timber-framed houses, then taking over whole facades.

The variety of materials led to distinctive localised styles: old-fashioned jetties at Blewbury, stone gables at Burford (12, O), and extraordinary coloured banding at Blisworth (10, N). During the 18th century, bricklayers in the Vales produced ever more sophisticated designs with gauged and glazed brick, as seen at Abingdon (7, O) and Brill. By then, however, the fashions of polite society were beginning to produce a more universal veneer of sashes, cornices and, above all, symmetry. The lopsided three-bay house of the 17th century gave way to the two-bay house with central door and matching chimneys at either end. The process is delightfully illustrated at the Old Red Lion, Marsh Gibbon and Town Mill, Amersham (8, BU).

Changes in fashion are never effected as easily in brick and stone as they are in dress. Wealthy owners moved on or built anew, and the less wealthy, particularly in towns or large villages like Amersham, rebuilt or refronted. The poorest either moved into discarded older buildings, dividing them into several units, or built as cheaply as possible in the old traditions. Labourers on the Claydon estate, in the Vale of Aylesbury, were still building themselves timber-framed houses in the mid-19th century, at a time when landowners were 'reviving' the technique as picturesque. The 18th- and 19th-century cob hovels of The College at Marsh Gibbon give some idea of the basic living conditions in such places, and Flora Thompson graphically portrays the lifestyle in *Lark Rise to Candleford*.

22

Amersham Museum, Buckinghamshire
Mid-15th century

SU 956973. The museum is at 49 High Street, Old Amersham, 14 miles (23 km) SE of Aylesbury, off A413

[A]

You little suspect, from the outside, that Amersham Museum is a fine timber-framed hall house of the 15th century. Like many buildings in crowded towns, it has been split up, into two storeys and three properties. The service end is still part of no. 47, and hides behind a late 18th-century front extension, while part of the upper cross-wing now belongs to the 19th-century post office. The central hall is almost completely concealed behind a modern shop, and only a narrow entrance remains visible.

Inside, behind this disguise, you find yourself in the former cross-passage, now separated from the hall by a chimney-stack of *c*. 1600. If you mentally take this and the contemporary upper floor away, you can recreate the space of the medieval hall, as shown in the diagram. Smoke from an open fire, lit on the cobbled stone hearth, originally rose free right up into the roof, blackening the wattle and daub in the end wall with soot. The roof itself made an imposing superstructure, and its fine details, now visible close-to upstairs, reflect the great importance of the room for the medieval household. At the far end, the roof rests on a simple truss with queen struts, only moulded along the tiebeam. But the central truss is a much more impressive affair, all its timbers handsomely edged with hollow chamfering, its collar braced so as to make a splendid arch above the hall.

The house has other signs of quality too. The rear window is richly detailed

Jettied framing and brick panels at Forge House, Blewbury. JAC

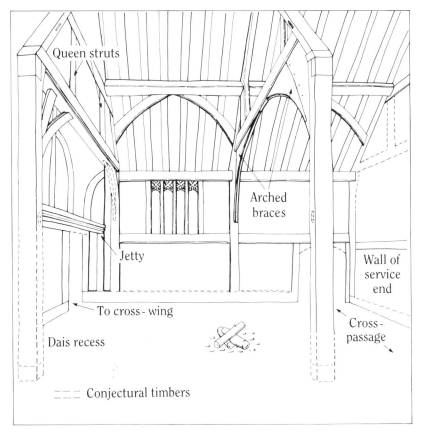

Amersham Museum: a reconstructed view of the 15th-century hall (derived from survey by J Chenevix Trench). EH

The building has recently been restored by the Amersham Society and makes a fine setting for its display of bygones, old photographs and maps of the town.

23

Bell Inn, Waltham St Lawrence, Berkshire
15th century

SU 829769. Near village church at Waltham St Lawrence, 4½ miles (7 km) SW of Maidenhead, off B3024 between White Waltham and Twyford

[C]

This attractive pub provides a rare opportunity to enjoy a 15th-century 'Wealden' house, unusual in this area but common in Kent and Sussex. Like the example reconstructed at the Weald and Downland Open Air Museum, near Chichester, it has jettied end bays that leave the former hall recessed in the centre behind large curved braces. A single half-hipped roof with gablet vents covers the whole. The structure is a little more basic here than in the south-east, with local clasped purlins instead of fancy crown-posts, and the hall has only one bay, but it represented a very

with ogee wooden tracery and moulded mullions, and the two-storey cross-wing is jettied out into the hall so as to form a shallow canopy over the dais area, where the owner would have sat. Fronting the jetty is a beautifully moulded beam that emphasises the superior status of this part of the hall, while at the north end are traces of a doorway that led to family chambers or parlours within the wing.

As usual, the hall was divided into two storeys *c.* 1600, and a new dormer window, nice and wide, gave plenty of light to the main upper room. Open fires were no longer possible, and a chimney was built of narrow brick and flint, rising to a fine T-plan shaft. Downstairs it had a wide inglenook with wooden lintel and side seats, upstairs a smaller fireplace with a chamfered brick arch. Life was becoming much more comfortable.

The Bell Inn, Waltham St Lawrence. CM

superior fashion. It was certainly one up on the Joneses!

As with any building intended for show, many of the best features are on the outside. The jetties are carried on impressively hefty beams with curved bracing, and there are shadows of large tension braces behind the plasterwork above. Deeply coved eaves gracefully bring the recessed hall bay into line. The windows and flimsy wall studs are not original, but there are two fine doorways with pointed wooden arches: a wide one in the left bay leads into the cross-passage at the end of the hall and has an old plank door, while a smaller one to the right may have led into a shop or office.

Inside the cross-passage, another archway in the left wall opens into the service end. This, true to function, now houses the beer cellar. Traces of a second arch suggest an original pantry/buttery division. To the right of the passage is the back of the hall fireplace, inserted in the 17th century when the hall was divided into two storeys. This made the hall much cosier (it is now the main bar), but sadly prevents you from seeing its arching wall-braces and sooty roof. The roof is remarkably complete, and even has rafters halved to carry the louvre that once let out smoke from the open fire.

More original detail can be seen in the far bar, to the right, where there are massive joists with rough Roman numerals. The stairs are in their original position, but the fireplace and partition, with 16th-century panelling, are much later.

24

Leadenporch House, Deddington, Oxfordshire
Early 14th and 17th centuries

SP 466314. On E side of New Street (A4260) near S end of town, 5½ miles (9 km) S of Banbury

[D]

Deddington is a small town built, like Great Tew (13, O), of local orange-brown marlstone. It was a place of some importance in medieval times, and the

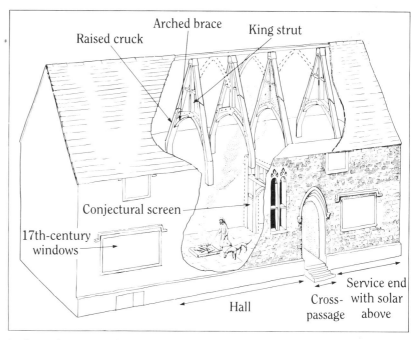

Leadenporch House, Deddington, opened up to show how the hall might have looked in the 14th century (derived from survey by R B Wood-Jones). EH

large earthworks of Deddington Castle can still be explored to the east. Leadenporch House is one of the few smaller buildings that recognisably belong to the same period.

At first sight it looks more like a 17th-century house, three rooms long and two storeys high. The windows have ovolo-moulded mullions and Tudor hoodmoulds of this date, and are of a pale limestone that wears better than the marl walling. However, the arched doorway and adjacent tall blocked-up window, both of darker brown stone, are clear evidence of a much earlier history. The doorway is finely moulded, with remnants of carved head stops, and leads into a cross-passage. The tall window breaks through the later storey division and shows that there was once a full-height central hall. Its cusped lights and blind tracery heads suggest an early 14th-century date.

Leadenporch House is a private house, so the spectacular roof is not generally open to view. It has, however, been recorded by R B Wood-Jones in his book *Traditional Domestic Architecture of the Banbury Region*. The extravagant

arrangement of arched braces, unusual king struts and massive cruck trusses, (here raised and set high into the stone walls), confirm the 14th-century date and reflect the distinctly up-market nature of the house. Sadly we know nothing of the man who built it, but the structure does allow us to imagine how he might have used it. A possible layout is shown in the diagram.

The four great cruck trusses are all numbered and variously blackened. The first two, set impressively close and thickly encrusted with soot from the open hearth, must have spanned the hall, dividing it into three narrow bays. The third truss has a partition above the collar, and marks the end of the hall. Beyond, to the right, are two wider bays with less smoke-blackening but just as fine a central truss. This may well have graced a solar, used as a family living and sleeping room, set on an upper floor above the cross-passage and service end.

What happened at the left end of the hall is less sure. There were no 14th-century trusses here, but the plinth on the front wall runs on through the present left bay. This was substantially rebuilt in the 17th century and has a wide parlour window on the ground floor. Similar windows show that the hall was divided into two storeys at much the same time, with a large new chimney-stack built back-up against the cross-passage.

25

Queen's Head, Crowmarsh Gifford, Oxfordshire
Mid-14th century

SU 616892. 12½ miles (20 km) SE of Oxford, off A4074, across the bridge from Wallingford

[C]

From the front the Queen's Head looks unspectacular, but a glance at the gable end soon tells you that this is no ordinary pub. It has lots of roof, low eaves, and a timber frame like that of a barn. What makes its resemblance to a barn so striking is its aisled structure, with tall arcade posts defining a central 'nave'. On a much smaller scale, the principle is the same as that of the 'tithe barn' at Great Coxwell (76, O). The Queen's Head, however, is not a barn but a domestic aisled hall. The long diagonal braces that pass from the aisle walls to the arcade posts are an early feature, and tree-ring analysis has

produced a remarkably consistent date of 1341.

The aisled hall is one of the earliest forms of house for which substantial evidence survives, and is mostly found in 'lowland' England, south of the Jurassic ridge. It was a luxurious class of house, covering a large household area with a single roof held up by wooden arcades of posts and braces. Inside, this modest example shows a common Midland improvement to the basic form, for there is no arcade post to impede the central space. Instead, the roof rests on a base cruck, which leans inward from the aisle wall and is braced to make a great central arch. A further arch supports the collar above. Sadly only half of this major truss survived the rebuilding of the front wall.

The far end of the hall has arcade posts again, grooved on the outside to take small screens. It therefore served as a spere truss, and probably divided the living space of the hall from a cross passage. The original plan is obscured by a restructuring of the area beyond, where there are now two parallel cross-wings with 17th-century chimneys and fragments of timber framing.

The structure of the hall itself is now easy to appreciate, thanks to recent restoration work. This involved the removal, all but for side galleries, of a later upper floor. As you sit with your

pint, you can now look straight up into the roof and admire, free from the smoke of the original open fire, the fine chamfering of the timbers and the elegant curves of the braces.

26

39 The Causeway, Steventon, Oxfordshire
14th century

SU 469919. 9 miles (15 km) S of Oxford, off A34, to W of B4017

[B]

Steventon has a remarkable gallery of timber-framed houses lined up along its raised medieval causeway. Laid out on display are the halls and cross-wings of wealthy tenant farmers and cloth workers, with jetties, rare crown posts, and a wealth of fancy detail dating from the 14th to the 17th centuries. No. 39 is an especially good example of a cruck hall combined with a box-framed cross-wing, and dates mostly to the 14th century.

A cruck truss is clearly visible in the gable end of the hall, its blades rising in a triangle from the low stone plinth. It supported a steeply pitched roof with low eaves that survive at the rear but were raised at the front in the 19th century. Inside, to the left of the door, another cruck truss spanned the centre of the hall, with elbowed braces once forming a rough arch under the collar. Smoke from the open hearth blackened the timbers until the 17th century, when an upper floor was inserted and a chimney built, with bread oven bulging from the gable. Beyond the central truss is a cross-passage with doorways to front and rear.

An arched doorway leads through from the passage into the side of the cross-wing. This had two storeys right from the start, with long three-bay rooms, now divided, on each floor. The upper floor rests on heavy 6 in (15 cm) joists, typical of the early date, and the room above was open to the roof. There are no crucks here, but simple collar and tiebeam trusses, clasped purlins and steep curved windbraces. The bare

The Queen's Head, Crowmarsh Gifford. CM

39 The Causeway, Steventon. CM

comfort of the wing was later improved by a side chimney, probably added in the 16th century, when a front room with Tudor arched doorway was partitioned off on the ground floor. A 15th-century kitchen (?) bay, once slightly detached, and a lower 17th-century extension were built on at the far end.

This straightforward explanation ignores a perplexing contrast between the rough-and-ready hall and the grand cross-wing, with its fine cusped bargeboards and showy cross-bracing. An awkward join between the two suggests a possible difference in date, but both are built of the same slight

timbers and have 14th-century features. Was the wing built in a superior way simply because of its higher status? Was it added on in a period of prosperity? Or could the hall even be a later rebuild when times were hard? Happily for the amateur sleuth, the question remains unanswered.

4

Country Houses and Castles

It is not hard to see why this area is so gloriously endowed with country houses. Fine landed estates provided a ready income and a sound long-term investment, and the area became particularly attractive as ready access to London grew ever more desirable. It was London, of course, that provided the model for the quality and variety of building styles in the area, as country seats strove to follow city fashions.

Royal influence goes back to 1066 and the strongholds of Norman domination. **Windsor Castle** (40, BE) has retained its royal link, but less obvious today are the royal origins of Rockingham Castle (N). Dramatically sited above the Welland Valley, it too was first built by William the Conqueror on a motte-and-bailey plan. Other Norman castles have almost completely disappeared, Northampton's beneath the railway, Oxford's into the prison. The area was not a frontier one, and disuse has left us only fragments and earthworks. There are, however, a number of smaller, later castles that survive in part. Barnwell (N), said to date from 1266, is a very early example of a square courtyard plan with round corner towers, a smaller version of which can be seen at **Donnington Castle** (35, BE). Early 14th-century gatehouses survive from similar castles at Boarstall (BU) and Bampton (O).

Broughton Castle (30, O) is more a manor house with fortifications than a fully fledged castle, and is considerably less forbidding than the great blank medieval walls of Drayton House (N). In both these houses the primary concern was living space, at first protected but later extended and embellished without fear. The great hall is found elsewhere without defence and continued to serve as the heart of the house. Early 16th-century examples can be seen from the park at Fawsley (N), where there is a magnificent oriel window, and in much restored form at Dorney (BU). Here there is also an upper end with parlours

and chambers, and a more basic service end, while at Chenies (BU) there is a lodgings range of *c*.1530 with splendidly elaborate brick chimneys. By the late 16th century these traditional elements had been moulded into the Elizabethan E- or U-plan, as at Mapledurham (O), or Castle Ashby (N). At Canons Ashby (N), a courtyard plan evolved, and it was this plan that was formalised at **Chastleton House** (31, O).

Deene Park (34, N) also grew round a courtyard but in the process acquired some fascinating Renaissance detail. It finds parallels in contemporary work of the 1570s at **Kirby Hall** (36, N) and Holdenby (N), the former 'prodigy' house, now reduced to a few fragments, that was built for Elizabeth's chancellor, Sir Christopher Hatton. Classical taste at court, in particular that of former courtiers of the Protector Somerset, must have provided the inspiration. A similar case is the appearance at Broughton Castle of classical stucco decoration of the type used at Henry VIII's long-vanished palace of Nonsuch.

The fashion for classicism gathered momentum at the Stuart court during the early 17th century, and influenced local landowners to build or remodel in the style of Inigo Jones. There are claims that he designed both the screen at Castle Ashby and the Stoke Park Pavilions (N), where curving colonnades quote from the villas of Palladio. More certain is the employment of Jones's pupil, John Webb, at Lamport (N). Provincial versions of the style can be found at Milton (O) and Princes Risborough (BU).

From the Restoration onwards there are countless houses of the elegant box type that seems so quintessentially English. In fact they owe much to the French and Flemish experiences of the court in exile. **Ashdown House** (27, O) and **Wotton House** (41, BU) are probably by William Winde, as was the original Cliveden (BU). Wren supervised the accounts at Winslow Hall (BU), and may

Blenheim Palace. AL

41

Chastleton House. ES

have contributed to the design of Fawley Court (BU). The style is alertly upright but regular, and was soon enlivened by Baroque flair. A pedimented centre-piece breaks up through the facade at Kingston Bagpuize (O), while parapets thrust skywards at **Chicheley Hall** (32, BU). More stunningly Baroque are the magnificent flourishes of **Blenheim Palace** (29, O), the compact force of Hawksmoor's Easton Neston (N), and the dense sculptural richness of

Talman's new work at Drayton, tightly packed with scrolls, busts and pediments.

The Palladian reaction of London's intelligensia was slow to take hold in the face of such exuberance. Kent's Wakefield Lodge at Potterspury (N) is unusually austere for the area, while **West Wycombe Park** (39, BU) has all the experimental idiosyncrasies of its dilettante owner. Truly professional Palladianism did not become popular until later in the 18th century, as at **Basildon Park** (28, BE) or Buscot (O). Instead a more informal approach was preferred, either keeping to the safe and well-tried box, or dabbling with a little Rococo ornament. **Claydon House** (33, BU) boasts superb examples of this in rocaille, Gothick and Chinese vein.

Gardens presented even more scope for architectural fancy, and this area has some of the best. Fascinating glimpses of the 17th-century formal gardens at Hartwell (BU) are provided by paintings in the County Museum at Aylesbury, but in several cases outstanding gardens have themselves survived to illustrate 18th-century principles of design. The classically staged landscape at Rousham (O), by Kent, is one of the earliest of its type and is little altered, while **Stowe** (38, BU) went on to develop idealised nature on the grandest of scales.

The hall at Mentmore Towers, before the sale of 1978. RCHME

Landscapes at Blenheim and Wotton were likewise remodelled by Capability Brown, as was West Wycombe by one of his pupils. Bridgeman's earlier work at Cliveden survived to become the basis for a formal Victorian garden.

A Thames-side situation, even without Cliveden's spectacular views,

The entrance front at Basildon Park. NT/JONATHON GIBSON

found increasing favour with owners seeking a pleasant retreat from the city. The villa at Harleyford (BU), by Sir Robert Taylor, is an early example, from 1755, but 19th- and early 20th-century houses were much more substantial. Danesfield, near Medmenham (15, BU), can be seen looming above the river as a chalky Tudor ghost, while its hidden neighbour, Wittington, is William and Mary. The Rothschilds preferred hunting country to river valley and peppered the Vale of Aylesbury with the pseudo-noble mansions of **Mentmore** (37, BU), Waddesdon, Ascott and Halton. These, like the vast house at Bear Wood (BE), are the ostentatious and commodious homes of the Victorian *nouveaux riches*.

More recent versions of the country seat evince greater subtlety. Lutyens built several houses in the area, including Deanery Garden, Sonning (BE) and Middleton Park (O), one of the last (1938) great mansions. Just as significant, especially in the London orbit, were the smaller villas of the late 1920s and 30s, such as High and Over at Amersham (8, BU).

27

Ashdown House, Oxfordshire
1660s?

SU 281820. 3 miles (5 km) NW of Lambourn, signposted off B4000

[A] NT

Ashdown is a delightful box of a house. Built of local chalk, it stands like a creamy-white dolls' house in the middle of the Downs, neat, compact and strangely tall. It was designed as a hunting lodge rather than a mansion, and affords splendid views of the surrounding parkland from its high roof leads.

It was built for William, 1st Earl of Craven, probably soon after the Restoration. Craven had spent the Interregnum in Royalist exile and returned strongly influenced by the architectural styles of Holland and France. This led him to employ for his mansion at Hamstead Marshall the Dutch-born Sir Balthasar Gerbier and

Ashdown House. AFK

his pupil William Winde, a fellow exile. It is highly likely that these two also designed Ashdown, though Winde's straightforward style predominates.

Ashdown's design has parallels with houses by François Mansart, particularly with that at Balleroy in Normandy, but there were also exciting local leads to follow. In many ways Ashdown was similar to the house built by Sir Roger Pratt at nearby Coleshill in the 1650s, which tragically burnt down in 1952. Both houses had the same sense of classical order, imposed by quoins, string courses, plinth and cornice, and both had the same hipped roofs, with tall chimneys, balustraded leads and cupolas. Both also relied for dramatic effect on their windows, but with very different results: tightly spaced end windows at Coleshill made a long facade satisfyingly compact, whereas the careful graduation to small top windows helps the facade at Ashdown soar upwards.

Although Winde had used small service pavilions elsewhere (possibly at Wotton (41, BU), for example), those at Ashdown seem less substantial than the main block and may well be an afterthought. Accommodation in the main block was certainly limited, despite the use of the compact 'double-pile' plan so favoured by Pratt. A quarter of its square, and the only part now open, is

taken up by the splendidly massive chestnut staircase which provides such an impressive ascent to the roof leads.

The pictures on the staircase walls tell of the romance of Ashdown. Craven is said to have consecrated the house to Elizabeth, sister of Charles I, whose winter reign as Queen of Bohemia ended in a life of poverty-stricken exile. Craven became her selflessly devoted champion, and possibly intended Ashdown as a country retreat for her. Sadly she died in his house in Drury Lane in 1662, leaving him her collection of antlers and pictures, before Ashdown could ever have been finished.

28

Basildon Park, Berkshire
1776–84

SU 610781. 7 miles (11 km) NW of Reading, between Streatley and Pangbourne. Signposted to W of A329

[A] NT

Basildon Park is one of the two important Palladian houses in this area to be featured in this book. Whereas the other house, West Wycombe Park (39, BU) was the work of a dilettante, Basildon Park demonstrates the style as perfected by a true architect. It was designed by John Carr of York for a former Yorkshire gentleman, Sir Francis Sykes, and financed by a fortune made in the East India Company.

The house is a beautifully balanced Palladian composition in Bath stone, dominated by a three-storey central villa with typical ground-floor rustication and pedimented portico. Less usual is the loggia recess behind the portico, also used by Carr at Constable Burton, Yorkshire. It was probably inspired by Italian examples such as Palladio's Villa Emo at Fanzolo. To either side of the villa are two-storey service pavilions flanked by linking courtyards with single-storey screen walls. The whole is a series of clear-cut elements tied together by the pyramidal composition and the repeated motifs of first-floor balustrading.

As usual with English Palladian buildings, the entrance presents a problem. Front doors do not go well below porticoes, and in any case the reception rooms are all grandly set on the first floor. Carr's solution here was to place a symmetrical pair of winder stairs behind the ground-floor arcade. The ascent from low Doric lobby to spacious Ionic loggia is ingeniously elegant, but a trifle cramped in comparison with the scale of the house. It also contrasts with the impressive stature of the great central stair hall, formerly vaulted and lit by thermal lunette windows. Here a splendid stone staircase with delicate wrought-iron balustrade winds in a leisurely way up to the heavy arcade of the vaulted bedroom passage. What with the adjacent flights for family use and the servants' tiny spiral, the staircase arrangements are one of the most fascinating features at Basildon.

Early 18th-century Palladian houses can be almost as severe inside as they are outside, but in this late example the interiors are softened by the Adam style. Delicate plaster ceilings are based on designs published by George Richardson, a former employee of Robert Adam, and feature husk garlands, Neoclassical motifs and cross-stitch ribbing. Griffins abound, especially in the plaster-panelled hall. Not all the rooms are complete, however. Some,

Basildon Park, the portico stairs. NT/JB

such as the Octagonal Drawing Room, were finished by J B Papworth in the 1840s, while others suffered during and between the First and Second World Wars. Original details have been supplemented with fittings from Panton House, Lincolnshire, also by Carr and now demolished. The restoration was carried out in the 1950s by Lord and Lady Iliffe.

29
Blenheim Palace, Oxfordshire
1705–1730s

SP 441160. At Woodstock, 7½ miles (12 km) NW of Oxford, off A44

[A]

Nothing in the country, not even its sister at Castle Howard, is quite so magnificent as Blenheim Palace, birthplace of Winston Churchill.

Blenheim Palace, the north portico. BLENHEIM PALACE

Ostensibly it was built as the gift of Queen Anne and the nation to John Churchill, Duke of Marlborough, in gratitude for his great victory at Blenheim. In fact it was not so much a home as a monument to Britannia, who stands high above the entrance. Perhaps it also stood proxy for the royal palace that the Stuarts lacked the cash and confidence to build. Kensington and Wren's work at Hampton Court are small fry in comparison.

Suitable grandeur was achieved only by ironic homage to Marlborough's vanquished foe, Louis XIV. The hugely impressive perspective of the entrance front at Blenheim and the rather useless suites of great state rooms, owe much to Versailles. They were not, however, a servile copy, but the work of two of the most imaginative geniuses in English architecture. Sir John Vanbrugh, playwright turned architect, was responsible for the grand conception, while Nicholas Hawksmoor (see All Souls College, Oxford (66, O), saw to the practicalities. Their palace may not be as vast as Versailles, but it is more satisfyingly unified and much more vigorously Baroque.

Four massive corner towers, with cornices like medieval corbel tables, give the palace all the aggressive assertion of a castle, while the wings between bulge with bays or porticoes. On the north front blind colonnades cave in towards the giant centre-piece, with the hall rising majestically above the richly carved pediment. To either side, further colonnades lead forwards to princely service courts: kitchens to the left, stables (incomplete) to the right. Crowning the whole is an exotic skyline of statuary, trophies and fantastic finials carved by the workshop of Grinling Gibbons. A theatrical set could not be more exciting.

Inside, a monumental stone hall with lofty clerestory leads through to the saloon and the symmetrical suites of state rooms. Painted decoration by Thornhill and Laguerre portrays the Duke in allegorical glory, while tapestries tell of his victories, and Rysbrack's huge marble tomb provides a fitting climax. This grand scheme, however, falls far short of the splendours

of Versailles. Much of it belongs to the penny-pinching years that followed the Duchess's fall from royal favour. Vanbrugh departed in a huff after constant complaints about his extravagance, and projected ceiling paintings for the long gallery were abandoned, perhaps happily, as we now have a noble room by Hawksmoor instead.

The glories of Blenheim extend beyond the palace to the surrounding parkland. This was originally laid out in formal parterres and avenues by Henry Wise, with Vanbrugh's Grand Bridge leading to the Column of Victory. The bridge is now not quite so grand as part of it is submerged, but the gracefulness of the lake – created by Capability Brown – makes it churlish to complain.

30
Broughton Castle, Oxfordshire
14th–16th century

SP 418381. 2½ miles (4 km) SW of Banbury, off B4035

[A]

Broughton Castle is not a castle, but a fortified manor transformed by successive owners into a comfortable mansion of fashionable refinement.

Its medieval history is complex but intriguing. The great hall, built in the early 14th century for Sir John de Broughton, is still there, but has an 18th-century 'Tudor' ceiling by Sanderson Miller. The entrance has also been changed around: archways and hatches show that the cross-passage and services were originally at the far end. The original upper end, to the left of the present entrance, has chambers and a chapel (licensed in 1331) above a series of vaulted undercrofts. These can only be entered from an extraordinarily tortuous set of richly vaulted passages and a narrow spiral stair. Were they planned for internal defence or might they just be an awkward link between hall and older cross-wing (perhaps with an earlier hall on the first floor)?

Defence was obviously of some

Renaissance fireplace in the Star Chamber, Broughton Castle. CL

concern. The site is moated and the gatehouse is 14th century in origin, although the embattled curtain walls date only to 1406. Also apparently defensive is the later 14th-century tower just discernible to the right of the garden front.

By the mid 16th century, Richard Fiennes and his family were more concerned with style and standards of living. The old kitchens were replaced by a new wing with spacious parlour and great chamber above. The entrance was altered and additional accommodation, including a long gallery, was added above the hall, with access via two rear stair turrets. All this was contained behind a newly symmetrical front with large regular windows and gables. The central chimney is dated 1554, while the oriel below is a rare early example of Renaissance court fashion. Its mullions are constructed as Ionic and Corinthian columns.

More extraordinary classical detail is found inside. The fireplace in 'Queen Anne's Room' has delightfully stumpy Corinthian columns and a Renaissance frieze, but is crudely carved. Heraldry dates it to the early 1550s. Far more sophisticated is the fireplace in the 'Star Chamber', which has a stucco overmantel with dryads dancing round an oak tree and an inscription from Ovid! The style is that of Rosso's work in the Galerie François I at Fontainebleau, emulated by his craftsmen for Henry VIII at Nonsuch. Very few instances of it survive.

Later decorative schemes were also very fine, with splendid plaster ceilings and panelling of 1599 in the west wing and 1760s Gothick in the long gallery. There were, however, intervals of neglect, and the present beauty of the house owes much to restoration work by George Gilbert Scott (son of Sir George) and recent owners.

31

Chastleton House, Oxfordshire
c.1603–9

SP 248290. 4½ miles (7 km) NW of Chipping Norton, signposted to SW of A44

[A] NT

When the National Trust acquired Chastleton House in 1991 they took on a first-class building in desperate need of basic maintenance. It was, however, still a real home, and visitors were treated to an intimate view both of its wonderful treasures and its obvious problems. Along with the tapestries and well-used four-posters (a recent visit found a cat fast asleep on an 18th-century quilt), went the cold, the damp patches and the flaking plaster. It was a revealing experience, unhampered by rope-ways and without a sniff of pot-pourri. May the trust preserve something of this spirit along with the building.

The house was built for Walter Jones, a wealthy wool merchant who bought the property in c.1602–3 from Robert Catesby of gunpowder plot fame. The new building belonged to the local Cotswold tradition with its limestone rubble walling and multi-gabled front, but its bold mass and novel plan suggest a surprising debt to the more northerly

The Great Chamber at Chastleton House. AFK

work of Robert Smythson. The strongly projecting bays hark back to Hardwick Hall (Derbyshire), while the side entry to the screens passage was used by Smythson at Burton Agnes (Humberside). This arrangement deprives the house of a grand entry, but allows exact symmetry by balancing the passage and oriel windows. These huge hall windows, however, disrupt the storey division in a most unSmythson-like manner. Although Smythson's influence is clear, it therefore seems unlikely that he had any direct hand in the design.

Inside, the house is made up of a circuit of rooms around a small courtyard, again not unlike Burton Agnes. An inventory taken after the death of Walter Jones in 1632 gives fascinating insight as to how the rooms were used. Kitchen, dairy and 'pastry' were housed in the basement, while on the ground floor there were the hall, great parlour, and family living rooms, including the nursery and one chamber. The great chamber, or main reception room, was on the first floor, along with family bedchambers and accompanying 'little chambers' or closets. On the second floor were the long gallery, more chambers and sleeping accommodation

for the servants. The stairs are housed in great towers at the sides of the house, the main east stairs with fine balustrading and pierced finials, the west service stairs with a plainly enclosed well.

Many of the rooms retain splendid Jacobean interiors with hangings, panelling, elaborate ceiling friezes, and armorial bearings set into the carved stone fireplaces. Most spectacular are the great hall, its screen richly crested with strapwork, and the great chamber, with arcaded panelling and a most elaborate pendant ceiling. The long gallery, which has a continuous plaster barrel vault completely covered with interlace and rosettes, is equally magnificent but perhaps more gracious.

32

Chicheley Hall, Buckinghamshire
1719–23

SP 905458. 2 miles (3 km) NE of Newport Pagnell, off A422

[A]

Chicheley is a Baroque curiosity. Building accounts prove that it was the work of Francis Smith of Warwick, and not Thomas Archer, as formerly supposed. However, correspondence and peculiar quirks of style suggest that the owner, Sir John Chester, played no small part in the design. The result is strikingly unorthodox.

The basic form of the house, with giant pilasters rising through the storeys, looks back to the style of Wotton (41, BU) and other houses of the early 1700s. At Chicheley, however, the main front is dramatised: the cornice and attic storey are swept up over the centre bays and a richly carved frieze is introduced; the pilasters are clustered so as to exaggerate the slight central projection, and arched windows with carved surrounds give the centre a sculptural weight. These windows derive from engravings of Italian Baroque buildings by Rainaldi and Soria, while the massive front pediment has been daringly added to a doorcase by Bernini.

The side and rear elevations are carefully subordinate. The side has Doric pilasters, as opposed to Corinthian at the front, and is more even in layout, with a quieter doorcase inspired by Borromini. The U-plan rear is even less pretentious and has Tuscan pilasters, of brick instead of stone. Large stair windows and squeezed-in niches distort the

composition and reinforce a general uneasiness of detail: the cornice is strangely thin, with no proper entablature; the corner links between the different facades are fudged, and the central parapet of the garden front disappears unhappily. Perhaps co-operation between architect and patron did not always produce smooth results.

Design problems apart, however, the house is beautifully constructed. Finely jointed brickwork and richly carved pale stone make for a very attractive exterior, while the woodwork inside is of exceptionally high quality. The oak staircase is a real gem. The treads and handrail are inlaid, the soffit elegantly scrolled and the balusters grouped in threes, one fluted, one twisted and one corkscrew. Many of the rooms have rich panelling that may well have been designed by Francis Smith. His particular trait was to frame each marble fireplace with giant pilasters. Not to be missed on the attic floor are the hidden library, with bookshelves concealed behind hinged panelling, and the steep stairs with split treads. These give access to the roof leads, from which the formal gardens laid out by George London could originally have been viewed. Only a U-plan canal now survives.

33

Claydon House, Buckinghamshire
1754–71

SP 718253. At Middle Claydon, 5½ miles (9 km) S of Buckingham, on minor roads signposted from the A41, A413 and A421

[A] NT

The great attraction of Claydon House lies not in any grand exterior, nor in its family mementoes of Florence Nightingale, but in the exuberant Rococo decoration and exquisite craftsmanship to be found inside.

The house as it now stands is the surviving remnant of a very grand scheme devised in emulation of Stowe (38, BU) for Ralph, 2nd Earl Verney. If the west front has the rather modest air of something lacking, it is because it originally served as side pavilion to a grandly domed rotunda with colonnaded portico, which, together with a matching ballroom pavilion, stood to the north of it. Both these buildings were demolished in 1792 after the earl's bankruptcy and death.

The restrained Palladian detail of the ashlar facade is probably the work of Thomas Robinson, the amateur gentleman architect who claimed to be working on the front in 1769. However, the building was well advanced by then and Luke Lightfoot was already decorating the state rooms. Lightfoot had been employed as carver-cum-surveyor since the mid-1750s, possibly implementing the earl's own ideas for the house, and he was undisputably responsible for the Rococo extravaganza inside. This is, amazingly, executed in carved wood rather than plaster. Robinson greatly disapproved of it and got Lightfoot dismissed in 1769. His are the rather more staid schemes of the saloon and library, with fine plaster ceilings by Joseph Rose, well known for his association with Robert Adam.

On the ground floor are three vast reception rooms, formerly serving as dining room, saloon and drawing room. The first, now the North Hall,

Chicheley Hall. CHICHELEY HALL

The Chinese Room, Claydon House. JB

establishes Lightfoot's Rococo tone with wildly scrolling foliage, exotic beasts and long-necked birds. Several motifs, including the uptilted curve of the doorcase pediments, have a distinctly Chinese flavour, reminiscent of Chippendale's *Director*. The classical ceiling trophy and Doric frieze do little to sober the frivolity.

Upstairs in the former bedroom suites, more of the same can be found, but this time in Gothick and Chinese styles. The Chinese Room is particularly playful. The doorheads become delicate pagodas with trellis fences, resting on scrolled jambs with Chinese heads. The dado has matching fretwork and the centre-piece is a fantastic alcove pagoda with lush foliage decoration.

Lightfoot's staircase relies not on thematic ornament but sheer quality of craftsmanship. The steps are beautifully inlaid all over, as is the handrail,

while the wrought-iron balustrade is composed of wonderfully delicate scrolls linked by husk garlands and wheatears. This is complemented by Rose's delicate plaster wall medallions, and crowned by his coffered ceiling with glazed dome.

34

Deene Park, Northamptonshire
16th century and later

SP 949927. 4 miles (6 km) NE of Corby, off A43

[A]

Deene Park was home to the 7th Earl of Cardigan, who led the charge of the Light Brigade at Balaclava. It deserves to be better known as one of the most romantic houses in the area, lovingly

'modernised' by almost every generation of the Brudenell family'since they took on the lease in 1514. Built of pale limestone ashlar, it grew and shrank in turn, engulfing a small medieval house and surrounding a delightfully intimate courtyard. The early 19th-century 'Tudor' of the south front happily failed to make everything too neat and tidy.

The most appealing parts of the house are those that are genuinely Tudor. To either side of the courtyard are ranges of lodgings and parlours with arched-light windows of the early to mid-16th century. The south-east wing is of similar date and can still be seen to the right of the south front, with battlements and buttresses as original, but 19th-century windows. The octagonal corner towers had high prospect rooms and ogee domes but were shortened in the 18th century. Inside this wing is a small chamber of *c.*1530–40, beautifully panelled with single linenfolds.

The Renaissance arrived at Deene in 1572, when Edmund Brudenell rebuilt the hall, complete with oriel window and porch. The window lights are still arched, in keeping with the older work, but there are charmingly rounded battlements and a porch with richly carved Ionic and Corinthian pilasters. Decorating the lower entablature are

delicate foliage scrolls and winged figures with heraldry of Edmund and his wife Agnes. The quality and choice of motifs are reminiscent of contemporary Renaissance work at nearby Kirby Hall (36, N) and Dingley, but the interior of the hall comes as a surprise. The magnificent hammerbeam roof smacks more of Hampton Court, and is perhaps consciously antiquarian, just like the hall at nearby Burghley, on the

Cambridgeshire/Lincolnshire border.

The striking bay window on the east front also bears the initials of Edmund and Agnes and has Ionic mullions, as at Broughton Castle (30, O). The work here is cruder than that of the hall, however, and puzzling in date. The bay was moved to its present site in the early 17th century by Thomas Brudenell, and the trefoil badges of his wife, Mary Tresham, appear carved into the lower panels. Thomas also remodelled the suite of state reception rooms, giving them splendid plaster ceilings with broad foliated ribs and pendants.

Alterations continued. The entrance range, with first-floor gallery and upright cross-windows, was built after the Restoration. Sash windows were introduced in the 18th century and replaced in the 19th, and an impressive suite of dining and drawing rooms was added *c.*1810–20. These lie behind the extended south front that gives such a misleadingly simple version of the 'Tudor' style.

35

Donnington Castle, Berkshire
1386

SU 461694. 1¼ miles (2 km) N of Newbury, signposted off B4494
[A] EH

The tall gatehouse of Donnington Castle stands high on a spur of land overlooking the River Lambourn and Newbury. This excellent site was already in use in 1386, when Richard de Adderbury, a royal chamberlain, was given licence to 'build anew and fortify'. His new castle of flint and stone probably replaced an earlier timber structure.

The regular plan of the castle is like a very modest version of Bodiam (East Sussex, also 1380s) and reflects the advances made by late 13th-century castles such as Harlech. Windsor's straggling baileys are replaced by a compact rectangular court surrounded by a curtain wall with towers. Foundations at Donnington show that the corner towers were round and the intermediate towers square. Built up against the curtain wall on the inside

Hall porch at Deene Park. RCHME

were the living quarters, of which only a few low walls and fireplaces remain. One side of the court is curiously canted, while the opposite side is dominated by the great gatehouse projecting in front.

The gatehouse is the strong point of the castle, obviating any need for a separate keep. It is three storeys high with a pair of even taller round towers either side of the entrance. Military features include the battlements, small slit windows, portcullis groove and narrow barbican, originally approached only by drawbridge. However, it was also a place of abode. Windows over the entrance arch, strings carved with heads and fleurons, and the decoratively cusped lierne vault all help to relieve its severity.

By the end of the 16th century the castle had been modified for a visit by Elizabeth I. The description in Camden's *Britannia* goes so far as to call it 'a small but very neat castle . . . having a fair prospect and windows in all sides very lightsome'. These must have been

Donnington Castle. AFK

regretted in the troubled times of the Civil War. Under the leadership of Sir John Boys, royalist forces withstood intermittent siege by the Parliamentarians from July 1644 right through to April 1646. The curtain wall and towers suffered much in the process, and there are large repairs in the gatehouse walls. Still faintly discernible around the castle are the rare star-shaped earthworks that were built as emplacements for royalist guns.

36

Kirby Hall, Northamptonshire
1570–1640

SP 926927. 3 miles (5 km) NE of Corby. Off A6116 or A43, on minor road between Corby and Deene

[A] EH

Do not go to Kirby to see family portraits and furnishings – the house is a roofless

Kirby Hall courtyard, with hall porch. JB

shell that lies quietly at rest after long neglect. Enjoy instead the freedom to explore every nook and cranny of a house glorious with rare Renaissance inspiration.

Built of the finest Weldon limestone, Kirby Hall was conceived on a grand scale for the surprisingly minor figure of Sir Humphrey Stafford. Its spacious courtyard, complete by his death in 1575, is unusually dignified for its date, with symmetry and regularity enhanced by ambitious classicism. Much of the decorative detail is influenced by the French Renaissance, but there is a daringly novel use of giant Ionic pilasters to articulate all four facades. Proportions may be somewhat awry, but the attempt to impose a classical sense of order is unmistakable.

This is especially true of the shorter end ranges. The north range has an arcaded loggia with close-set pilasters, those flanking the central entrance richly carved with Italianate colonnettes, acanthus and putti. To the south, a grandiose symmetry is achieved by matching the fenestration of the service end to that of the hall. The only clue to its humbler function is a row of blind lights that formerly masked an upper floor. Marking the central axis is the splendid three-tier porch, while to either side are even ranges of lodgings.

Such order and classicism put Kirby in the vanguard of English Renaissance architecture, and it would be fascinating to know who was responsible for it. The surveyor John Thorpe laid the first stone as a child in 1570, but it is more likely that his family were masons at Kirby rather than designers. Possibly the design was influenced by Sir Humphrey himself, inspired by the classical taste of the Somerset Protectorate. This taste was revived elsewhere in the locality in the 1570s, by William Cecil at Burghley (Cambridgeshire) and by the Brudenells at Deene Park (34, N). Also local and classical was Sir Christopher Hatton's great house at Holdenby, built as a 'shrine' for Queen Elizabeth and demolished as a white elephant in the 1650s.

It was Hatton who acquired Kirby after Sir Humphrey's death, and his successors who updated its Renaissance

Mentmore Towers, the entrance front. RCHME

image. Flemish strapwork gables and handsome bow windows of *c.*1600 gave way in 1638–40 to the pediments and pergolas (balconies) of 'artisan mannerism'. The remodelling of the north range in this style is possibly the work of Nicolas Stone.

37

Mentmore Towers, Buckinghamshire
1851–4

SP 902196. At Mentmore, 6 miles (10 km) NE of Aylesbury, via minor roads to S of A418

[A]

Mentmore Towers was built for Meyer Amschel de Rothschild by Sir Joseph Paxton and his son-in-law G H Stokes. Vast banking profits brought wealth but not respectability, and a country seat was needed to right the balance. Mentmore was chosen as good hunting country, the design was picked from a range of reputable historical models, and Paxton was employed to ensure that everything was up to date. Expense was no object.

Externally the building is a flagrant copy of Wollaton House, Nottingham, designed in the 1580s by Robert Smythson. Both houses have the same square plan with enclosed central hall and projecting corner towers, the same mannered Doric, Ionic and Corinthian orders, and the same fantastic skyline of strapwork gables and obelisks. Highclere Castle, in Hampshire, had earlier followed the same lead but far less fruitily.

In no way, however, did Wollaton suit 19th-century living standards. At Mentmore the ground floor is made taller to accommodate a luxurious succession of reception rooms, and the house sprouts an additional wing with a conservatory and suitably distant smoking room. This balances the facade of the service courtyard, now far too vast and complex to fit in the basement.

Opulent interiors made great show of Rothschild wealth. The hall is monumental. It has a first-floor gallery with massive arcading in Caen stone, and a large black and white marble fireplace said to come from Rubens's house in Antwerp. The grand imperial staircase is all of marble, and the reception rooms are in the 18th-century

French style, with gilt plaster ceilings. Some have boiseries from Parisian *hôtels*. Even the bathroom fittings are adapted from fine 18th-century French commodes.

There were eight bathrooms on the first floor, a remarkable number for the 1850s, demonstrating the new importance of modern conveniences. Mentmore was one of the earliest houses to have a hot water system and central heating via underfloor pipes. There was also a ventilation system and plenty of light. The hall doorways and south-east entrance had large sheets of plate glass (then newly available), and the hall roof was impressively glazed with technology fresh from Paxton's Crystal Palace.

The Rothschilds sold Mentmore Towers in 1978 – it became the British Capital of the Age of Enlightenment, and a centre for transcendental meditation. Sadly the contents of the house were not part of the transaction. For an idea of their sumptuous style it is best to visit another of the area's great Rothschild mansions, the fabulous French chateau that Baron Ferdinand built in 1874–89 at Waddesdon Manor (BU), now a National Trust treasure house.

38

Stowe Landscape Gardens, Buckinghamshire
18th century

SP 6737. 3 miles (5 km) NW of Buckingham, off A422

[A] NT

This is the most glorious landscape garden in the country. Praised by Rousseau and copied by Catherine the Great, it has always been a major tourist attraction. Its first guide book was published in 1744! The garden was created by Sir Richard Temple, Viscount Cobham, and his nephew Richard Grenville, Earl Temple. Under their supervision, Stowe led 18th-century gardening away from geometric formality, through classical arcadia, to idealised natural beauty.

Lord Cobham's first garden designer was Charles Bridgeman, employed

The Gothick Temple at Stowe. CM

1714–33. Bridgeman enlarged the existing terraced garden on a formal plan, with a canal on the north axis, a parterre, avenue and octagonal pond to the south, and a network of hedged paths to the west. The main diagonal paths converged on a rotunda by Vanbrugh, who also designed a fountain and the pair of Doric pavilions by the pond. The rotunda and pavilions still stand in modified form, but the formal plan was slowly naturalised.

By the late 1720s the garden had spread west to enclose an area of pasture and an irregular new Eleven-Acre Lake. These marked the beginnings of a less formal approach enhanced by Bridgeman's pioneering use of the ha-ha, which allowed unimpeded views of the parkland beyond. The corner bastions are perhaps a reference to Cobham's former military career. Within the new area were various eyecatchers. James Gibbs designed the Boycott Pavilions, originally with pyramid roofs, and a Fane of Pastoral Poetry, now re-sited. Overlooking the lake are the rustic Hermitage and the severely Palladian Temple of Venus, both by William Kent.

Kent's major contribution was the creation of the Elysian Fields in the 1730s. This is the most intimate part of the garden, designed as an informal arcadia in the manner of Claude and Poussin. A stream flows from a grotto into pools separated by a shell-bridge

dam, similar to that at Rousham (O). On the gentle slopes stand allegorical buildings alluding to Cobham's Whig ideology and anti-Walpole politics: one is a round, perfectly classical Temple of Ancient Virtue; another displays a pantheon of British Worthies with busts by Rysbrack and Scheemakers.

The political theme continued in the adjacent Hawkwell Field with the Temple of Friendship (1739) and the Gothick Temple of Liberty (1744–48), both by Gibbs. The latter is a fascinatingly robust version of early Gothic Revival, in brown ironstone with Saxon iconography. The field itself served as idealised farmland with picturesque haycocks and cattle, and could be viewed from a carriage drive which led to the Palladian Bridge. This is perhaps the most attractive building at Stowe, and was built in 1738, a year after the one at Wilton.

From *c.*1740 the garden became increasingly 'natural'. The Grecian Valley, constructed in 1746, presents a seemingly artless sweep of idyllic landscape with only a Neoclassical temple at its head. Elsewhere earlier paths and yew hedges gave way to expanses of lawn tastefully punctuated by clusters of trees. The new style was probably instigated by Richard Grenville, but left a permanent influence on Capability Brown, who was head gardener from 1741 to 1751.

Grenville continued the work in the 1760s and 70s, naturalising the octagonal pond, widening the south vista and extending it to a monumental Corinthian Arch. Grand avenues beyond and towards Oxford vastly enlarged the scale of the garden, while new buildings and remodellings by Borra and Valdre brought it architecturally up to date. The house followed suit, with embellishments by Vanbrugh, Leoni and Kent giving way to palatial facades by Valdre, Adam, and Thomas Pitt, Lord Camelford. The expense crippled family fortunes, and the house is now Stowe School.

39

West Wycombe Park, Buckinghamshire
1740s–1781

SU 829943. 2 miles (3 km) NW of High Wycombe, on A40

[A] NT

West Wycombe Park is the creation of Sir Francis Dashwood, notorious for the debauchery of his Hell-Fire Club, but respected as a founder member of the Society of Dilettanti. He was also a fellow of the Royal Society and of the Society of Antiquaries, and it was his gentlemanly interest in classical aesthetics that shaped this house and its grounds.

Fresh from a series of grand tours, Sir Francis set about remodelling the family mansion in the Italian manner of Palladio. To supervise the work, he chose John Donowell, former draughtsman to that ace Palladian, Lord Burlington, but the ideas were probably his own or those of his friends. The architecture shows the somewhat piecemeal approach of an amateur. Each front has a separate quality, and trees are necessary to disguise awkward corners.

The north front, of c.1748–50, is the most reticent. With its pedimented centre, rustication, and advanced end bays it is typical of the English Palladianism of Campbell and Kent. The east and south fronts, both in existence by 1755, are much more distinctive.

West Wycombe Park, south and east fronts. CM

Tacked on to the east front is a bold Doric portico, probably inspired by the Ionic porticoes of Palladio's Villa Rotonda – Sir Francis's uncle had already followed the precedent at Mereworth Castle in Kent. Even bolder are the two-tier colonnades of the south front, which derive from the Palazzo Chiericati at Vicenza. They are pure theatre, with plastered wooden columns that make an unorthodox leap straight from Tuscan to Corinthian.

By 1770, the date of the absurdly magnificent west portico, such architectural inexactitudes had become unacceptable. Classical motif was no longer to be modelled on Palladio but on accurate architectural investigation. The new portico was by Nicholas Revett and was based on his own drawings of the Greek Temple of Bacchus at Telos.

Inside the house there was a similar change from Italianate to Neoclassical. Florid Baroque ceilings were painted by Giuseppe Borgnis in the 1750s, with gods and goddesses after Raphael and Caracci. Henry Cheere supplied richly carved marble fireplaces. Then, in the 1760s, came ceilings in the manner of ancient Rome and Pompeii, by William Hannan. Finally came the splendid hall of c.1770–1, Greek-inspired with mock marbling and ceilings based on Robert Wood's *Ruins of Palmyra*.

Outside there is not only a landscape garden enhanced with temples by Revett, but the historic village of West Wycombe and the extraordinary Dashwood Mausoleum (illustrated in chapter 9). This vast flint edifice was built by Sir Francis in 1763–4, next to the church that he remodelled in equally eccentric fashion. Sadly these two buildings are now kept locked, but they command a dramatic hilltop site with lovely views over the park and down the A40 to High Wycombe.

40

Windsor Castle, Berkshire
c.1080 onwards

SU 968768. In Windsor, signposted from M4

[A]

Windsor Castle is all that a Hollywood set-maker could wish for – grim castle walls, a palace, cosy corners of domesticity, and a magnificent chapel with cloisters. It even comes equipped with queen, princes, guardsmen, clergy and crowds of extras. But, far more exciting than any celluloid sham, it is real, and results from nine centuries of royal use as stronghold, hunting lodge, family home and stage for state ceremonial.

The castle's earliest role was obviously a military one. William the Conqueror chose the site for its

Windsor Castle from the air. AL

dominance over the Thames Valley, and built a large earthen motte with an enclosure and two outer baileys, strung out along a high escarpment. His wooden defences were replaced in stone a century later by Henry II, who built a shell keep (the Round Tower) on the motte, and set square towers at strategic intervals along the bailey walls. The east wall, facing the town, was completed by Henry III in the 13th century, with the latest semi-circular towers, and the gateway was rebuilt by Henry VIII in 1509.

These medieval walls and towers still determine the form of the castle today, but their Romantic possibilities were recognised and elaborated in the late 18th and 19th centuries. The most notable alterations were carried out by Jeffry Wyatville for George IV. Between 1824 and 1831 the Round Tower was heightened, and Upper Ward (the far bailey) 'restored' with a delightful fantasy of traceried windows, arrow slits and machicolated battlements. Lower Ward remained more severe, especially after Salvin saw to the east end in the

1860s. His steep French roof on top of Henry III's Curfew Tower added the final touch to the castle's new picturesque skyline.

Inside, Lower Ward is almost entirely given over to the College of St George, founded in 1348 by Edward III in conjunction with his famous Order of the Garter. The magnificence of St George's Chapel (50, BE) dominates this area, in which there are also many humbler buildings that house the clergy. Canons' Cloister, behind the chapel, was built immediately after the college's foundation and is now a pleasing jumble of walks and chimneys. Horseshoe Cloister, much restored by Sir George Gilbert Scott in 1870, is more primly quaint, with ogee timbers and herringbone brick. The modest ashlar terraces opposite the chapel housed the Poor Knights, who attended services on behalf of their Garter counterparts.

The royal apartments are in the Upper Ward. Much of their genuine medieval detail disappeared in 1675–80, when Charles II had Hugh May turn everything Baroque, but the transformation was short-lived. Only three of Charles's splendid rooms, with ceilings painted by Verrio and panelling enriched by Grinling Gibbons, survive. The rest were re-Gothicised, luxuriously rather than authentically, for George III and George IV. Wyatville opened up the castle walls with new window tracery and a gateway into Home Park, provided enclosed cloister passages for shivering ladies-in-waiting, and re-decked St George's Hall with arches and armour. For his other state rooms, the architect settled on a gracious but less inspiring mix of gilt, flock and crystal. It was these 19th-century interiors that were so severely damaged by fire in 1992, the royal '*annus horribilis*'. While some people still sincerely mourn their loss, others are already relishing the opportunity to take this ever-adaptable fortress into the 21st century.

41

Wotton House, Buckinghamshire
1704–14 and 1820s

SP 685162. At Wotton Underwood, 8 miles (13 km) W of Aylesbury, on minor roads to S of A41

[A]

Partially rebuilt after a fire in 1820, Wotton House is still the closest thing we have to the original building that later became Buckingham Palace. The

Wotton House, drawn by Sir James Thornhill in the early 18th century.
BUCKINGHAMSHIRE COUNTY MUSEUM

Queen has lost out. Wotton is grand but not brash, and intimately English, not aloofly imperial. It has exquisite pavilions, exciting interiors by Sir John Soane, and an overgrown landscape by Capability Brown.

The drawing by Sir James Thornhill shows Wotton House as first built for Richard Grenville in the early 18th century. Parallels with the then Buckingham House suggest that the architect was William Winde. Both houses had similar plans, with curved links to flanking service pavilions, and a grand screen, providing a *cour d'honneur* in the Versailles manner. The type is also seen at nearby Chilton House, a more provincial example dating from the 1740s. At Wotton the screen has graceful stone piers and splendid ironwork by Thomas Robinson.

Wotton's pavilions happily survived the fire and provide a delightful air of domesticity. Hipped roofs with dormer windows, lanterns and tall chimneys are reminiscent of Ashdown House (27, O), but here they crown walls of warm red brick. Doric doorcases and tall windows with original mullions and transoms balance each other beautifully across the courtyard, and conceal the very different functions of coach-house (left) and kitchen (right).

The centre block was rebuilt by Soane with great respect for the

original. The same giant order of Corinthian pilasters was used, and the front doorcase is still dated 1704. The attic storey, however, was reduced to a hefty entablature with windows squeezed into the frieze, and all windows were converted to sashes.

Internally the changes were more drastic. Soane filled the house with ingenious vistas – through archways, along passages, and up to balconies. One arch, mysteriously floating above the hall fireplace, gives a fleeting view of the delicate stone staircase, while the chimney flue is diverted to provide hidden heating. Ornament is typically restrained, so as not to impinge upon the light airy spaces. Lesser rooms have shallow reed mouldings and beading, while grander ones indulge in a little honeysuckle or Greek fret.

The gardens at Wotton can usually be viewed only from a distance, but even a glimpse is well worth it. In the early 1700s George London, Royal Gardener, laid out the kitchen garden and the grand avenues leading north and south. The rest of the landscape park, with informal lakes, meadows and woodlands, dates to 1757–60, and is the work of Capability Brown. The picturesque buildings include a pair of Tuscan Pavilions, a round domed temple and a Turkey Building (Turkish, and not for poultry).

5

Churches and Chapels

This is not an area for devotees of the great abbey church or cathedral. Oxford's Christ Church (see 19, O), built to serve the Priory of St Frideswide, became a cathedral in 1546, but otherwise, monastic remains are few and insubstantial. Instead, we are offered an excellent collection of privately endowed chapels, including St George's (50, BE) at Windsor and the college chapels at Oxford (see chapter 6) and Eton (60, BE), and a rich heritage of parish churches. Some of these are bold and blatant, such as All Saints, Northampton (see 16, N), but many, such as All Saints, Hillesden (45, BU), hidden away in a remote village, or St John the Baptist, Shottesbrooke (52, BE) and St Peter, Gayhurst (57, BU), secreted in country parks, make marvellous 'finds'.

Two churches, All Saints, Brixworth (43, N) and All Saints, Wing (46, BU) are especially exciting for their rare evidence of very early Christianity. During the 7th century the area was converted in a two-pronged attack: the south by Birinus, who based his bishopric at Dorchester (O), the north by monks from the abbey of Medehamstede, at modern Peterborough. Brixworth was an early daughter house of Medehamstede, and is an amazingly ancient survival. Its brick tiles take us back to the Roman period, and its basilican plan to Early Christian Italy. A number of unusual features suggest that its 'northern' foundation was tempered, as has happened so often in this area, by 'southern' and other influences. Firstly there are the side chambers ('porticus'), which resemble those of Augustine's churches in Kent, and then there is the extraordinary crypt, similar in purpose to those built by Wilfrid at Hexham (Northumberland) and Ripon (North Yorkshire), but uniquely designed at Brixworth as a ring passage round the apse. The crypt at Wing, another rare basilica, temptingly suggests a 7th-century date for this church too.

From the later Saxon period comes the herringbone stonework and rounded stair turrets at Brixworth and Brigstock (N), but the most remarkable building of the 10th century to be found in this area is the tower at All Saints, Earls Barton (44, N), with its famous strip decoration and window balusters. Its massive, defensive character ties in with early Norman work, found in plainer form at the lovely church of St Bartholomew, Fingest (49, BU). In both cases the tower is at the west end, and may have doubled as nave. More elaborate churches had the tower in the centre, with nave and chancel to either side. This is the form found at Langford (O), where there are carved Saxon figures and strip decoration, and later at St Michael and All Angels, Stewkley (56, BU) and Iffley (O), both mid-12th-century churches with exceptionally lavish zigzag, chevron and beakhead ornamentation. The small but delightful church at Avington (BE), has more of the same.

Two Norman churches in Northampton (16, N) deserve a special mention: St Peter's is a grand town church with decorative arcading and coloured stone bands; Holy Sepulchre a round crusaders' church of sterner style. Scores of other churches go back as far, but few remain unaltered. At Burford (12, O), for instance, the west end and tower clearly retain 12th-century features, but the rest is greatly confused by additional aisles, transepts and chapels. Here these early accretions were unified by a magnificent remodelling in 15th-century Perpendicular, financed by the wool trade, but usually the process of transformation remained modest and gradual. More typical is the delightful mix of 14th-century window tracery and 15th-century pinnacles that disguise the earlier origins of St Peter ad Vincula, South Newington (58, O), better known for its outstanding wall paintings. Gradual alteration, however, makes for complex building history, so this

All Saints, Brixworth. AFK

chapter concentrates on churches that illustrate more clearly the distinctive phases of gothic development – Early English, Decorated and Perpendicular.

St Mary, Warmington (54, N) is an exceptionally fine church of the 13th century. It shows Early English lancet windows developing into simple tracery, and is highly decorated with dogtooth, intricate roll mouldings and clustered shafts. There is similar work at neighbouring Polebrook, and gaunt arcading in the same style not far away at Raunds. All three churches have early spires and herald the spire tradition that is such a feature of the Northamptonshire/north Oxfordshire stone belt. These early spires are distinguished by semi-pyramidal broaches that ease the transition from octagon to square tower top. In the 14th century these give way to a more elegant, recessed form, with ribs and crockets, as at Olney (18, BU) and Higham Ferrers (N). This last church is also well known for its extraordinary 13th-century porch, designed in a frenchified style akin to that of Westminster Abbey, and carved with delightful figured roundels – an extreme case of courtliness in the countryside.

During the 14th century, window tracery became more flowing, and carved decoration more elaborate. A supreme example is the choir at Dorchester Abbey (O), where one of the windows has tracery bars carved with foliage trails and statuettes that illustrate the Tree of Jesse. Spirited carving from this period is also a particular feature of a small group of north Oxfordshire churches, including those at Bloxham, Adderbury, Alkerton and Hanwell. This century was a time of beautification and church extension rather than new building. Shottesbrooke, an exception, is included here for its compact perfection.

Vast windows with grid-like tracery belong to the late 14th and 15th centuries, and the Perpendicular style. They appear to especial advantage at Hillesden and Lowick (N), and can be found, on a smaller scale, in almost every clerestory. The style was long-lived, and was given a great boost by the Oxford colleges, who derived it from

St Mary, Higham Ferrers. ES

royal sources – William of Wykeham had used royal masons from Windsor for his seminal work at New College (68, O) in the 1380s. The most fabulous Perpendicular buildings – the chapels at Windsor and Eton, and the great church of St Mary and All Saints, Fotheringhay (53, N) – were all direct royal commissions.

St Peter, Gayhurst. CM

After the chaos of the Reformation, London fashion took greater hold. There are delightful idiosyncrasies of the early 17th century, such as the fantastic pews at Rycote Chapel (48, O) and Langley Marish (BE), but then the sequence becomes more recognisably conformist. The barley-sugar porch columns at St Mary the Virgin, Oxford (70, O), reflect Laudian Mannerism of the 1640s, while the 'Wren' style appears in the 1670s and 80s at Willen (BU), by Robert Hooke, and at All Saints, Northampton, probably by Henry Bell. It was still around in the 1720s at Gayhurst, complete with sumptuous plasterwork and fittings, and in the 1750s at Daventry (N). By 1800, however, St Mary's, Banbury (O), was being rebuilt in a distinctly severe and Neoclassical manner.

Gothick Revival made a delicate impact in the 18th century, at Hartwell and Stony Stratford in Buckinghamshire and Wicken in Northamptonshire, but was taken more seriously in the 19th. To begin with, the economy-minded Church Commissioners favoured the plain Perpendicular of St Lawrence's, Hungerford (BE), and rarely tolerated the brave Early English of Theale (BE). Then, in the Victorian era, Gothic was given much more punch and purpose. The High Church enthusiasms of the Oxford Movement, and the spirit of Ruskin, fathered the amazing polychrome style of Butterfield (Keble College Chapel (67, O)) and G E Street (All Saints, Boyne Hill (42, BE)). Street, as Diocesan Architect, disseminated it throughout the Oxford area. Churches by H Woodyer, in Berkshire, and by Sir George Gilbert Scott, born and bred near Buckingham, are less aggressively historical, but also less eye-catching. They lack the excitement of more radical experiments of the time – S S Teulon's church of St James, Leckampstead (51, BE), A Blomfield's St Barnabas in Jericho, Oxford, and the unorthodoxly Byzantine St James at Gerrards Cross (BU), by Sir William Tite. The wonderful freshness of St Mary, Wellingborough (55, N), by Sir Ninian Comper, brings us into the 20th century.

It would be misleading to suppose that the area remained staunchly

Church of England. A quiet but persistent strain of Nonconformism is reflected in the peaceful domesticity of the **Friends' Meeting House, Jordans** (47, BU). Keach's Meeting House at Winslow (BU), also of the late 17th century, is even more modest, but equally worth a visit. There are many chapels of simple, Georgian-box design throughout the area, and a good selection of showier 'church' types from the late 19th to the early 20th centuries. Of these, the ovoid Congregational Chapel of 1875 at Wellingborough (N) is perhaps the most extravagant.

42

All Saints, Boyne Hill, Maidenhead, Berkshire
1854–65 and 1911

SU 877808. On Boyn Hill Road, left turn off A4, ¾ mile (1.2 km) W of Maidenhead town centre

[C]

The stripy belfry and spire of All Saints stand out high on the top of Boyn Hill, like a beacon of High Victorian righteousness. They draw you to a small complex built at the expense of a few high-minded ladies, the Misses Hulme and the Misses Lamotte, who foresaw the growth of a suburban parish here, and determined to provide for all aspects of its spiritual development. They began with a church, vicarage and school (1854–7), and added almshouses (1858) and infant school and clergy house (1859). The bell tower was not completed until 1865. The buildings, designed by George Edmund Street with 'more than ordinary success', were highly praised by the *Ecclesiologist* in 1854, and are fascinating today for their comprehensiveness of purpose and punchy High Church style.

Street grouped all the buildings except for the almshouses round a loose quadrangle. They are all made of red brick, with bands of black brick and creamy Bath stone, but each part is given a distinct, appropriate character. The church and tower, separate until the nave was extended in 1911 by Street's

All Saints, Boyne Hill, as illustrated in the *Builder*, 1860. BL

son, Arthur Edmund, dominate the north side of the quadrangle. On the east side is the vicarage, looking like a medieval manor house with buttresses and cross-wings. Its former offices and stables are hidden in the south-east corner behind a round stair turret, charmingly complete with spire, which turns the angle into the south range. Here there is the schoolmaster's house, and then long schoolrooms distinguished by steep gables, tapering chimneys and windows with wooden plate tracery. At the west end is the infant school, while the simpler domestic block at right-angles, with hipped dormers, is the clergy house. A gateway with a stepped Tudor parapet rounds off the whole and contributes to an appropriate sense of picturesque informality.

Street's polychrome style shows a debt to Butterfield's All Saints at Margaret Street, in Westminster, but the direct influence of High Church ritualism, as expounded by the Oxford Movement (see Keble College, Oxford (67, O)) and the Ecclesiological Society, becomes apparent inside the church. This sombre interior aims at all the holy richness of gothic catholicism. Decorated tracery is filled with stained glass by Hardman; patterned brick walls are broken by arcades with nailhead ornament; tightly detailed carvings by Thomas Earp of Lambeth enliven spandrels, font and pulpit. Most extravagant of all is the chancel, where the walls are densely patterned with stencilled arcading and richly coloured bands of brick. Yellow, green and purple glazes add to the usual red and black, and, on the east wall, alabaster competes with black enamel inlay. You may not like it, but you can hardly fail to be impressed!

All Saints, Brixworth, the nave, looking west. ES

enormous great church, with its walls still reaching right up to the top of the original clerestory, really be so old? Experts continue to argue, but there does seem to be a strong possibility that it is.

Structural evidence certainly tallies with an early date, as some features hark back to Roman methods of construction. The round arches of the clerestory windows and massive nave arcades are all made of narrow Roman tiles, and excavation has revealed floors of 'opus signinum', a hard mortar made with pounded brick. By contrast, the herringbone masonry of the tower and stair turret show up as 'only' 10th century, as do the chunky 'Saxon' balusters of the internal tower window. The latter are clearly an alteration, as they cut through the original gallery arch.

The plan form is even more significant, for All Saints is a rare basilican church, of the type mentioned by Bede. Its basic composition of entrance narthex, arcaded nave and apse, was inspired by the Early Christian basilicas of Italy, and is usually associated with those missionary bishops who had paid visits to or been sent by Rome. Here it may have been influenced by Wilfrid, the strong-minded Bishop of York, who was to die not far away in his monastery near Oundle.

43

All Saints, Brixworth, Northamptonshire
Late 7th century

SP 747712. At N end of village, 7 miles (11 km) N of Northampton, to west of A508

[C]

Standing in the nave of Brixworth church, you cannot but feel a sense of awe, for this is the grandest church of its period in the whole country. It takes us right back to the very distant and hazy times described by the Venerable Bede, when King Peada of the Middle Angles began the conversion of Mercia to Christianity. Peada established a monastery at Medehamstede (Peterborough), and this, according to 12th-century chronicles, set up daughter houses, including one at Brixworth, soon after AD 675. Can this

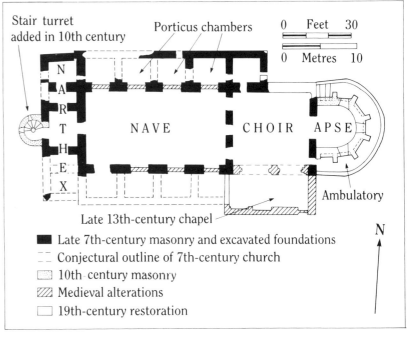

The Saxon church at Brixworth (after M Audouy). EH

The basilica plan may need a little interpretation. The narthex survives only as the base of the later Saxon tower (now topped by a 14th-century spire), but once extended to either side, as the small side arches show. The original west door now opens into the 10th-century stair turret. The nave and clerestory are much more complete, but the great arches have been blocked up. Excavation shows that they opened not into aisles but into side chambers, or 'porticus'. These were divided by cross-walls of very early if not contemporary date, and were possibly used for side altars. Bede describes the burial of St Augustine in a similar chamber at Canterbury.

The east end of the church was altered in the 15th century, when the triple Saxon arches that divided nave and choir were replaced by a single wide arch, and a chancel built in place of the original apse. Happily we now have the apse back again – it was reconstructed in 1864–5 by the Revd C F Watkins, who demolished the offending chancel with a confident enthusiasm that few would venture today. He based his rebuild on two surviving sides of the original polygon, and on excavations that revealed a sunken ambulatory or ring crypt. This was entered through two low archways in the east wall of the choir, and presumably allowed pilgrims a glimpse of a treasured relic. Strangely there is no firm evidence for a central crypt chapel, such as the one at Wing (46, BU).

44

All Saints, Earls Barton, Northamptonshire
10th century and later medieval

SP 852637. In village centre, 7 miles (11 km) E of Northampton, off A45 or A4500

[C]

The 10th-century tower at Earls Barton is a classic of Saxon architecture, but a very idiosyncratic one. It has the strange long and short quoins that distinguish

All Saints, Earls Barton. The Saxon tower. AFK

many other Saxon buildings, and an impressive array of chunky stone balusters in its bell chamber. These balusters are so thick, and so closely packed, that there is scarcely any opening between. Even more excitingly, the tower is decorated with narrow stone strips (lesenes) that divide the walls into tall panels, and make arch and criss-cross patterns. It is all delightfully unsophisticated. The strips were probably inspired by traditional decoration on timber buildings, and look like matchsticks, stuck on with great enthusiasm but scant respect for the massive bulk of the stone walls.

The tower is truly massive, and may have been built so soundly because it

served more than the one purpose. The ground floor, with its arched west door, probably served as the nave of the church, perhaps with a narrow chancel extending eastwards on the site of the present nave. A similar arrangement survives at Fingest (49, BU). However, the stage above is reminiscent of a refuge tower, designed for defence, with a high narrow entrance and tiny windows. Even the 'nave' windows, grand on the outside with balusters and shallow arches, are set very high up and are mostly blocked by slabs with cross-slits. The bell chamber lights, way up out of danger, are much more generous, and no doubt doubled as a look-out. The Normans also saw the defensive possibilities of the site, and built a motte immediately to the north.

By the 12th century, the Saxon building was no longer regarded as a proper church. A new nave and chancel were built to the east, and the church was extended again in the 13th and 14th centuries. Its most eye-catching features are the elaborately carved details added in the late 12th century: the chancel has blind arcades and sedilia superbly adorned with chevron; the tower arch has lots of re-set billet; and the south door is resplendent with zigzag and spiral columns and chevron and beakhead decoration.

45

All Saints, Hillesden, Buckinghamshire
c.*1493*

SP 685287. At far end of village, 3 miles (5 km) S of Buckingham. Hillesden is signposted from minor road between Gawcott and Grendon Underwood

[C]

Hillesden church is a finely wrought Perpendicular jewel. Except for the mid-15th-century west tower, it was rebuilt all of a piece, in proud ashlar, shortly after 1493. It owes its original splendour to the patronage of Notley Abbey, and its present excellent condition to Sir George Gilbert Scott, who lovingly restored the fabric in 1874–5. Scott had admired the church since childhood, when he had lived nearby at Gawcott, and he paid personally for work on the porch vault and four of the pinnacles.

It is easy to see why he liked the building so much, for it is all lightness and delicacy. The nave has a lantern clerestory, continuously glazed but for the slenderest of mullions, and the main windows become larger and ever more intricate as they go eastwards. Moulded battlements and spiky pinnacles make for a cheery skyline, and two exquisite details catch the eye. The first is the north porch, with its dainty fan vault and panelled walls. The second is the octagonal stair turret, which rises from vestry to study, then up again to finish

All Saints, Hillesden. The nave, looking through into the chancel and north chapel. CM

in a coronet of traceried battlements, pinnacles and arching buttresses.

The interior is kept light and open by graceful arcades of four-centred arches. Like the windows, they are carefully graded to create a hierarchy of structure, with taller transept arches and even taller chancel arch. Mouldings and wall surfaces also become more elaborate. Plain ashlar gives way to traceried wall panels, and the chancel revels in a glorious frieze of carved stone half-angels. These still have traces of their original colouring, and the four on the east wall play organs or lutes.

The flat ceilings with wooden ribs

strike a slightly discordant note, and some of the fittings are over-restored – the linenfold panels are very spruce and the canopy over the screen is too good to be true – but there are some lovely touches. A window in the south transept illustrates the life of St Nicholas in brightly stained glass of c.1500, and the Denton family pew has later 17th-century panels with fine strapwork and pedimented cartouches. There are Denton tombs, including one by Henry Cheere, and what are reputed to be bullet holes in the church door. These were supposedly inflicted during the family's defence of the royalist cause in the Civil War.

46

All Saints, Wing, Buckinghamshire
7th?–10th century and later

SP 880226. In Church Street, Wing, 7 miles (11 km) NE of Aylesbury, to N of A418

[C]

Saxon churches are tantalising because so little can be said about them with any certainty. This church at Wing is a fascinating case in point. It is an outstanding building of the same basilican type as Brixworth (43, N), apparently complete and of a piece. Historians would have us believe that it was built in the 10th century, perhaps by Wing's royal landlady, Aelfgifu, who died in AD 975. Yet close inspection reveals that its building history is very far from simple, and might take us further back than first seems possible.

Doubts begin with the nave. Its massive arcades have been assigned to the 10th century, perhaps because the wide round arches have a Norman feel about them. Yet they are cut, unmoulded, out of the wall thickness just like the much earlier ones at Brixworth. Only the impost blocks are slightly different. Whether there were 'porticus' divisions beyond is difficult to say – there are no obvious traces even in the Saxon north aisle – but above the western arches there are high blocked doorways that once gave access to a gallery. Could it be that all this is 7th century? The only features that are definitely not are the very wide chancel arch and the window above, with its stone baluster.

The polygonal apse seems even more undeniably 10th century, at first. Externally it is finely decorated, with narrow raised strips (lesenes) similar to those at Earls Barton (44, N). Here they are arranged to form a blind arcade with pilasters at the corners and gablet motifs above. Three low arched windows, one enlarged into a doorway, light a vaulted crypt below, revealing an ambulatory or ring passage as at Brixworth, but with side recesses and a central chapel for relics. This was no doubt the shrine mentioned in Lady Aelfgifu's will, but it sits oddly below the elaborate walls of her apse above. Its openings do not tally with the 10th-century arcading, and its vaults have been inserted into an earlier structure. Perhaps what we have here after all is a 7th-century building with a 10th-century facelift?

Other features are obviously later medieval. The south aisle was rebuilt in the 14th century, the tower, porch and clerestory added in the 15th. This involved a splendid new roof over the nave, with carved angels spreading their wings in the roof trusses and wooden saints, kings and musicians crouching as corbels. Another attraction is the chastely classical monument to Sir Robert Dormer, in the north aisle. It is dated 1552 and is a rare example of early Renaissance work, as found also at Broughton Castle (30, O). It has no effigy, just a sarcophagus with ox skulls and fruit swags, and a canopy supported by fine Corinthian columns.

47

Friends' Meeting House, Jordans, Buckinghamshire
1688

SU 974910. 2 miles (3 km) E of Beaconsfield, on minor road between A40 and Chalfont St Giles, by turning to Chalfont St Peter

[C]

The Meeting House at Jordans has a wonderful sense of peace and serenity. It stands at a remote crossroads, far away from worldly concerns, with all the gentle modesty of a late 17th-century home. There is no fancy stonework or window tracery, just a simple box of chequer brick, with cornice and hipped roof, wooden mullions and shutters. In front are neat lawns and immaculate flower beds. From the lawns, however, rise small headstones, one marking the burial in 1718 of no less a person than William Penn, founder of Pennsylvania.

There are, of course, reasons for its reticence. Quakerism had been founded by George Fox in the mid-17th century as a reaction against High Church paraphernalia. Everyone might find the 'Inner Light' of Christ in their own soul, and had no need of church or clergyman in order to worship. A meeting place had only to offer simple shelter and a sense

All Saints, Wing, with Saxon arcading round the apse. AFK

Friends' Meeting House, Jordans. AFK

48

Rycote Chapel, Oxfordshire
15th and 17th century

SP 667046. Signposted off A329
between Thame and M40 Junction 7.
(Southbound traffic should leave
M40 at Junction 8 and first follow
A40)

[A] EH

There is a sense of unreality about
Rycote Chapel. Consecrated in 1449, it
was built of fine ashlar on the scale of a
parish church, with a tall west tower and
continuous nave-cum-chancel. In fact it
was a mere chantry chapel, and stands
isolated in the grassy grounds of a
mansion that was largely burnt down in
1745. You might expect to find it full of
family tombs, but Richard
Quatremayne, who built it, and later
owners, preferred more ostentatious
burial in the church at Thame. Instead,
you are confronted with a series of
outlandish fittings that speak more of
fantasy than devotion.

Early in the 17th century the Norreys
family decided that the chapel, already

of community. Simplicity was honest,
but also safely unobtrusive, for early
Quakers were persecuted with fines and
imprisonment. Local Friends had been
meeting illegally at Old Jordans Farm,
higher up the hill, since the late
1660s, but it was not until 1688, when
a frightened James II made his
Declaration of Indulgence, that they felt
free to build a proper meeting house. It
was John Penington, a relative by
marriage of William Penn, who acquired
the site.

The meeting house looks now much
as it did when first built. Two tall cross-
windows light the meeting room, while
smaller windows to the right mark the
two storeys formerly used as a
caretaker's cottage. This cottage part
still has a cosy kitchen fireplace, but
could always be opened up, by the
removal of wooden screens, to provide
extra meeting space. It now serves
permanently as lobby and gallery, and
the caretaker lives in a rear extension
built in 1958.

The meeting room itself is very plain,
with whitewashed walls and brick floor.
Simple wooden dado panelling, probably
added in 1733, incorporates a long
bench along each side, and rises, at the
far end, over a raised bench for the
elders. Occasional pegs protrude for
hats. The open-back benches, formerly
arranged to face the elders, are of later
date, but some of the early ones have
been placed in the gallery. The complete
absence of fuss or pretension make the
room a perfect place for quiet
contemplation.

One of the Norreys family pews in Rycote Chapel. EH

resplendent with 15th-century pews and choir stalls, needed some redecoration. They had the waggon roof repainted, with red marbling on the ribs and gold stars stuck on to the blue panels between. They also had a gallery built across the west end, on Ionic columns darkened to look like ebony. The sturdy columns of the gallery balustrade, and the elaborate split-baluster decoration on the piers, were similarly treated, while the ceiling below was painted as a fairy-tale blue sky, with bubbly white clouds and more gold stars.

Alterations to the rood screen were equally elaborate. A new arcade with strapwork cresting was set on top of the lower 15th-century panels, and an amazing pair of covered box pews were built in front. The left pew has the same arcading as the screen, and is exquisitely decorated inside – it has another cloudy sky, and wooden panelling painted with scenes and figures in oval frames. The roof of the pew served as a gallery, probably for musicians, and had pierced fretwork panels, so delicate that many had to be renewed during a general restoration early this century. The right-hand pew was added later, perhaps for a visit by Charles I in 1625, and has a splendid ogee canopy with crocketed ribs. In front of it stand the pulpit and reader's desk.

The early 17th-century reredos now hangs in the tower. It was ousted in 1682 by a superb Baroque replacement with beautifully carved festoons of naturalistic fruit and foliage in the pediment. Elegantly twisted altar rails separate sophistication here from the earlier exuberance of the rest of the church.

49

St Bartholomew, Fingest, Buckinghamshire
Early 12th century and later

SU 776911. At Fingest, 5½ miles (9 km) W of High Wycombe, on minor roads between A40 and A4155 [C]

Fingest church is unforgettable, both for its simple Norman bulk and the remote

St Bartholomew, Fingest. AFK

beauty of its setting. Its massive tower stands guard over a small cluster of houses down in the valley bottom, and the Chiltern Hills, with their hanging beechwoods, shut out the rest of the world. Only the rooks, cawing in the beech trees that line the churchyard, disturb the peace.

The tower dominates everything, just as the earlier one at Earls Barton (44, N) does. At Fingest, however, there is no fancy decoration. The 12th-century flint and rubble walls are plainly covered with rough plaster, and look very, very solid. They are nearly 4 ft (1.2 m) thick, and were pierced in the lower stage only by tiny round-headed windows. (The larger west window, with plate tracery, was inserted early in the 13th century.) Perhaps defence was an important consideration. At the safe height of the bell chamber the building suddenly becomes more gracious. Here, there are two large openings in each side, with round arches and roll-mouldings, columns and cushion capitals, and even a little billet. 14th-century twin gables rise like eyebrows above.

Twin roofs were a sensible way of covering the great girth of the tower. At 27 ft (8.2 m) square, it is wider than the rest of the church, and provides a considerable proportion of the internal space. It is possible that it originally served as a nave, and that the present nave was built as a chancel. This could

account for the very wide arch between the two, and again takes us back to the plan form of Earls Barton.

Whatever its intended function, the nave has the same simple massiveness as the tower. Inside, it feels like a tunnel: tall, narrow and dark. Originally it must have been even darker, for the thick north wall has only one small window. More light was provided by enlarging the corresponding south window in the 14th century and by adding another to match in the 19th. High above the tunnel is a suitably unfussy roof of the 14th or early 15th century, with windbraces and wide arch-braced collars.

The Norman church probably stopped at the east end of the nave, for the present chancel was not built until the 13th century. It never had a proper chancel arch, but the heavy, dark-stained screen of 1867, appropriately solid, makes a satisfying substitute.

50

St George's Chapel, Windsor, Berkshire
1475–1528

SU 968769. In Lower Ward of Windsor Castle (40, BE) [A]

St George's Chapel is one of the most splendid Perpendicular monuments in

65

St George's Chapel, Windsor, the west end.
AFK

England. Edward IV began it in 1475, determined to outdo the great chapels of his former rival, Henry VI, at Eton (60, BE) and Cambridge. The imposing grid of vast Perpendicular windows, flying buttresses and slender pinnacles was probably the work of his master mason, Henry Jenyngs. The magnificent vaults of the nave and chancel, with their branching ribs, star-patterned liernes, and rich heraldic bosses, were not completed until 1509, by William Vertue and John Hylmer. A more majestic setting for royal worship and ceremonial could hardly be imagined.

The trappings of royal pageantry are at their most fabulous in the choir. Here the sovereign and his/her Knights of the Garter have always sat, in stalls exotically carved with miniature scenes and grotesques, below canopies that rise in fantastic tiers of flamboyant woodwork. The occupant of the stall is identified by the dummy bust set on top, complete with helm, mantling and sword, by the banner hanging above, and by a small gilded plate. Most of the carving was directed by William Berkeley in 1478–85, but some of the scenes show frock coats lurking amidst the medieval jerkins. These newer stalls were made in the late 1780s by Henry Emlyn, for George III's excess of knightly sons.

As well as a home for the Order of the Garter, the chapel was, inevitably, built to serve a chantry foundation. Shortly after founding the order in 1348, Edward III established the College of St

George. Eight times a day, its clergy and choristers were to conduct services for the founder's soul, in an older chapel that Henry III had begun in 1240. The fine doorway to this building survives in the east wall behind the choir, and there are more of its arches in Dean's Cloister, which Edward III remodelled. He also built Canons' Cloister to house the collegiate clergy. The present chapel would have remained incomplete but for further chantry endowments, served by side chapels in the polygonal transept and end bays. The chapel at the north-east corner has appropriate prayers inscribed on the front wall.

The presence of royals at rest within the chapel might pass almost unnoticed. Henry VI, Edward IV, Henry VIII and Charles I (with head) all lie here, but the only substantial royal monument is Matthew Wyatt's romantic vision of Princess Charlotte rising from her shroud. George III loved Windsor and had a burial crypt excavated below the old chapel of Henry III. This chapel, usually closed to public view, was itself transformed by Victoria into yet another lavish memorial to Prince Albert. Its decoration rivals that of the Royal Mausoleum, Frogmore (96, BE).

51
St James, Leckhampstead, Berkshire
1859–60

SU 439759. At Leckhampstead, midway between Wantage and Newbury, to W of B4494

[C]

This is a completely new Victorian church, built to save the parishioners the mile-long tramp to a chapel of ease at Chapel Farm. It was paid for by public subscription and had perforce to be cheap. The architect, Samuel Saunders Teulon, rose to the challenge with his usual idiosyncrasy. The flat polychrome style may remind you of Ruskin, Butterfield and Street (Keble College, Oxford (67, O) and All Saints, Boyne Hill (42, BE)), but the spatial arrangements have a novelty that is all Teulon's own.

Externally, the church is built of local knapped flint with a rigid pattern of red brick bands. There are few expensive stone dressings, and no fussy buttresses or pinnacles to interrupt the wall plane. Even the Decorated window tracery plays a subordinate role. Much more important is the massing of the building, suggesting a complex hierarchy of parts over a very simple ground plan. The steep nave roof sweeps down over the single aisle, but is dramatically broken by a high cross-ridge, with 'transept' windows looming out of huge dormer gables. A simple wooden bell turret marks the 'crossing'. The sense of upward climax and aspiration seems far beyond the expectation of such a modest building.

The inside comes as rather a shock, as it is economically but aggressively faced with red and white brick in vivid diaper patterns. Black bricks emphasise the highlights. This colour scheme is used to distinguish the various parts of the church – red diapers on white in the nave, and an enriched pattern of white diapers on red to mark the superiority of the chancel. Even more emphatic are the different spatial qualities of each part of the building. The low south aisle is

St James, Leckhampstead. CM

cut off by severe pointed arches on stumpy piers, while the nave beyond soars high up to a roof of steeply arched trusses. Cusped trusses and high windows define the transept bay, which seems extraordinarily lofty for its narrow width. By contrast the compact chancel appears a precious inner sanctum.

Presumably the subscribers were happy with all this, but they chose to re-use fittings from the old church rather than commission new ones. The font is a medieval stone tub with acanthus and vine trails, while the pulpit and altar rails are 17th and 18th century. Parts of the 17th-century screen were built into the new porch.

52

St John the Baptist, Shottesbrooke, Berkshire
Mid-14th century

SU 841771. In Shottesbrooke Park, 4 miles (6 km) SW of Maidenhead, on N side of B3024 between White Waltham and Waltham St Lawrence

[A] For key, see details in porch

This is an absolutely perfect English church. Perfect as an ornament in an idyllic country park, with spire rising high above the tree-tops, and cattle grazing peacefully round the nearby lake. Perfect also in its form, tightly composed and consistently Decorated, with pretty flowing tracery and neat little buttresses. Victorian architects such as Butterfield and Benjamin Ferrey loved it, especially Ferrey, who built a close replica at Kingswood in Surrey. Shottesbrooke has a sad side too – the congregation dwindled with the clearing of the park, and the church now stands empty – but this detracts surprisingly little from the pleasure of visiting it.

The beautiful unity of the church derives from the fact that it was built virtually all in one go, to serve a college of chantry priests founded by Sir William Trussell in 1337. The college consisted of a warden, five chaplains and two clerks, who lived in buildings to the south, on the site now occupied by the offices of the Landmark Trust. A blocked door in the south transept originally gave

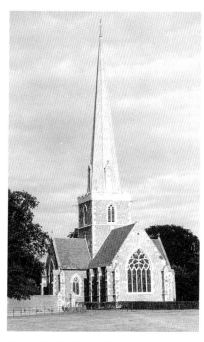

St John the Baptist, Shottesbrooke. PM

them direct access to the church, where they dutifully prayed for Trussell's soul.

The collegiate function also helps explain the shape of the church. It is a compact cross, with central tower and transepts, but has a peculiarly short, aisle-less nave and a larger chancel for the priests. In fact the chancel is bigger and better in every way – its five-light east window is much more glorious than the three-light end windows of nave and transepts, and its flint walls are painstakingly squared and coursed instead of plainly knapped. The tall spire gracefully ties everything together and pulls the whole church heavenwards.

Inside, the north transept is dominated by a superb double tomb, presumably for Trussell and his wife, which almost exceeds the length of the north wall. Perhaps it had been intended for another site? It is composed of two altar-like recesses, sumptuously carved in chalk with traceried panels, fan-type vaults and hanging ogee arches. There are also several very fine brasses and, in the chancel, a more peculiar stone monument, showing an effigy of one of the college wardens squeezed into a coffin on the wall.

53

St Mary and All Saints, Fotheringhay, Northamptonshire
1434–c.1441

TL 059931. At Fotheringhay, 3 miles (5 km) N of Oundle, on minor roads to NW of A605

[C]

Fotheringhay lies in the north-east tip of Northamptonshire, almost in fen country, and has a church to suit. It is a magnificent Perpendicular building, with great traceried windows, tall orderly pinnacles and the slenderest of flying buttresses. A more specific debt to East Anglia is the Ely-inspired octagonal lantern that gracefully crowns the tower. It is one of several in the area, and has a very pretty rival at Lowick. Inside the church, everything is light, airy and open. The wide nave is divided from the aisles only by narrow piers with fluid mouldings, and is delicately roofed with slight arching trusses.

There is, however, a peculiar feel about the church. Externally it looks stunted and too short for its grand style, and internally it is more than a little bare. The elaborate fan vault of 1529, under the tower, and the bright colours on the pulpit, repainted in 1967, cannot make up for a sense of something missing. In fact there is a great deal missing – a vast choir with aisles and lady chapel to the east, and the cloisters of a priestly college to the south. To explain the rise and fall of this once enormous building we have to explore Fotheringhay's connections with the royal House of York.

Fotheringhay once had a great castle. Like the church, it stood above the River Nene, and traces of it can be seen as lumps and bumps on the far side of the road. It became notorious for the trial and execution of Mary Queen of Scots in 1587, but is relevant here because it was given, in the late 14th century, to Edmund Langley, 1st Duke of York. His son refounded the castle's college of chantry priests in 1411, and amalgamated it with the parish church.

St Mary and All Saints, Fotheringhay. RCHME

Members of the family were to be buried in an impressive new choir, where the collegiate clergy and choristers would pray for their souls. We know what the choir must have looked like because a contract of 1434, issued to William Horwode, mason, required the nave to be built to much the same design.

All this grandeur was very short-lived. The college went the way of all chantries and was dissolved in 1548. The splendid choir, first stripped of its lead roof and left to decay, was demolished in 1573, and the cloister buildings failed to last out the 17th century. Only the nave survived, a majestic orphan, saved by its subordinate role as parish church. It had always been strictly divided from the choir by stone screens, and these were now crudely built up into a new east wall. Two 16th-century tombs, built to re-accommodate the 2nd and 3rd dukes of York, are the only clues to the building's noble parenthood.

54

St Mary, Warmington, Northamptonshire
Mid-13th century

TL 077910. At Warmington, 3 miles (5 km) NE of Oundle, on minor road to E of A605

[C]

There is no denying that St Mary's is a very neat and tidy church – it was restored very thoroughly in 1876 by Sir George Gilbert Scott and B Ferrey – but do not be put off. For this is an excellent piece of Early English architecture, pure in form, with simple geometric shapes, but wonderfully rich in decoration, with dogtooth, complex roll-mouldings and dense clusters of shafts.

This decoration belongs to the mid-13th century, when an earlier church of *c.*1200 was extensively remodelled. The tower, built of creamy-grey rubble stone, was raised in fine ashlar, and crowned with an early form of broach spire, dumpy and comfortably solid, with hefty lucarnes. Immediately below the spire are large bell chamber openings with distinctive plate tracery – each opening has two arched lights with a quatrefoil cut out of the solid spandrel above. There are more quatrefoils below, and an even more distinctive west door. This has a trefoil arch, numerous shafts, and outer bands with roll-mouldings, crisp dogtooth and puffy rosettes.

The south aisle was widened and rebuilt at about the same time. It boasts another doorway with elaborate roll-mouldings, and a very grand vaulted porch (rebuilt in 1876). The windows are also very fine, but show signs of a slight change in style. They each have three lancets, with a taller central light, but the earlier eastern windows are enriched with dogtooth, shafts and stiff-leaf

St Mary, Warmington. RCHME

capitals, while the western windows are plain. The progression follows through into the slightly later clerestory and north aisle, where the windows have more delicate tracery but no decoration.

Inside, you are confronted by a most extraordinary roof. The 13th-century rebuilders kept the earlier nave arcades, with their scalloped and waterleaf capitals, but inserted narrow wall shafts between the arches. On these they rested a series of groin vaults, astonishingly made not of stone but wood. There is no structural reason for building a wooden roof in vault form – it would be far more economical to assemble trusses and purlins – so this was pure affectation. It made a grand church seem even grander, but without undue expense. Perhaps funds were running low!

Lastly, look down as well as up, for there are some lovely 15th–16th-century benches with scrolled fleur-de-lis at each end. They come in a children's size too.

55

St Mary, Wellingborough, Northamptonshire
1906–30

SP 901680. ⅔ mile (1 km) E of town centre, on corner of Knox Road and B573 (eastern ring route)

[C]

From the outside, this church may seem a little dull. It is a great hulk of tawny Lias ashlar, surprisingly heavy for its Perpendicular style, surrounded by routine red-brick terraces. But if you borrow the key and go in, you find yourself in a fabulous world of light and vision. Grand spaces, exquisite furnishings and ethereal blues and golds seem to recreate a little of God's heavenly glory here on earth.

A new parish was formed here in 1904, and the Misses Sharman promptly gave £5,000 for a church. This was begun in 1906, and grew slowly, like a medieval building. The north chapel was consecrated in 1908, and the chancel in 1915, but the nave was not finished until 1930. The painted decoration is still incomplete, and the remaining extent of

The nave of St Mary, Wellingborough. CM

chancel. Both styles contribute without conflict, and Comper mixes them unreservedly. Even within the screens you find that Tuscan columns, carved lunettes, and thin Italianate balusters all blend in with gothic tracery patterns. More obviously Renaissance is the gilded baldacchino over the altar. It has Corinthian corner columns and putti surrounding the figure of Christ Risen.

The dramatic rood screen belongs to a more medieval, Catholic tradition. It has a proper rood loft, reached via a delightful flying passage across the north aisle, and a proper Crucifixion scene, all gilt, with seraphim to either side. The most impressive part, however, is the wonderfully youthful figure of Christ in Glory that hangs above. This has nothing to do with medieval doom and gloom, nor with the sombre seriousness of Victorian ritual. Rather it radiates pure hope and happiness.

56

St Michael and All Angels, Stewkley, Buckinghamshire
Mid-12th century

SP 852261. At centre of Stewkley village, 8 miles (13 km) N of Aylesbury, on B4032 between Winslow and Leighton Buzzard
[C]

This church is Romanesque at its best – massively sound, straightforward in function, and consistently decorated with rich carving. It has been little altered, and shows what many other 12th-century churches must have been like before they grew aisles, transepts and chapels. Of contemporary churches in this area, only St Mary's at Iffley, near Oxford, is as fine and undisturbed.

Like Iffley, St Michael's has an alluringly simple plan. Nave, central tower and chancel are set out in a single line, all built of a piece, with thick stone walls and small round-arched windows. Inside, the windows splay to more generous proportions and all have borders of carved chevron. The same motif recurs throughout the church, decorating archways and forming a

bare white perhaps gives an unintentional freshness. Otherwise, the church has a remarkable consistency, for it was completely designed, fittings and all, by Sir Ninian Comper.

Comper chose the Perpendicular style for both its generosity of space and its decorative grandeur. Tall arcades, of four-centred arches on slender piers, emphasise the ample width of the

church, and make a long run through nave and chancel. Equally long, and spectacularly gorgeous, is the fan-vaulted ceiling, a fantastic plaster creation of flowing ribs, star-like bosses and deep pendants. Two bays show the intended blue and gold decoration.

Below this medieval magnificence, delicate Renaissance screens make a jewelled cage around the sanctity of the

St Michael and All Angels, Stewkley. JB

splendid blind arcade around the top of the tower. Below the windows runs a zigzag string that ties the whole building together, inside and out.

Against this homogeneous background, the church's key features look all the more spectacular. The triple-arched west portal has impressive quantities of chevron, and a particularly grand central doorway with cabled columns. There are whirly-tailed dragons carved in shallow relief on the strangely shaped tympanum. The north and south doorways are less elaborate, but have interesting mouldings, especially the south one with its band of small balls and fierce head stop. Inside, the arches to the tower and the chancel are massive and magnificently carved, not only with chevron and zigzag but with beakhead as well – small grotesque heads curl beaks, beards or tongues round the roll moulding below.

The chancel is vaulted, and still has its 12th-century ribs with carved lozenge patterns. The vault itself, however, was reconstructed in 1844 and decorated with painted scrolls. In the 1860s, the church was restored by G E Street, with great feeling for its monumentality if not its detail. The beakhead ornament lost a little liveliness

in recutting, and the 'Norman' pulpit is weightily uninspiring, but Street refused to cut through the massive walls to make new aisles or transepts. Instead he merely added the south porch, rebuilt the top of the west gable, and recreated the steeply pitched roofs. In the process he found the delightful alabaster carving of the Madonna and Angels that is now mounted in the chancel.

57
St Peter, Gayhurst, Buckinghamshire
1728

SP 846462. In grounds of Gayhurst House, 2½ miles (4 km) NW of Newport Pagnell, to W of B526

[C]

St Peter's stands in an idyllic country park like a grand chapel to Gayhurst House (c.1600 and now private flats). In fact, it is a parish church, but the village was moved tidily out of sight in the late 1730s. The owner of the house, George Wrighte, had the church completely rebuilt between 1724 and 1728 in ambitious classical style, with golden

ashlar masonry and superb furnishings. A slightly provincial interpretation relieves the grandeur and makes it all the more attractive.

Wrighte's anonymous architect was probably an imaginative local builder, for the classical motifs are handled with charm rather than expertise. Heavy rustication suddenly gives way to a delicate Ionic order, while classical round-arched windows in the tower have gothic Y-tracery. On top of the tower sits a delightful but diminutive cupola with leaded dome and arcading. To the north and south are grand symmetrical facades, the south dramatised by a crescendo of corner strips, pilasters and central columns, the north featuring an aggressively rusticated centre with curious floating pediment. The effect is whimsically elegant, rather than full-blown Baroque.

The light, open interior also has a classical order, this time Corinthian. There are slight problems in accommodating it at the corners, but the glorious plaster ceilings make all forgivable. The nave has richly moulded compartments, while the grander chancel has coving with foliage trails and baskets of flowers. Over the altar is a beautifully unsophisticated sunburst with cloud whorls and cherub heads.

Original fittings include a complete set of panelled box pews, including a capacious one for the Wrightes, and a magnificent two-decker pulpit. This boasts a tester with inlaid decoration and a discreet curving stair with the most delicately turned balusters. In the chancel, steps rise to an altar area with a black and white marble floor and finely carved wooden reredos. This glows with gilded classical ornament and painted texts of the credo, ten commandments and Lord's prayer.

The crowning glory of Gayhurst, however, is the Wrighte monument. George and his father Sir Nathan Wrighte, Keeper of the Great Seal, stand in elegantly relaxed poses, glorious in frock coats, mantles and periwigs, below tented draperies. The pedimented surround enhances the sense of noble ease. Roubiliac has been suggested as a possible sculptor, but the early date makes such an attribution unlikely.

Plate 1 *Garter heraldry in the choir of St George's Chapel, Windsor.* AFK

Plate 2 *Market Place, Abingdon, with the County Hall.* JB

Plate 3 *Timber framing at 39 The Causeway, Steventon.* CM

Plate 4 *Palladian Bridge, Stowe.* NT/JERRY HARPUR

Plate 5 *Broughton Castle, its 16th-century front reflected in the medieval moat.* JB

Plate 6 *Friends' Meeting House at Jordans.* JB

Plate 7 *Wall paintings in the church at South Newington: St Margaret slaying a dragon.* EBENEZER PICTURES/CHRISTOPHER PHILLIPS

Plate 8 *The Radcliffe Camera, Oxford.* JB

Plate 9   *School Yard at Eton, looking towards Lupton's Tower.* ETON COLLEGE

Plate 10   *Maidenhead Railway Viaduct.* CM

Plate 11 *Rushton Triangular Lodge.* EH

58

St Peter ad Vincula, South Newington, Oxfordshire
14th and 15th century

SP 407333. At South Newington, 5 miles (8 km) SW of Banbury, to E of A361

[C]

This church appeals at first sight. It is built of warm iron-tinted Lias and is charming rather than grand. The windows have lovely Decorated tracery of *c.*1300, with intersecting 'Y's and cusped trefoils, and the Perpendicular porch has delightful pinnacles that stick up from the middle of the battlements. The church's chief glories, however, are the marvellous wall paintings inside. A series in the north aisle dates back to the mid-14th century, while above the north arcade (mid-12th-century in part) runs a late 15th-century Passion frieze. Over the chancel arch are the remains of a Doom.

The paintings in the north aisle are the most fascinating and unusual. Alongside the martyrdom of Thomas à Becket appears that of the little-known Thomas of Lancaster, sanctified by some as the credited murderer of Edward II's favourite, Piers Gaveston. Both martyrdoms are fragmentary but excitingly vigorous: Becket kneels calmly at the altar amidst a flurry of knightly swords and surcoats; Lancaster's assassin stands sprung above his victim, ready to put his whole weight behind the blow. Delicate details, such as the fine links in the chain mail, or the embroidery on the altar cloth, ennoble the butchery, and reflect a general elegance more usually associated with fine altar panels or manuscript illumination. The deep reds and greens are also exceptional, oil paint making for a far richer, more sensuous colour scheme than the usual fresco.

Towards the east end of the aisle the paintings are more complete. A graceful, swaying Virgin stands in a cusped arch against a background of delicate leafy tendrils, while smaller figures of the donors, Thomas Gifford and his wife Margaret Mortayne, kneel to one side. Thomas appears again, next to St James, below the Annunciation. On the jamb of the east window stands St Margaret, effortlessly slaying a dainty dragon with her slender spear (see Plate 7).

The later paintings in the nave are crude by contrast, though enjoyably so. The spandrels between the arches are adorned with chunky, triple-branched trees that symbolise the Trinity, and the scenes above show stunted little figures enacting the Passion with gruesome jollity. The muted ochres and variously diapered backgrounds look decidely homespun, and make the courtly elegance of the aisle even more remarkable.

Interior of St Peter, Gayhurst, with the Wrighte monument and a view into the chancel. ES

6

Educational and Charitable Institutions

All the buildings in this chapter share a common charitable intent. Almost all were paid for by wealthy individuals anxious to improve the lot of the needy, but perhaps also with other considerations in mind. A fine college, school or almshouse, suitably adorned with family heraldry and inscriptions, might secure both a fitting earthly memorial and immortality in the hereafter. This last belief prompted the chantry provisions of most medieval charities – the beneficiaries being obliged to spend much of their time in prayer for the soul of the founder, and so ease his path to heaven. Even after the chantries were dissolved in the 1530s and 40s, the principle lived on.

Oxford has figured large in the field of education since the late 12th century. Although many of the colleges began as individual chantry foundations, the university itself grew from informal gatherings of clerical teachers and students. They were perhaps attracted to the city by its ecclesiastical courts and by the patronage of Henry II and the great religious houses. Until the 15th century, the only focal point for this 'studium universale' was the church of St Mary the Virgin. The complex of specialised University Buildings (70, O) then evolved to the north, with libraries, lecture rooms and a ceremonial theatre.

Students boarded at first in lodgings and later in halls supervised by masters. The name of St Edmund Hall still refers to the latter system, but original hall buildings are hard to find. An early 14th-century example, known as Tackley's Inn, survives to the south of the High Street, behind nos. 106–7.

Colleges were at first for graduate fellows only. Some colleges, such as Gloucester (now part of Worcester) and Durham (now part of Trinity) were tied to monastic houses, but others were intended to educate secular clergy and civil servants. Merton, University College and Balliol each claim the first foundation, but Merton has the oldest

statutes (1263) and the earliest surviving buildings: its chapel choir dates to the 1290s, and Mob Quad to 1304–78. New College (68, O) is featured here, partly because it was the first to cater for undergraduates, but mainly because it established the model quadrangular plan that so many later colleges were to follow.

This plan, along with appropriate late medieval detail, continued to be repeated well into the 17th century. It set such a strong tradition of college design that later builders found it difficult to break away. Hawksmoor came up with a brilliantly imaginative re-interpretation at All Souls College (66, O), and also tried out a classical version at Queen's. Another good classical ensemble from the early 18th century can be found at Christ Church, with Peckwater Quadrangle by Henry Aldrich and the library by George Clarke. Nineteenth-century extensions reverted to the original idiom, adding tall gables and fancy tracery, but only Keble College (67, O) posed the question of how to design a completely new college. Butterfield's answer was spunky but decidedly not Oxford. St Catherine's College (69, O) faced the same problem in the 1960s.

Outside Oxford, the area has a splendid network of schools. The earliest of these taught the Latin grammar that was so essential for a university education. Just as William of Wykeham established a school at Winchester to prepare scholars for his foundation at New College, Oxford so Henry VI founded both Eton College (60, BE) and King's College, Cambridge. Although Eton is now a famous public school, it set out (in 1440) to give free education to twenty-five scholars. It was only a small part of a chantry foundation that also allowed for priests, an almshouse and a pilgrimage church. Slightly earlier foundations at Higham Ferrers (59, N) and Ewelme (61, O) had made similar arrangements on a less ambitious scale.

The Divinity School, Oxford. AFK

Duke Humphrey's Library, in the Bodleian, Oxford. AFK

After the Dissolution, foundations were more moderate. Only rarely were schools and almshouses combined, as at Clipston and Cottesbrooke in Northamptonshire. It was quite usual to provide only a single schoolroom. Uffington (21, O) has a delightfully tiny building near the church, and Burton Latimer (N) a slightly larger one dating from 1622. Other schools had lodgings for the master attached. At Bampton (O, c.1650, now a public library) these were in the attic, while at Witney (O, 1660) master and assistant were lodged in wings to either side. A grand range was provided at Guilsborough (N, 1668), with accommodation for pupils as well. A rare interior of c.1680, complete with benches and desks running round the walls, survives on the estate at Courteenhall (N), but is usually inaccessible to the public.

The school at Ewelme. CM

By the time these 17th-century schools were founded, there was increasing distinction between 'grammar' schools and free schools of humbler character. Whereas Witney and Guilsborough taught Latin, Greek and Hebrew, the little school at **Weekley** (65, N) aimed only to teach writing and reading. 18th-century charity schools, like the one at **Soulbury** (63, BU), developed this practical approach. The handsome school at Blewbury (9, O), built in 1709, added arithmetic to the list of subjects, along with spinning, weaving, sewing and knitting. These were 'taught' in an adjacent workshop. A practical education was still considered appropriate in 1900, when the school at Medmenham (15, BU) was conveniently sited for girls to work in the laundry and boys to labour out in the fields.

During the 19th century, education became more widespread and standardised. Many of the small village schools were established either by the National Society (Church of England) or the British and Foreign School Society (Nonconformist), and common principles of design permeated through to independent schools like that at Soulbury. Here the new school building also shows the legacy of the Oxford Movement (see Keble) and the Ecclesiologists. Its brick patterns and Gothic details are similar in inspiration to those of G E Street's buildings at All Saints', Boyne Hill (42, BE).

Provision for the aged was often linked with education in medieval chantry foundations, and remained a charitable option long afterwards. Elderly bedesmen prayed for their benefactor in return for a small allowance, and housing in a bedehouse or almshouse. The almshouses here are chosen to illustrate the wide variety of types in the area. The Chichele Bedehouse at Higham Ferrers is a medieval infirmary hall, formerly with cubicles, while the bedehouse that now serves as the **White Hart Inn, Fyfield** (73, O) adopted a domestic plan. At Ewelme and **Jesus Hospital, Bray** (62, BE) the almshouses are arranged like a college round a courtyard, while at Abingdon there is a fine group of variously designed single ranges around **St Helen's Churchyard** (72, O). Weekley has a smaller single range. The U-plan was also popular, as at Amersham (8, BU), Tomkins' Almshouses, Abingdon (7, O), and at **Lucas Hospital, Wokingham** (64, BE), included here because it is so complete.

Archbishop Chichele's bedehouse, Higham Ferrers. CM

59

Chichele College, Bedehouse and School, Higham Ferrers, Northamptonshire
1422–mid-15th century

College SP 960687. In College Street (A6) to N of Market Square
[A]

Bedehouse and school SP 961685. In churchyard, off Market Square
Bedehouse [D], school [C]

Higham Ferrers is well known for the church of St Mary, with its beautiful spire and unusual 13th-century porch (see introduction to chapter 5). It is also known as the birthplace of Henry Chichele, Archbishop of Canterbury and founder of All Souls College, Oxford (66, O). In 1422 Chichele showed his gratitude to the town by establishing a chantry with provision for the school and bedehouse in the churchyard. His purpose was similar to that of Dame Alice at Ewelme (61, O), but his ambition was much greater – a great man required a whole college, not just one priest, to secure his heavenly future.

The college was the key element of the foundation. It was to house eight chaplains, four clerks and six choristers, all of whom were to celebrate daily services for the souls of Chichele and Henry V, their families and 'all the faithful departed'. The chaplains and clerks were also to administer the bedehouse and act as schoolmaster and choirmaster. It is sad that, of the group, the college buildings have survived the least well. Only the entrance wall and the south range of the original quadrangle stand above foundation level, and even these are partly rebuilt. Above the entrance arch, however, survive three canopied niches that once held figures of the college's patron saints.

The bedehouse is a striking building of striped limestone and ironstone. It is not at all like Ewelme, for it resembles a small church, with buttresses and traceried windows. As at St Mary's Hospital, Chichester (West Sussex), the bedesmen were housed in the 'nave', which was partitioned into small cubicles, each with a cupboard let into the wall thickness. The cupboards in the south wall have been restored but the 'nave' has been cleared and serves as a parish hall. It retains the large communal fireplace and a fine roof.

At the east end of the bedehouse is a chancel arch and a much restored chapel. The twelve bedesmen were required to spend at least four hours a day in prayer, either here or in the church, and at the end of their life passed into the crypt below. While living, they were looked after by one old woman, and received an allowance of one penny a day.

The history of Chichele's school is less clear. Although he made new provision for a grammar master in 1422, a school already existed in the town. By 1542, when the chantry was dissolved, the school was held in the Jesus Chapel by the church. This is a later 15th-century building, completely different in style to either the bedehouse or the college. It is built of fine ashlar limestone and is elegantly Perpendicular. There are wide traceried windows, delightful pierced battlements, and tall crocketed pinnacles. Inside, the rood-loft stairs prove its origins as a chapel, but the graffiti and wooden lobby, dated 1636, date from its use as a school. Now it is a chapel once more.

60

Eton College, Berkshire
From 1440

SU 967779. At N end of Eton High Street
[A]

Eton College Chapel is clearly visible from the terrace of Windsor Castle. It stands out as a great bulk of pale stone, proud with pinnacles and huge Perpendicular windows, and was built, like the castle, by craftsmen of the Royal Works. The dominance of the chapel reflects the primary purpose of the college's foundation in 1440.

It was then that Henry VI decided to celebrate his majority and his

Lower School at Eton. ETON COLLEGE

Wooden posts inserted in the early 17th century divide it into aisles, and help support Long Chamber, above. Now partitioned, this dormitory once slept all seventy scholars and became infamous for all the worst public school excesses.

The chapel is altogether more dignified. The choir glows with modern stained glass by Evie Hone and the Piper/Reyntiens partnership, while above the stalls run wonderful wall paintings dating from 1479–88. These are executed in grisaille, and are full of Flemish curves and detail. The fan vaults are concrete, erected in 1956–9 in place of a humbler wooden roof, and serve as a reminder of the glories that Henry intended but never quite achieved. Only the choir of his great minster was ever built, and even that had to be finished by a former provost, Bishop Waynflete. Henry was deposed in 1461. He ended his days, stickily, in the Tower, and must have hoped very much that the prayers of his college would be heard.

assumption of full regal powers with a magnificent church, to which pilgrims would flock to see relics and receive indulgences, and in which masses would be said many times daily for the soul of the founder. Services would be led by a college of clerics, and prayers augmented by twenty-five almsmen and twenty-five scholars. Provision for the almsmen rapidly dwindled, but the number of scholars soon rose to seventy. Henry gave them statutes modelled on William of Wykeham's college at Winchester (see also New College, Oxford (68, O)), and established King's College, Cambridge for their further education. From this chantry by-product grew England's most renowned public school.

The original college buildings, apart from the stone hall and kitchen, are modest ranges of warm red brick, with blue diaper patterning and arched stone window lights. They are grouped around two courtyards. The vast School Yard is entered through a range of 1689–91, which houses Upper School above a handsome Tuscan arcade. To the right is the chapel, to the left Lower School (in use by 1485), with the even windows of

Long Chamber above. Opposite is the range rebuilt by Provost Lupton in the early 16th century. Its central tower, splendid with octagonal turrets and two-storey oriel, is the only serious rival to the magnificence of the chapel. To its left, on the first floor, are the close-set windows of Lupton's library, now Election Hall.

The tower arch leads through to the cloisters. Here, small twin doorways and an upper gallery gave access to rooms for the clerical fellows. An ashlar top storey of 1758 now sits incongruously on top of the 15th-century brickwork, and a gracious library of 1725–9 masks the original hall.

The most evocative parts of the college are undoubtedly the schoolrooms: benches are worn and polished by centuries of restless wriggling, and hundreds of names are carved into panelling and shutters. The enormously long Upper School is an impressive relic of the system of mass education, with masters' desks raised like a throne at one end, and lesser desks for assistants placed half-way down. Lower School still has some of the early scholars' desks, and is more compact.

61

Ewelme Almshouses, School and Church, Oxfordshire
1437–c.1450

SU 646914. At SE end of Ewelme village, 13 miles (21 km) SE of Oxford, off B4009 between Benson and Watlington

[C]

This outstanding group of charitable buildings, all still in use, straggles picturesquely down the hillside as a perpetual reminder of the piety and beneficence of Alice Chaucer, granddaughter to Geoffrey Chaucer, and her husband, William de la Pole, Earl of Suffolk. The foundations compare with those of Henry Chichele at Higham Ferrers (59, N) but are very different in plan and appearance. A special delight at Ewelme is the very early use of brick, also found nearby at Shirburn Castle and Stonor.

The almshouses, licensed in 1437, housed thirteen poor men who were all to pray twice daily for the souls of the founders. Handsome endowments catered for an annual stipend, fuel allowance and black uniform with a red cross, but there was also a firm code of conduct. In charge were two chaplains, one to serve as master of the almshouses, the other to teach grammar in the school.

The almshouse buildings are arranged like a college around a quadrangle, each almsman having one room and an attic. The master's lodgings and muniment room occupy the first floor of the north-east range and are separated by a passage to the church. The buildings have been much restored, most recently in 1970, but still retain their original character. Outer walls are of chalky limestone rubble with brick chimneys, but courtyard walls are timber-framed with brick infill, mostly laid in herringbone pattern. The steep roofs, originally thatched, extend over a cloister passage, each side of which has a splendid gabled entry with traceried wooden lights and intricately carved bargeboards. The entrance to the whole, with its blind tracery and stepped gable, is a particularly fine example of Flemish-style brickwork.

South-west of the almshouses is the teacher's house, with 15th-century brickwork but altered fenestration. Then comes the tall, two-storey school, built

slightly later than the almshouses. This is more completely constructed of bricks – long narrow ones are used – and only the window details are of stone. The imposing south-west front has especially grand windows with cinquefoil tracery and square hoodmoulds, two with carved figures bearing shields. The two tall chimneys formerly heated the schoolroom, down below, and a large upper room that probably served as a dormitory. This has a surprisingly splendid roof, with graceful arch-braced collars and arched windbraces. A small study occupies the upper storey of the porch, which now has traceried doors from the church.

Dame Alice and her husband also rebuilt the church in Perpendicular style. Some of its features have a distinct flavour of Suffolk about them. The chantry chapel is splendidly decorated with painted IHS monograms and carved wooden ceiling angels, and contains the stern alabaster effigy of Alice herself. Her buildings serve as a kinder memorial.

Jesus Hospital, Bray. PM

The almshouses at Ewelme. CM

62

Jesus Hospital, Bray, Berkshire
1627–8

SU 902793. At S end of Bray village, 1¼ miles (2 km) SE of Maidenhead, on B3028

[C] Visits on application to the Chaplain

Jesus Hospital is a large and ostentatious set of almshouses founded in 1627 in fulfillment of the will of William Goddard. It was to house forty poor and aged people, thirty-four of them from the village, and six drawn from former members of the Company of Fishmongers, to which Goddard himself belonged. A painted statue of Goddard stands prominently above the entrance, while below the windows on either side are the family and company arms.

The almshouses are built of brick, laid in English bond, and are ranged in a single storey around a large courtyard. They give the same sense of enclosed

community as at Ewelme (61, O). Each resident had his own room, with stone mullion window and tall rear chimney, but shared an entrance with his neighbour. Above the doorways, with their old board doors and four-centred stone arches, are renewed dormers that formerly lit small communal hallways. The attic space was for storage and could only be reached by ladder.

Marking the central axis of the courtyard are the high gables of entrance and chapel. The entrance bay housed the chaplain in first-floor rooms graced with tall cross-windows, but later his accommodation spread into the raised bays either side. Below, an imposing stone arch opens into a passage which contains an almsbox, firmly strapped on to its post. A stone tablet above, dated 1633, reads: 'He that giveth to the poore lendeth to the Lord'.

The chapel, like the rest of the hospital, has been much restored and has a completely new roof and bellcote. Its traceried windows, however, still boast some 17th-century glass, and arched panels from the original screen have been reset in the new.

63

Lovett House and The Old School House, Soulbury, Buckinghamshire
1724 and 1863

SP 882271. 8 miles (13 km) S of Milton Keynes, in Soulbury, on the corner of B4032 and Chapel Lane

[D]

It might well escape the casual observer that both of these buildings formerly served as the village school. Whereas The Old School House is obviously purpose-built, Lovett House looks very much like an ordinary Georgian home. The two beautifully illustrate a dramatic change in attitudes to education.

The school originally held in Lovett House was an independent charity school, founded in 1728 in accordance with the will of Robert Lovett. His endowment paid for a master to teach twenty-four poor boys and girls of Soulbury to read, write, cast accounts and say the church catechism. He also left money for apprenticeships. The building, erected in 1724, was given by the Revd John Sambee, and was large enough to house both the master and additional fee-paying boarders.

The design of Lovett House has been attributed to Thomas Harris from nearby Cublington. It is a handsome but straightforward, homely building, of local red and vitreous brick, with details picked out in soft red. The leaded cross-windows have been renewed, but are true to the original pattern, and the two doorways have segmental hoods on scrolled acanthus brackets. Only the plaque and the extra doorway distinguish the building as a school. The left door led into the schoolmaster's house and the right into the schoolroom.

By 1863 there were more village children to be educated, and a new school, much more standardised, was built with £700 taken from the original endowment. It was designed by Mr R Durley of Aylesbury in accordance with principles established by the National and British School Societies,

The Old School House, Soulbury. CM

and its educational function is much more clearly expressed than at Lovett House. The entrance is distinguished by a small tower with bellcote and spire, and has an adjacent small cloakroom. A long schoolroom runs behind, marked by large windows at either end, and a classroom for smaller groups or infants projects to the left.

The style is distinctly churchy, as thought suitable for the pious, altruistic function of a school. It is supposed to be 'Early English', with buttresses and plate-traceried windows, but the free interpretation is influenced by the work of the diocesan architect, G E Street. Walls are richly patterned in red and black brick with Bath stone details, and the roof has coloured bands of fishscale tiles. Bargeboards are intricately cusped

or scalloped, and there is delightful floral decoration incised around the windows. In 1847 the *Ecclesiologist* had expressed the desire that the school be 'the prettiest building in the village, next to the church'. This school certainly does its best.

64

Lucas Hospital, Wokingham, Berkshire
1660s

SU 812674. 1 mile (1.6 km) S of Wokingham. Turn left off A321 into Luckley Road, continue under railway, then fork left

[C] Visits on application to the Matron

This is a very handsome Restoration building, remarkably intact in detail, and fascinating for its original arrangements. It was endowed by Henry Lucas (d. 1663) to house a master, or chaplain, and sixteen aged bachelors who had formerly resided in the Forest of Windsor. His trustees, the Drapers' Company, chose the site, obtained a licence in 1667, and still manage the hospital today.

The building has more the air of a country house than an institution. It

Lucas Hospital, Wokingham. JB

was built in warm red brick on a wide U-plan, with fashionably hipped tile roof, wooden eaves cornice and rusticated brick quoins. The centre is marked by a small cupola and a wide pediment-gable with heraldic shield and cornucopias carved in stone. Even the brick screen across the forecourt rises grandly to central rusticated gate piers. Only the rather widely spaced horizontal windows, with their wooden mullions and leaded lights, restore a sense of the vernacular.

The sixteen rooms are arranged on two storeys in sets of four, with doors opening onto shared staircases. These are complete with original balustrades. Each bachelor also had his own shed in a low range at the rear, and an allotment in the walled garden beyond.

The communal parts of the building are in the side wings and are distinguished by large front windows with arched heads and raised brick surrounds. In the side walls facing the forecourt are tall double-panelled doors with architrave frames and round windows above. The right door is inscribed 'VENITE' and leads into the chapel. The left door is more ominously inscribed 'REQUIES' and leads to the mortuary below the hall.

The chapel has beautiful original detail, with high-backed pews and three-sided altar rails. The chancel arch has a classical wooden frame with segmental pediment and Corinthian pilasters, and the arms of Charles II, usually placed above, are relegated to stained glass in the east window.

65

Montagu Hospital and the Free School, Weekley, Northamptonshire
1611 and 1624

SP 888809. 2 miles (3 km) NE of Kettering, to E of A43, in Weekley village on road to church

[D]

There are two small charitable buildings in Weekley – a gracious almshouse founded by Sir Edward Montagu of

Montagu Hospital, Weekley. CM

neighbouring Boughton, and a humble free school founded by a parson, Nicholas Latham. Although both buildings belong to the early 17th century, they are markedly different in character, and reflect all too obviously the different aspirations of their founders.

The Montagu Hospital is now a private house, but used to provide comfortable accommodation for six brethren and a master. It enjoys a lovely site overlooking a small green by the back gates to Boughton Park, and is very much an adjunct to the Montagu estate. Sir Edward Montagu, who is commemorated in the church next door, was a man with puritan leanings, who believed that he was accountable to God for the well-being of his tenants. He no doubt intended the hospital to be a great comfort to them in their old age, but he was not averse to his generosity making a fine show. The building has an extremely handsome ashlar front, with stone mullion windows arranged symmetrically about a splendid centrepiece. Fancy gable curves, obelisks and shell motifs all catch the eye, and the Montagu arms, set above the fine doorcase, clearly signal the identity of the founder. The painted sundial was added in 1631.

Latham's school, by contrast, is a very modest building of rubble stone, almost dwarfed by the 19th-century extension that projects in front. When first built, in 1624, it consisted of a single room with large stone mullion windows. The small arched doorway may have been altered, but still has the original inscription tablet above. This records that the building was a free school for Weekley and Warkton, founded 'to teach theire children to write and read'. There is no mention of prestigious grammar-school Latin. Latham founded similar schools at Barnwell St Andrew, where he was parson, and also at Brigstock and Luddington. He seems to have been genuinely concerned not with show but with providing basic education for the local people.

66

Oxford Colleges: All Souls College, Oxford, Oxfordshire
1438–43 and 1715–34

SP 516063. On corner of High Street and Catte Street. See map of Oxford (19, O)

[A]

All Souls College was founded in 1438 by Henry Chichele, Archbishop of Canterbury, with the blessing of Henry VI. Chichele had already founded the college, school and bedehouse at Higham Ferrers (59, N), but was here concerned with higher education for future clergy and clerical civil servants. The forty fellows were to pray daily for the souls of Chichele, Henry V and all the faithful departed, especially those who died in the Hundred Years War. No undergraduates have ever been admitted. By the 18th century, wealthy aristocratic fellows required more space, and financed one of Oxford's grandest architectural achievements, a stunning Gothick extension by Hawksmoor.

The original buildings around Front Quadrangle were erected in 1438–43. Details may have been designed by the master mason, Richard Chevynton, but the plan was inspired by New College, where Chichele had been an

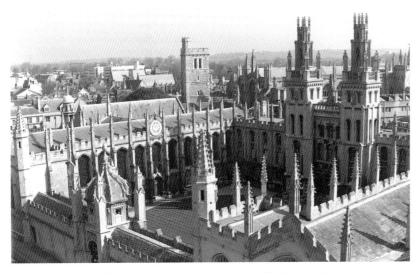

North Quadrangle at All Souls, Oxford, seen from the tower of St Mary the Virgin. BTA

67

Oxford Colleges: Keble College, Oxford, Oxfordshire
1868–82, 1970–7

SP 513069. Parks Road. (See map of Oxford (19, O))

[C]

Keble is often regarded as an Oxford horror: its aggressively polychrome brickwork jars hideously against the city's customary mellow limestone; its gaunt forms lack grace or charm, and its open quadrangles defy traditional college planning. Despite this, the buildings have great presence, and their perversity intrigues even the most ardent critic.

The college was founded in 1870 by a group of Tractarians (also known as the Oxford Movement) anxious to educate future Anglican clergy according to the High Church ideology of Keble, Pusey and Newman. The new college was also to serve as a memorial to Keble, and was funded by a public appeal after his death in 1866. It had to be reasonably cheap, as it lacked the wealthy endowments of medieval foundations. Whereas the latter had become worldly establishments, the new college aimed to provide a very different life-style, one of piety and disciplined austerity.

The architect chosen to provide a fit environment was William Butterfield, a protagonist of the similarly inspired Ecclesiological Society, for whom he had designed All Saints, Margaret Street in Westminster. His use of brick suited Keble's limited budget and dramatically emphasised the special nature of the new college. Instead of the usual smooth ashlar and carved detail, Keble displays a riot of flat Ruskinian pattern. Basic redbrick walls are striped with courses of blue and white, window heads emphasised by zigzags, and gables decorated with diapers or chequering.

The patterning helps denote the different forms and functions of the buildings. Lodging ranges are long and even, reflecting the novel corridor arrangement, and are punctuated by the taller gatehouse, staircases and gabled

undergraduate. Both colleges have entrance towers, first-floor libraries with even fenestration, and staircases giving access to lodgings with study cubicles. Whereas New College can seem rather vast, however, All Souls is intimately compact, and retains more original detail. The windows giving out over the quadrangle are still 15th-century, and the splendid Perpendicular chapel, which takes up the whole of the narrow north range, has its original hammerbeam roof with gilded angels. The ante-chapel plan is copied from New College, and there is even a very similar stone reredos, but here only the figures have been restored – the reredos itself survived various remodellings and still bears traces of 15th-century colouring.

The original hall and cloisters lay to the north of Front Quadrangle. They were demolished in 1703, leaving the site free for the grand extensions envisaged by Dr George Clark, then Warden of the college. Clarke drew up designs himself, but also reviewed schemes by Hawksmoor, Talman, William Townesend and Dean Aldrich of Christ Church. Hawksmoor's ideas were eventually accepted in 1715 and North Quadrangle was completed by 1734.

North Quadrangle dramatically recasts the traditional collegiate style in a fabulously monumental mould. Its

Gothick arches and pinnacles echo the details of the earlier buildings, but much more boldly and baldly, without any fussy tracery. And its layout incorporates the old work in a new composition of magnificent symmetry. The chapel and matching new hall on the south side are mirrored on the north by the Codrington Library, both ranges forceful in character with regimented buttresses and vast arched windows. These lead inexorably towards the climax of the composition – the twin towers that rise above the east lodgings like the west front of an unorthodox cathedral. Their fantastic lanterns, tiered like wedding cakes, make a splendidly Gothick counterbalance to the more serious majesty of the Radcliffe Camera opposite. The two were meant to be seen together, for all that divides the college from Radcliffe Square is a low arcade.

Access to the interior of Hawksmoor's buildings is more limited, and might give rather a surprise. For here all is classical. Window arches that look four-centred outside magically become round inside, and groin vaults alternate with domes. The hall has an Ionic screen, shell niches and a plaster barrel vault, and the library has later Doric and Ionic bookcases. Most exquisite of all is the buttery, superbly crowned by a coffered oval dome.

tutors' blocks. The hall and library range is dignified by traceried windows, buttresses and a grand staircase oriel, while the chapel dominates with its immense height. Here the patterns are compacted by tall pinnacled buttresses, and the great windows are set high up with intricate chequering above.

Even more dramatic is the interior of the chapel, where rich decoration reflects Tractarian ritual and the sanctity of the Sacrament. The floor rises in ever more elaborately patterned steps towards the altar. Blind arcading becomes enriched with coloured marble inlay, and mosaic panels and stained glass compete with patterned brick above. Lofty painted groin vaults provide its crowning glory. Holman Hunt's *Light of the World* is discreetly set in a side chapel.

Any form of extension to such a distinctive college causes immediate design problems. These have been splendidly overcome by Ahrends, Burton and Koralek in the Hayward and de Breyne Quadrangles of 1970–7. The outer walls of yellow brick, with tall slit windows and staircase buttresses, suggest a sympathetic cross between castle and monastery. To the college, the new buildings present a vast expanse of window glass, a giant screen coiled in at either end.

68
Oxford Colleges: New College, Oxford, Oxfordshire
1379–1403 and later

SP 517064. Entrance in New College Lane (See map of Oxford, (19,O))

[A]

New College was the first Oxford college to be built as an entity, and provided a model for many later medieval foundations such as All Souls and Magdalen. It was founded in 1379 by William of Wykeham, Bishop of Winchester, together with a school at Winchester, for the education of future clergy, and broke precedent by admitting undergraduate fellows as well as graduates. Besides the seventy fellows and warden, the statutes also provided for ten chaplains, three clerks and sixteen choristers to celebrate mass for the founder's soul in the college chapel.

Front Quadrangle was finished by 1386, and the cloisters and bell tower added 1396–1403, all under Wykeham's supervision. He had assembled a team of craftsmen while acting as Surveyor of the Royal Works at Windsor, and the quadrangular plan with hall and chapel in line owed much to the then arrangement of Lower Ward. The designer was probably the master mason, William Wynford.

The fellows were housed in two-storey lodging ranges. Small arched doors give on to staircases with four sets of chambers, each originally holding three or four beds and the same number of corner study cubicles. Senior fellows shared with and supervised juniors. The fenestration still gives the rhythm of large chamber windows and narrow study lights, but cusped heads and mullions gave way to larger sashes in 1718–21. Ashlar masonry distinguishes the later top storey (added 1674–5) from the rubble stone of the older buildings.

The library, with nine close-set windows, occupied the first floor of the east range. Underneath to the left was the bursary, next to the four-storey muniment tower with strongrooms for college monies, statutes, deeds and plate. The tower has a star-vaulted stairway to the hall, and statuary that is echoed on the entrance tower in the west range. This tower, together with adjacent rooms, housed the Warden's Lodgings. The warden also enjoyed the use of a garden and barn on the far side of New College Lane, to which a connecting bridge was built in the 1670s.

The north range is magnificent, with ashlar masonry and an even row of buttresses and pinnacles. Smaller windows carefully distinguish the hall from the vast expanses of Perpendicular chapel tracery. Inside there is much restoration work of the 1860s and 70s by Sir George Gilbert Scott and his sons, George Gilbert and John Oldrid, but also some earlier treasures. The hall is beautifully decked with 1530s linenfold panelling, while the antechapel has glorious original glass and a great west window designed by Reynolds. The chapel adopted the truncated plan of Merton Chapel and established the T-plan as an Oxford standard. Its cloisters served for ceremony and study but also for the burial of departed fellows.

By the later 17th century, superior accommodation was required for senior fellows and fee-paying noble commoners. New ranges were built out into the gardens on an open courtyard plan influenced by royal palaces. The

The chapel at Keble College, Oxford. AFK

inner wings, by William Byrd, were built in 1678–84, and gracefully masked the old kitchen and latrines. Outer wings were added 1700–10 and were closed with an extremely handsome wrought-iron screen by Thomas Robinson. The present screen is a copy of 1894. Beyond, the gardens are still enclosed by the old city wall (see chapter 2), and contain a late 16th-century artificial mound, originally used for viewing formal patterns in the beds below.

Further expansion in 1857 led to new ranges along Holywell Street. The initial buildings by Scott are bluntly Gothic, while extensions by Basil Champneys are more softly Tudor. The most striking recent addition is the Sacher Building of 1961–3, by David Roberts.

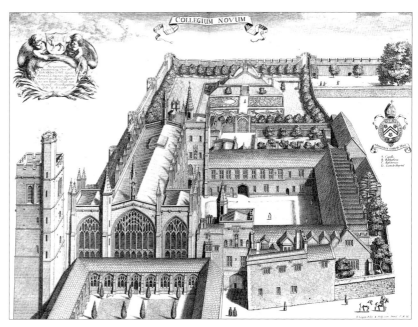

New College, Oxford, as illustrated in David Loggan's *Oxonia Illustrata*, 1675. BL

69

Oxford Colleges: St Catherine's College, Oxford, Oxfordshire
1960–64

SP 522067. At far end of Manor Road, off St Cross Road. (See map of Oxford (19, O))

[C]

Are Oxford colleges all about tradition, or should they keep up to date with new talent and novel ideas? Old colleges can do both, as at All Souls (66, O), but new colleges must make a choice. Nuffield (founded 1937) went in for traditional limestone and quadrangles, but St Catherine's, safely distant in the loop of the River Cherwell, went boldly 'Modern'.

A Danish architect, Arne Jacobsen, was appointed in 1959. His buildings are elegant pieces of engineering, with frames expressed in smooth concrete and clad in sheeny glass or narrow brick. The brick is precision-laid and neatly pointed, its soft yellow reminiscent of the more usual limestone. Careful planting is an essential part of the scheme, adding more than a little green and softening the clean, fine lines.

The entrance comes as rather a shock. Gone is the traditional archway and gate-tower. Instead, the visitor wanders casually past the bicycle shed and in through a gap in the wall. After that, everything is more calculated and gracious. Beyond a wide lawn and a delightful water garden of a moat lies a long, even range with two storeys of study-bedrooms floating above a terrace. The recessed ground floor is

The Bernard Sunley Building, St Catherine's College, Oxford. CM

continuously glazed, but slender concrete uprights soar through the upper storeys to give the great length a tight verticality.

Glass doorways lead through to an open quadrangle, incompletely enclosed by a matching range on the far side and by the blocks of communal buildings that lie between. To the left of the perfectly circular green are the brick walls of the hall, made massive by wide, flat buttresses and high windows squeezed in under the roof. Beyond are single-storey ranges with Junior and Senior Common Rooms. To the right of the green are the Wolfson Library, with glazed and bronze panels, and the lecture rooms of the Bernard Sunley Building, shaded by suspended metal louvres. Between the two rises a tall concrete bell tower.

All the functional elements of an Oxford college are clearly present, but the form is barely recognisable and the sense of order is slightly oppressive. This extends to the strips of garden between the ranges, formally bound by brick screens and yew hedges neatly clipped to match. They may provide perfect havens for logical thought, but one questions whether they inspire the imagination.

70

Oxford University Buildings: Divinity School, Schools Quadrangle and Bodleian Library (c.1420–1624); Radcliffe Camera (1737–49); St Mary the Virgin (c.1300–1510); Sheldonian Theatre (1663–9). Oxford, Oxfordshire

SP 515062. Between Broad Street, Catte Street and High Street

[A]

Whereas most Oxford colleges were private foundations properly housed in purpose-built premises, the university itself was a much more amorphous entity. Only gradually did it acquire a formal structure and the funds to erect its own buildings. Featured here are the most significant ones – impressive for their architectural style, but equally fascinating for the peculiarity of their function.

The University Church of *St Mary the Virgin* boasts one of Oxford's most romantic spires (14th-century Decorated with plenty of pinnacles) and perhaps its most exotic porch – a Rubensian gem with barleysugar columns, built in 1637 by Nicholas Stone. The bulk of the church was remodelled in 1462–1510 and became splendidly Perpendicular, but its importance to the university goes back long before. From the very late 12th century, when Oxford first became noted for its academic activities, the church provided a meeting place for scholars, and it was soon serving the fledgling university as a centre for administration and ceremony. The de Brome chapel, added c.1320, is still arranged as the Chancellor's Courtroom, and another contemporary extension, to the north-east, housed meetings of Congregation in the vaulted chamber below, and the university's first library, bequeathed by Bishop Cobham, in the room above.

Teaching, by such early Oxford masters as Roger Bacon, Duns Scotus and William of Occam, took place in small schools dispersed throughout the town. *Schools Quadrangle* was later to provide more organised facilities. It was built in 1613–24, in handsome Oxford Tudor, with a grand five-tier centre-piece of Renaissance columns and strapwork. The names over the doorways form a roll-call of medieval and Renaissance education – there were schools for the Seven Liberal Arts, Law, Languages (Greek and Hebrew), Natural and Moral Philosophy, and Metaphysics. The supremely important faculty of Theology, however, was housed in a much earlier and more magnificent building beyond the main entrance. The *Divinity School*, begun in the 1420s, is a superb Perpendicular lecture hall, with beautiful large traceried windows. But what makes it sublime is its gorgeous vault, built in 1480–3 by William Orchard. Delicate stone fans and pendants hang above the space as if by a miracle, all fabulously enriched with ornate ribs and a multitude of bosses. On the bosses are carved religious symbols and the badges of the School's benefactors.

On top of the Divinity School was built a new library (now part of the

Schools Quadrangle, Oxford. AFK

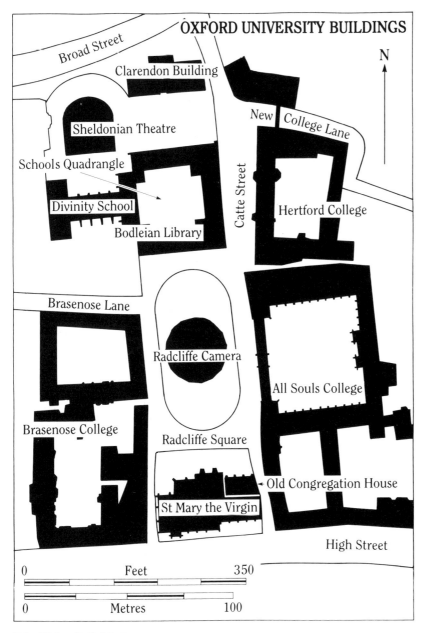

OXFORD UNIVERSITY BUILDINGS

N

Broad Street

Clarendon Building

Sheldonian Theatre

New College Lane

Schools Quadrangle

Catte Street

Divinity School

Hertford College

Bodleian Library

Brasenose Lane

Radcliffe Camera

All Souls College

Brasenose College

Radcliffe Square

Old Congregation House

St Mary the Virgin

High Street

0	Feet	350
0	Metres	100

Oxford University Buildings. EH

Bodleian Library), to hold books and manuscripts left by Humphrey, Duke of Gloucester in 1447. His collection did not survive the Reformation, but the library was refitted and opened again in 1602, by Sir Thomas Bodley. Visitors can still see desks and bookshelves of this date, and a restored painted ceiling. Bodley negotiated a copyright deal with

the Stationers' Company in 1610, and the library immediately began to expand. An extension was built across the front in 1610–13, and another across the far end in 1634–7, above a new Convocation House and Court Room. Bodley's library also flowed into the top floors of Schools Quadrangle and then into the Radcliffe Camera. It is now a

vast institution, with a late 1930s extension by Sir Giles Gilbert Scott on the north side of Broad Street, and a separate branch in the Science Area off Parks Road.

The *Radcliffe Camera*, built in 1737–49 as a Physic Library endowed by Dr John Radcliffe, must rank as the finest, most satisfying piece of architecture in the whole of Oxford. Its conception as a domed rotunda, set in a grand square associated with the new buildings at All Souls College (66, O), came from Hawksmoor, but James Gibbs provided the final design. His forms are much more rounded and flowingly Baroque than Hawksmoor's work at All Souls and the Clarendon Building, and the building has a mature classical majesty that makes it a rare treat in amongst the familiar Oxford pinnacles.

By contrast, the *Sheldonian Theatre* is an intriguingly immature building, designed by Christopher Wren as early as 1663, shortly after he had been made Savilian Professor of Astronomy. By then, the university felt the need for a specialist building (rather than St Mary's) to serve as a theatre for degree and matriculation ceremonies. Gilbert Sheldon, Warden of All Souls, came up with the cash, Wren with a round-ended design based on the Roman Theatre of Marcellus. The flat ceiling, constructed with all Wren's ingenuity across a vast span, was painted by Robert Streeter as if to appear open to the sky. Canvas covers are seemingly drawn back to reveal an Oxford dream – the heavenly Triumph of Truth, Arts and Sciences.

71

Oxford University Museum, Oxford, Oxfordshire
1854–59

SP 514069. On Parks Road, opposite Keble College. (See map of Oxford (19, O))

[A]

The University Museum may look a little boring from the outside, but do not be misled. Inside, it is the most exciting 19th-century building in Oxford,

'Gothic' ironwork in the University Museum, Oxford. AFK

reconciling a new age of science and technology with all the virtues of tradition and historical precedent.

The museum owed its existence to Dr Henry Acland, later Regius Professor of Medicine and provider of the estate cottages at Marsh Gibbon (14, BU). Acland campaigned for a new centre to boost scientific studies, with research facilities and teaching rooms surrounding a glazed exhibition area. As regards design, Acland was strongly influenced by his friend, the great John Ruskin, and favoured a Gothic proposal put forward by Benjamin Woodward, of the Irish architectural firm Deane, Son and Woodward.

'Gothic' is a misleadingly simple term. Externally the museum is a Flemish cloth hall, with central tower and steeply pitched roof. (Northampton Guildhall (16, N) was to follow the same lead.) Cusped lancets and plate tracery add an 'Early English' tone, while smooth ashlar walling and coloured banding owe much to Ruskin's 'Venetian Gothic'. The unfinished scuptural decoration was also Ruskinian in that it was based on nature and the free expression of the craftsmen, in this case the Irish O'Shea brothers. It is perhaps curious, in the age of Charles Darwin, that the portal should feature Adam, Eve and the Creator.

Slightly apart, to the right, are the former chemistry laboratories, modelled on the Abbot's Kitchen at Glastonbury, while the central court is surrounded by a two-tier cloister of almost Sicilian richness, built of banded red and white brickwork. The arcades serve as an encyclopaedia of nature, with labelled columns of different rock, and capitals deeply carved with thistles, daisies, ivy and honeysuckle.

In the middle of all this rises an astonishing cathedral of iron and glass. Clusters of slender cast-iron shafts divide the court into nave and aisles, and support steeply pointed arches as gaunt and skeletal as the ribs of the dinosaurs below. Above are steep roofs of glass tiles, weightily held in place by diagonal wooden battens. Much lighter are the iron capitals and arcades, delicately wrought into leaves of palm, chestnut, sycamore or oak. Despite the daring

Long Alley Almshouses, St Helen's Churchyard, Abingdon. BTA

technology and total lack of precedent, this iron court, erected by Skidmore of Coventry, seems far more Gothic in imaginative spirit than its heavy, Ruskinian shell.

72

St Helen's Churchyard, Abingdon, Oxfordshire
1446–1608, 1707 and 1718

SU 496967. St Helen's Wharf. (See map of Abingdon (7, O))

[D] Apply to Matron for entry to Long Alley hall

Grouped around St Helen's churchyard is an attractive series of three almshouses known as Long Alley, Brick Alley and Twitty's Almshouses. They are all now administered as Christ's Hospital, but vary greatly in the style and manner of their foundation.

Long Alley was founded by the Fraternity of the Holy Cross, a self-help guild of local townsfolk responsible for the new bridge of 1416–17, a market cross and a fourth aisle for St Helen's Church. When the fraternity was incorporated, in 1441, it was required to provide for thirteen 'poor sick and impotent men and women'. Individual chantry-style endowments, like that of Sir John Golafre (see the White Hart

Inn, Fyfield (73, O) helped towards the cost, and Long Alley was built in 1446–7. It survived the fraternity's dissolution in 1547 to re-emerge, minus endowments, in 1553 as Christ's Hospital.

The buildings consist of a long row of single rooms opening on to a cloister passage. A central hall served as a meeting place for governors, but there was no chapel, as worship took place in St Helen's. The rear walls are stone, with tall brick chimneys and traces of original detail. Sadly, the only unaltered windows are the cusped lights of the south gable, which possibly lit rooms for the two chaplains stipulated in the foundation. As at Ewelme (61, O) the front wall is timber-framed, with old board doors in four-centred wooden arches. The passage in front has a delightful wooden arcade, the style suggesting a slightly later date.

Gabled wooden porches were added in 1605. These have paintings by Sampson Strong of Oxford illustrating themes of mercy and alms-giving. Strong also painted the market cross on the south gable. Other alterations of 1605–8 included the beautification of the hall with a stone bay window, a lantern, handsome panelling and a set of benefactors' portraits. Most prominent is a quaint pastiche of the bridge builders.

Brick Alley, originally founded in the 15th century by Geoffrey Barbour, was gradually taken over by Christ's Hospital. Poor, overcrowded buildings were replaced in 1718–20 by a splendid new range built of chequer brick with very fine gauged brick dressings. The design is novel. Single-room lodgings on two storeys are set back behind tall brick arcades with first-floor balconies. The stair projection makes a glorious centre-piece, with pedimented gable, urns and flowery Latin inscription.

By contrast, the smaller north range of almshouses was a private foundation. Charles Twitty of Abingdon, Deputy Auditor of the Exchequer, left £1,700 to cater for three poor men and as many women, all from his native town. Built in 1707 of chequer brick, these more modest almshouses have a simple symmetry, with central pediment-gable and square lantern.

73

White Hart Inn, Fyfield, Oxfordshire
Mid-15th century

SU 423987. At E end of Fyfield village, 9 miles (14 km) SW of Oxford, to N of A420

[C]

The White Hart was not built as an inn, but as a chantry house, and was known as the Hospital of St John the Baptist. It was founded in accordance with the will of Sir John Golafre (see also Long Alley, St Helen's Churchyard, Abingdon (72,

Interior of the hall at the White Hart Inn, Fyfield. CM

O)) who died in 1442 and was buried in the chantry chapel in the church. This was where the occupants of the chantry house, five poor bedesmen and a priest or master, were to pray for his soul in return for their upkeep.

The chantry house was sold at the Dissolution and altered in the 17th century, but expert work in 1962–3 has restored much of its original form. It is very like a small manor house, and the visitor can now choose to eat and drink in the hall, service end or upper cross-wing. The full-height hall, with arched

braces elegantly supporting the collar of the central truss, is a special treat.

At one end of the hall is a cross-passage with wide opposing doorways. The rear door could be made secure against the outside world, since there are slots in the jambs for a draw bar. Inside, two smaller wooden doorways with Tudor arches suggest that a pantry and buttery occupied the present bar area, with its heavy ceiling joists, while the room beyond is likely to have been the kitchen. Upstairs there was probably a dormitory for the bedesmen, and not the modern gallery you see today.

The other end of the hall was given finer treatment. Jambs of large windows survive in both side walls (the rear window was reconstructed in the 1960s), and the jetty of the cross-wing provides an inbuilt narrow canopy over a possible dais. Here the master would have sat in state, with his lodgings in the cross-wing behind him. Whereas the main building is of limestone rubble, now rendered over, the master's wing is distinguished by a timber-framed upper storey with tension bracing and a front gable.

Downstairs. the cross-wing seems to have had only one long room, with heavy chamfered joists, a wide front window, and confused fireplace arrangements. In a rear corner a stone spiral stair, now only visible from underneath, leads up to the two rooms and closet above. Here there are two blocked windows with original wooden mullions, one with a groove for a sliding shutter. Not even the master had the luxury of glass.

7

Living off the Land

These four counties are a land of farms, rich from crops grown in fertile valleys, and from sheep and cattle grazed on the hills. There are none of the mineral resources that make for heavy industry. Car plant at Cowley owes more to the local residence of William Morris (of Morris Motors, not the Arts and Crafts Movement) than to any geographical advantage, and the industrial estates around towns such as Northampton, Daventry and Banbury arise from modern ease of transport. This, and the decentralisation of London, also account for the office blocks and computers of Slough, Bracknell and Reading. The truly local buildings of this chapter are therefore all to do with farming, food production and associated manufacturing.

Medieval farming in this area, and throughout the country, was geared primarily to feeding the local population with grain, meat, and milk, and so kept a careful balance between arable land and livestock. A map with parish boundaries will show, for instance, long parishes like Uffington (21, O), which stretch from the valley bottom right up across the scarp of the Berkshire Downs to the high grazing land beyond. By the 16th century, however, farming had become more specialised. Sheep, kept on the chalk Downs in the south and the limestone uplands in the north, were big business, and crafty landowners, such as the Treshams of Rushton (see chapter 9) and the Spencers of Althorp, were enclosing large tracts of land for grazing. In the valleys, the emphasis was put on grain, and production peaked in the late 18th and early 19th centuries. It is to this period that the vast storage barns of the Thames Valley (e.g., at Ipsden (O) and near Benson (O) at Preston Crowmarsh and Fyfield Manor) belong.

The farm buildings at Cogges (75, O) clearly reflect these changes, and later fluctuations, on a smaller scale. Evidence for the grain boom is provided by two large early 18th-century barns and by stabling for the plough horses and oxen. When the boom ended and the agricultural decline of the mid-19th century set in, the farm resorted, like many others, to meat and dairy production – the yard was divided into various fold areas and new shelter sheds and pigsties were put up. They were built as cheaply as possible, not with stone as before, but with weatherboarding, brick and primitive bundle thatch.

Farmsteads similar to Cogges can be found throughout the area, but differ in guise according to the local building materials. Another example from the limestone belt of Northamptonshire/ north Buckinghamshire/north Oxfordshire, can be visited at Filkins (O), where a fine barn of c.1730 is now used as a weaving workshop. Chiltern farms are often built of chalk and flint, as at Medmenham (15, BU), whereas timber framing and weatherboard are usual in the Vales. There is a good collection of the timber-framed type at the Chiltern Open Air Museum (BU), where redundant buildings have been re-erected as a 19th-century farmstead. Visitors can also see a rare cruck barn of c.1500.

Whereas old farmsteads like Cogges were built piecemeal, usually within a village, new farms of the late 18th and 19th centuries were carefully planned and built all in one go, out in their newly enclosed fields. Estate farms could take model planning even further, as on the Grafton Estate in Northamptonshire, where the land agent, John Green, designed a uniform set of farms in the 1830s. Each has a symmetrical stone farmhouse with a Doric porch and recessed side wings, and formal yards behind. Two near Stoke Bruerne – Stoke Plain and Stoke Gap Lodge – can be glimpsed from the road. A more modest model farm, also of 1830, at Pitstone Green (see **Pitstone Windmill** (82, BU) is occasionally open to the public as a farm museum.

Inside Great Coxwell Barn. ES

The great medieval 'tithe barns' were not so much farm buildings as collection depots for large estates. **Great Coxwell Barn** (76, O) served the Abbey of Beaulieu, while the striped stone barn at Wellingborough (N) was built for Croyland Abbey. The large barn at Swalcliffe (O), splendid with gabled porches, buttresses and arch-braced crucks, was just one of several built for the New College estates in c.1400. Other barns of similar status are a timber-framed barn of c.1500 at Edlesborough (BU), with alternate cruck and post trusses, and a brick barn at Addington (BU), probably built in the early 17th century.

Of the buildings for processing food, the most important were mills for grinding and crushing cereals into flour and animal fodder. **Mapledurham** (79, O) is one of the most picturesque of the smaller watermills, and is kept in working order, as are those at Ford End near Ivinghoe in Buckinghamshire and Great Billing, Northampton. Many others survive as houses. Although they may pre-date Domesday in origin, few retain any structural detail earlier than the 17th century, and the larger mills are usually later in date. These include the now converted mill at Hambleden (BU), on the Thames, with fine weatherboarded buildings of the late 18th and early 19th centuries, and the Whitworth Mill at Wellingborough (N), on the Nene, built in brick in 1886.

Windmills are also well represented. There are 17th-century post mills at Pitstone and Brill (11, BU), the latter dramatically sited above the Oxford Plain, and early 19th-century tower mills at Great Haseley (O), Quainton (BU) and Bradwell (BU). The Chilterns boast picturesque smock mills (tower mills with tapering timber sides) at Lacey Green and above Turville.

Ale, brewed from barley, was almost as much a staple food as bread. There used to be small maltings and backyard brewhouses everywhere, but the most distinctive buildings belong to the late 18th and 19th centuries, when brewing became more specialised. **Hook Norton Brewery** (78, O) is a delightful example of a small-scale concern set up to meet local demand, but most of the larger

Blanket Hall, Witney. PM

breweries were concentrated in the Thames Valley. Here there was plenty of barley, and ready transport. Brakspear's was established at Henley-on-Thames (O) in 1779, and Morrell's at Oxford in 1782. Morland's at Abingdon (7, O) dates back to the 1860s, but has splendid tower buildings of 1911–12.

Apart from food, the main products of the area were wool, from the numerous sheep on the uplands, and leather, from the cattle that later took their place. The woollen cloth industry brought prosperity as early as the 12th century, and was still important in the 19th. Reading was a major centre in the south, as was Newbury, where the Wharf Road Museum, built in 1626–7, originally served as a weaving workshop. In Oxfordshire, Burford (12, O) became rich as a market town, while other centres went on to develop specialities: blankets at **Witney** (83, O), plush in the Banbury area, kerseys and tweed from the magnificent mill at **Chipping Norton** (74, O).

The leather trade has left a less dramatic heritage. Deer and sheep supplied a glove industry centred around Oxford and Woodstock, but this was small fry compared with the boots and shoes of **Northampton** (81, N). The hides of the cattle that grazed in the Nene Valley were already being used for

shoemaking in the Middle Ages, but the industry only became dominant after the Civil War. In Northampton it was to generate a 19th-century sprawl of brick factories and terraced housing, but you can also find small workshops and factories dotted about at Earls Barton (N), Higham Ferrers (N), Olney (18, BU) and other neighbouring villages.

Both weaving and shoemaking were slow to benefit from the Industrial Revolution, partly because there was no ready power supply other than water. Instead they continued to run on a small-scale cottage basis until well into the 19th century. An interesting parallel is the High Wycombe (BU) furniture industry – workshops can be seen at West Wycombe and the Chiltern Open Air Museum, but most of the initial work was carried out by 'bodgers', busily turning chair legs on makeshift lathes in the beechwoods. Even smaller in scale was the lace industry, with women and girls working at home or in dame schools. Acland saw one such 'school', with thirteen children squeezed into a tiny room, when he visited the squatter cottages at Marsh Gibbon (14, BU) in 1858. Olney has a small lace 'factory' dating from 1928, and a fine collection of lace in the Cowper and Newton Museum.

Small-scale industry and a predominantly agricultural economy were the inevitable products of an amenable but coal-less land. This is not to say that the land was totally devoid of useful minerals. The marlstones of Northamptonshire and north Oxfordshire were worked for their iron content at Hunsbury Camp (N) and elsewhere; clay from the Vales was transformed by small brickworks, such as the ones at **Great Linford** (77, BU) and Nettlebed (O), into bricks of a lovely soft red colour, the ends often glazed or vitrified by exposure in the kiln to an attractive purple-blue or grey; and the limestones of the Burford (O) and Weldon (N) areas (see map in introduction) earned a national reputation for their exceptionally fine quality. Wren used Burford stone for his City churches, and even head-hunted the masons who quarried it – the Strongs of Taynton and Christopher

Brick Kilns at Great Linford. CM

74
Bliss Tweed Mill, Chipping Norton, Oxfordshire
1872

SP 304266. 18 miles (29 km) NW of Oxford, off A44, immediately to W of town

[D]

Kempster of Upton. The lasting contribution of these building materials, however, was not so much the livelihood they provided but rather the beauty they bestowed on the area's architectural heritage.

This majestic mill is the most imposing industrial building in the area and is not to be missed, though it ceased working in 1980, and is now being converted into apartments. It was the grandest in a series of mills built for the Bliss family, and represents the climax of their fortunes.

Bliss Tweed Mill, Chipping Norton (before conversion). JAC

William Bliss II, for whom the surviving mill was built, wrote an account of the family business in 1877. It began in 1758 as a 'small manufactory' of woollen covers for horses and carts, expanded in the 1790s with popular kersey check designs, and won first class medals for its tweeds, serges and shawls at the Great Exhibition of 1851. As business grew, the initial practice of contracting out work proved inadequate and William Bliss I implemented a factory system, with large-scale machinery housed in two mills. Upper Mill, on the present site of Dunstan Avenue, was fitted up with new carding machines in 1804, and later with horse-driven spinning frames. Lower Mill, on the present site, was acquired in 1810 for water-powered spinning and fulling. Steam power was introduced in the mid-19th century, and a special branch line was built to bring the coal.

As at Witney, fire was to prove a major hazard. Lower Mill was rebuilt in 1863, but burned down almost immediately, in February 1872. Only a single-storey weaving shed, and a range with former office and boiler house, survived. The main building that you see today had to be begun from scratch and, amazingly, was completed within a year, while Upper Mill worked round the clock. The result was a vast building five to six storeys high, with large open floor spaces to take the newest carding and spinning machines, all powered by a steam engine in the basement. Future fire damage was minimised by using cast-iron columns and girders instead of wood, and by constructing the upper floors on shallow barrel vaults of brick. This fireproof technology, pioneered in 1797 at the Ditherington Flax Mill, Shrewsbury, had all too often been ignored in Oxfordshire.

In contrast with its factory interior, the outside of the mill has all the grandeur of a stately home. This owed much to the rising aspirations of the Bliss family, but was also influenced by the current palazzo style of Lancashire/West Yorkshire mill design. The architect was George Woodhouse of Bolton, and the round-arched top windows, heavy cornice and corner towers find parallels at Saltaire,

Bradford and Reddish. The most striking feature is the chimney, which rises as a tall Tuscan column from the dome of a semi-circular staircase tower.

Sadly the success of the mill was short-lived. A new fashion for loud Scotch plaid put sober tweed out of business, Upper Mill was sold off, and the Bliss family left Chipping Norton in 1896.

75

Cogges Manor Farm Museum, Oxfordshire
13th century to c.1900

SP 362096. Across the Windrush from Witney (see map for Witney's Blanket Industry (83, O)). Road access signposted from B4022

[A]

Manor Farm at Cogges is much more than just a farm museum – it presents the neatly packaged history of a small rural settlement. Clearly visible in its grounds are the moated site of a Norman manor house and the earthworks of a shrunken medieval village. Still standing are the remains of a 12th-century priory (now part of The Vicarage), and a 13th-century manor that was extended to form the present farmhouse. Its traceried lights make

very fine kitchen windows. The interior of the farmhouse has been set up as it would have been c.1900, but the gardens, orchards and farm buildings around it go back long before.

The farm buildings vary in date from the early 18th century to the late 19th. They also vary in function and style, in accordance with changing fortunes and patterns of farming. The two large barns that dominate the corner of the yard pre-date 1725, and were built at a time when cereal production was becoming more profitable than the former balance of sheep, dairy and arable farming. They are prosperous buildings, of local rubble stone, with ample facilities for housing large harvests of wheat and barley. Both barns are kept well ventilated by leaving the scaffold holes open, and both have porches and large rear doorways, so that carts could shelter, unload and exit without difficulty. The wheat barn, with the larger porch, also has its stone-flag threshing floor, the cart doors providing light and a through draught for winnowing. Unthreshed sheaves would have been stored on the earth floors to either side, and later in the small rickyard in front, while winnowed grain was transferred to a separate granary.

Cereal farming depended on plough horses and oxen, so more stabling was needed as well as more storage. A small, older barn was converted for the horses,

Cogges Manor Farm Museum, an aerial view.
© SKYSCAN BALLOON PHOTOGRAPHY

and is still arranged in basic early 19th-century fashion. It has mangers along each side, and racks that were filled with hay dropped straight down from the loft above, through slits in the ceiling. The later stalls for riding horses, at one end, are much finer.

Lowly oxen were kept in a humble byre, built probably in the late 18th century, when the farm was just beginning to feel the pinch. The byre walls are still of stone, but the roof is only bundle thatch – it has no expensive carpentry, just a low ceiling of rough logs, with bundles of twigs piled up on top so as to form a shallow pitch for the thatch. Inside are eight wide stalls with heavy plank partitions, stone troughs and a feeding passage.

By the mid-19th century, the grain boom was definitely over and the farm turned increasingly to livestock. The yard was gradually divided up into smaller fold areas, and new buildings were put up, as cheaply as possible. The weatherboarded cowshed probably came first, then open-fronted shelter sheds, built up against the older stone walls of the yard. One is roofed with bundle thatch, another with Bridgwater tiles. Last of all came the late 19th-century pigsties in the middle of the yard, their cheap brick walls and Welsh slate roofs looking very out of place amongst all the stone.

Most of these buildings now house either animals or displays of agricultural implements. Especially interesting is the collection of equipment in the dairy, a late medieval building conveniently close to the house. It is crammed full of large lead settling trays, butter churns and cheese presses.

76

Great Coxwell Barn, Oxfordshire
Mid-13th century–c.1300

SU 269940. At N end of Great Coxwell village, 2 miles (3 km) SW of Faringdon, between A420 and B4019

[A] NT

William Morris dubbed this barn 'the finest piece of architecture in England'.

Great Coxwell Barn from the west. AFK

It is indeed hard to beat. Inside the buttressed stone walls and gables, below the massive stone slate roof, the interior of the barn is vast and dark and quite as magnificent as any cathedral. What impresses the visitor is the honesty of its structure – a seeming forest of essential timbers marshalled into architectural order. Tall wooden posts, set proud on tall stone piers, rise to support the high roof trusses, and divide the barn into nave and aisles; extraordinary double braces link posts to tiebeams and arcade plates, forming a regular procession of huge gaunt arches. The connoisseur of such buildings will note the cruck supports here, rising between the main trusses direct from the aisle walls, and strengthening the barn without impinging on its space.

The enormous size of the building and its fine construction make it quite obvious that this was no ordinary barn. It was built by the Cistercians and was, for them, a comparatively modest affair. Their barn at Beaulieu, in Hampshire, had twice the capacity, and rivalled the mammoth Cluniac barn, sadly long-demolished, at Cholsey. The Cistercians had been given lands at Great Coxwell and Faringdon by King John in 1204, and retained them as an outlying agricultural estate, or grange, when the

monks settled at Beaulieu Abbey. Masonry details and radio-carbon dating suggest that they built the barn as early as the mid-13th century, but tree-ring technology provides a later date of c.1300–1310.

Inside the barn the monks would have stored their harvest of grain, possibly with oats in one half and wheat in the other, as was the practice elsewhere. The crops were kept ventilated by leaving the square scaffolding holes and the eaves open, while splayed wall slits provided light as well as air. The tall porches sheltered carts and allowed them to be driven right through the barn, for ease of unloading. Originally they were the only entrances – the doorways in the end gables were not cut through until the 18th century.

As regards function, the porches are the most interesting parts of the barn. Their opposing doorways provided a through draught for winnowing (separating the threshed grain from the chaff), and the east porch has a dovecot high inside its gable. The west porch probably served as an office for the bailiff or 'grangerius'. This porch has a small pedestrian side entrance, and is wider than the other, allowing for limited stabling to one side. Stairs led up from the internal doorway to a high loft.

77

Great Linford Brick Kilns, Milton Keynes, Buckinghamshire

1890s

SP 860415. Turn N from A422 (H3) at Linford Roundabout, then 2nd right into Marsh Drive and right into Willen Lane. At far end, go through gate on right-hand side, opposite car park, and follow path to kilns.

[A]

This small group of hidden kilns provides a discreet reminder that there was some industry in the area long before it was overtaken by the sprawl of Milton Keynes. The new railway towns of Wolverton and New Bradwell devoured bricks, creating a demand that Great Linford was ideally placed to meet. Clay could be dug on site, from pits that have now become ponds, while the canal alongside brought coal for firing and took away the finished bricks. The kilns functioned from the 1890s until 1911,

fired by a stoker who lived in the cottage by the gate.

The kilns are of the downdraught type, with shallow domes like brick beehives. Iron bands around the walls helped to prevent distortion as the whole kiln expanded in the intense heat of firing. As the diagram shows, heat rose from eight low arched fireholes up a narrow flue or 'bag' between the main structure and an inner wall, now missing. It was then deflected by the dome down through the bricks in the central firing chamber, and sucked out through a perforated floor along an underground flue to a separate chimney. Chimney, flue and floor are now gone.

This type of kiln represented a great advance on the simple roofless (scotch) kilns more commonly used by small-scale brickworks, and even on the traditional updraught pottery kilns, with their bottle-shaped chimneys. (A good 18th-century 'bottle' kiln survives at Nettlebed (O), and was used for firing bricks as well as coarse pottery.) The downdraught design gave much more control over firing, as draughts could be regulated by vents in the dome or

by a damper in the chimney flue. Temperatures could be kept more even, and different colours could be obtained more accurately by oxidation or reduction.

Two kilns survive at Great Linford, and low walls mark the site of another, all formerly served by the same chimney. This group of three allowed for a rotational system of firing, one kiln being fired while another cooled and the third was emptied and refilled. Each kiln had a capacity of 20,000–25,000 bricks.

78

Hook Norton Brewery, Oxfordshire

1872 and c.*1900*

SP 348332. In Brewery Lane at W end of Hook Norton village, 8 miles (13 km) SW of Banbury, via minor roads off A361

[D]

This is a small commercial brewery that still brews beer as it did in 1900, and has always been run by the Harris and Clarke families. Its distinctive beer is much appreciated by devotees of real ale, and its ironstone buildings are an equally distinctive blend of fortress and Chinese pagoda.

The business began in 1849 as a maltings for local barley. John Harris soon expanded into brewing and in 1872 built the four-storey brewing tower that stands to the right of the taller complex. Further expansion was required to meet the demands of railway navvies and the local ironstone works. A large stable block was added in 1894, and an office block with cellars below in 1896. The greatest investment, however, was the set of four- and six-storey towers of 1898–1901, designed by a specialist London architect, William Bradford. Together with a steam engine and other equipment from Buxton and Thornley of Burton-on-Trent, Bradford's bill came to £18,386 3s 9d.

The steam engine is housed at the base of the central four-storey tower and is complete with flywheel, belts and geared shafting. Now oil-fired, it still

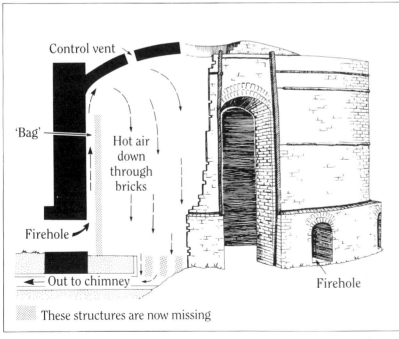

Control vent

'Bag'

Hot air down through bricks

Firehole

Out to chimney

Firehole

These structures are now missing

The downward flow of air through one of the brick kilns at Great Linford (after Milton Keynes Development Corporation). EH

94

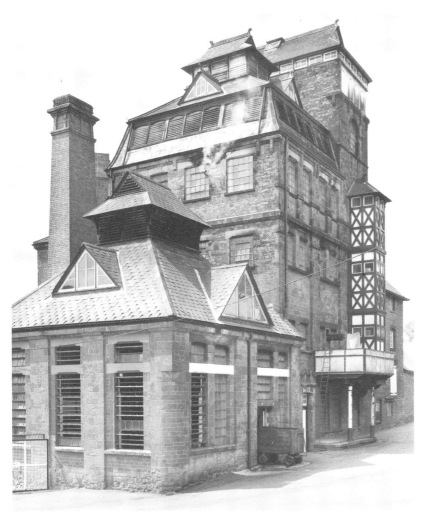

Hook Norton Brewery, the copper house and brewing towers. JB

the decorative half-timbering of the hoist shaft. Inside the brewery it is light, airy and spacious, with cast-iron columns and criss-cross wooden balustrading.

79

Mapledurham Watermill, Oxfordshire
15th–18th century

SU 669767. 3 miles (5 km) NW of Reading, signposted off A4074
[A]

Mapledurham is an idyllic little village of flint and brick cottages, close to Reading but so remotely tucked away, down by the Thames, that it almost seems preserved in a time warp. It comes complete with church, almshouses, 16th-century mansion, and an imposing house for the miller. The watermill itself, in the grounds of Mapledurham House, is as picturesque as you could imagine, and has been restored to working order. You can be mesmerised by the turning of the wheel, deafened by the rumble of the machinery, and tempted by the sweet smell into buying a bag of freshly ground flour.

The mellow brick and weatherboard exterior of the mill disguises a complex history. There has been a mill on the site since Domesday, but the earliest structural details are the remnants of a 15th-century timber frame that runs through the middle of the building. This still helps to enclose the present machinery but belonged to a lower mill, originally powered by a waterwheel at the far gable end. A second wheel was added at the near gable, where the present wheel works, probably in the later 17th century. At the same time the mill was extended on the upstream side, and the roof was raised to accommodate grain bins. These were filled with the aid of the sack hoist housed in the small wooden turret.

The mill's heyday came in the 18th and early 19th centuries. It continued to grind coarse flour and to crush feed as before, but also aimed to supply the new demand for fine white flour. Flour

pumps water from deep wells immediately below up to a tank in the top of the six-storey tower, and hoists malt sacks up to a mill on the fifth floor. Both ingredients, water and malt, then descend by gravity. The water is boiled on the third floor, and mixed with the ground malt in wooden mash tuns on the second floor. The resulting 'sweet wort' is then tapped off to be boiled with hops in the copper. The lower Copper House is easily recognisable to the left, where its louvred cast-iron windows and wooden roof vents gush with steam during boiling.

After the hops have settled, the wort is pumped back up to a large shallow tank at the top of the four-storey tower, where more wooden louvres and a central vent help it to cool. From here it descends through vertical refrigerators to the rear block, where it is fermented and casked. Finally the casks are rolled through tunnels to cellars under the offices.

The design of the buildings, especially the roofscape with its distinctive venting, is dictated by function, but style is not forgotten. The walling is severe with almost ashlar stonework, buttress-like pilasters and narrow corbels. Deep bracketed eaves, fancy ridge cresting and perky triangular dormers provide light relief, along with

95

Mapledurham Watermill. CM

dressers, which sifted out the bran, were installed in yet another extension on the downstream side of the building. By the end of the 18th century, production was so great that flour, bran and crushed oats were having to be stored in a barn on the island, before being loaded on to barges bound for London.

In the course of all this activity, the machinery has been steadily worn away and replaced piecemeal in traditional fashion. The undershot waterwheel is a modern reconstruction, made of oak with elm paddles, and the interior wheels are a mixture of wood and cast iron, wooden cogs making for easy, on-the-spot replacement. They power two sets of millstones and the sack hoist. Everything is clearly visible, and, if you can hear above the din, you can listen to a tape that explains how it all works!

80

Minster Lovell Dovecot, Oxfordshire
15th century?

SP 324114. At Minster Lovell Hall, 2 miles (3 km) NW of Witney, signposted off B4047. Access via Hall ruins

[A] EH

Medieval dovecots or pigeon houses were not the picturesque niceties that they became in the 19th century. They were functional buildings that ensured a supply of eggs, rich manure and fresh meat throughout the winter. They were

also symbols of privilege. As the birds fed on any nearby crop regardless of who grew it, the right to keep a dovecot was open only to lords of the manor and clergy, a restriction not lifted in theory until 1761/2.

The dovecot at Minster Lovell is a suitably fine example. It takes the form of a short round tower of limestone rubble, with offset eaves and a conical roof of stone slates, and is similar to other manorial dovecots that can be seen at Rousham House and Marcham, also in Oxfordshire. Birds entered through a simple glover (an open-sided turret) at the apex and were housed in nesting boxes built into the wall

thickness. There are about 650 of these boxes, arranged in rows with continuous stone ledges on which the birds could alight.

Human access was required for the collection of birds and eggs and for cleaning out the muck. Only a small doorway was provided, however, so as to inhibit any escape of the pigeons. Another necessity would have been a ladder for reaching the higher nesting boxes. It is likely, given the round form of the building, that this hung from a potence, a revolving arm attached to a central post. The collector could then have swung himself round along the rows without having to climb down.

Inside the dovecot at Minster Lovell. EH

Such an arrangement still exists in the dovecot at Kinwarton in Warwickshire.

The date of the Minster Lovell dovecot is a little uncertain. It is tempting to believe that it was built in the 1430s by William, Lord Lovell, at the same time as the new Hall – it stands in the Hall farmyard along with two barns, one of which has medieval buttressing. However, a later date is equally possible, for the round tower form remained common into the 17th century.

81

Northampton's Boot and Shoe Industry, Northamptonshire
Later 19th century

SP 7661

[D]

Northampton is renowned for its shoe industry, and houses a splendid collection of footwear in the Central Museum in Guildhall Road. There is also a Museum of Leathercraft (see map of Northampton (16, N). A more obvious reminder of the industry is the sea of red-brick factories and terraced housing to the northeast of the town centre, between the Kingsthorpe and Wellingborough Roads.

Although this area was not developed until the later 19th and early 20th centuries, it contains the earliest buildings that catered specifically for the shoe industry. Before then, shoemakers had worked at home, or in small workshops, requiring only light, skill, and a small kit of tools. They became very highly organised – the different processes of cutting out, stitching and assembling uppers and soles were all divided out among specialist workers – but there was no need for a factory system until the mid-19th century, when mechanisation began to take a belated hold. First came the Singer sewing machine, adapted for stitching uppers in 1856, followed by the Blake sole-sewer of 1864, a machine far too heavy and expensive to use at home. One of the first factories to install such machinery was the Manfield Warehouse

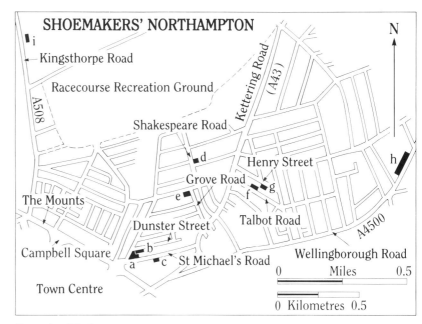

Shoemakers' Northampton. EH

of 1857, a grand Italianate palazzo, complete with bell tower, that used to ennoble Campbell Square. Why Northampton chose to obliterate this key heritage building for the sake of the present development is now hard to imagine!

One can only hope that the less glamorous but equally illuminating buildings beyond the Mounts do not all share the same fate. A concentration of them is to be found in St Michael's Road and Dunster Street. The Hawkins Building (a), inscribed 'Waukerz Boot Factory', sets the tone for the 1880s. It is a gaunt four-storey block of pale red brick with stone bands and cornice, cast-iron windows and slate roof. A pedimented doorcase and pilastered bays with pediment-like gables provide the main features. The building behind (b), now used by EMF Electrical, is slightly later, with brick window aprons and a shaped central gable. The premises of R E Tricker (c), faced with treacly-brown glazed brick, are more Art Nouveau in style, and have leaded windows with stained glass motifs and label for the office door.

Smaller concerns are to be found further north in Shakespeare Road. The best example is the Cowper Works (d),

three to four storeys high but with the owner's house-cum-office attached to one side. Not far away are the larger Grove Works (e), with the same pediment gables as at Hawkins. Similar dated examples are the Normal Boot and Shoe Factory (f) of 1889 in Talbot Road, and the Queen Boot Factory (g) of 1890 in Henry Street.

These buildings stand proud above even two-storey terraces of workers' housing. The earlier rows tend to have arched doorways, small tripartite sashes and simple rendered dressings. Later developments of the 1890s, east of Kettering Road, feature bay windows and fancier dressings. Sadly the homogeneous character of the area is beginning to suffer from a rash of plastic windows and inappropriate stone cladding.

More distinctive buildings characterise later approaches to the industry. Manfield's new factory (h) of 1890–2 on Wellingborough Road followed an American lead with a more efficient single-storey system. It was designed by Charles Dorman in an Arts and Crafts style with shaped and pedimented gables, mullion and transom windows and carved terracotta plaques. Barratt's Footshape Boot Works

Barratt's Footshape Bootworks, Northampton. CM

(i) of 1913, on Kingsthorpe Road, is still multi-storey but enjoyably Baroque with jolly stripes.

82

Pitstone Windmill, Buckinghamshire
1627?

SP 946157. 8 miles (13 km) E of Aylesbury, off B488 to S of Ivinghoe

[A] NT

Pitstone Windmill, the earliest known post mill in England, stands jauntily in the middle of a cornfield beneath the Chilterns. It was built in or before 1627, the date inscribed on one of the wall rails inside, and therefore pre-dates the very similar mill of the 1680s at Brill (11, BU). Like all such working buildings, it has been subjected to much wear and tear – further dates of 1749 and 1784 record just some of the necessary repairs – and in 1963 the mill and its machinery had to be restored after a long period of dereliction. Much of the basic 17th-century structure, however, survives, and demonstrates the sound simplicity of its engineering.

Post mills were beautifully efficient and adaptable. All the mill machinery was housed in the upper wooden body, which could easily be pushed round a central post by the tail pole, so as to bring the sails into the wind. The only difficulty lay in keeping the whole thing

Pitstone Windmill. CM

upright – hence the brick roundhouse below. This was rebuilt in 1895, but inside there are huge great braces with 17th-century mouldings. These support and steady the massive wooden post from which the whole framework of the upper body hangs. The post has a 17th-century moulded base, like a column, and many other timbers have stop-chamfering of the same date. Another period feature is the shaped bracket on the outside, at the slightly pointed sail end.

The working of the machinery is rather more complex but easily decipherable. The wooden lattice sails were designed to take canvas covers that could be reefed in high winds. They turned the windshaft and the great cogged wooden wheel on the top floor, which linked with a 19th-century iron wallower wheel and gearing, which turned two sets of millstones. The grain was fed into a hopper, shaken in between the millstones, ground, and directed down a chute into meal bins on the floor below. For fine flour it was then taken back up to the top of the mill and fed through a dresser, housed in a narrow extension at the entrance end of the wooden body. Other refinements to aid the miller included a braking system for the main wheel, tentering gear to control the speed and fineness of the grinding process, and a sack hoist.

The mill used to belong to Pitstone Green Farm, just across the field. This is run, in part, as a farm museum and is well worth visiting on open days. It is especially interesting as it was a model farm, built for the Ashridge estate in 1830.

83

Witney's Blanket Industry, Oxfordshire

SP 3510. 11 miles (18 km) W of Oxford, off A40

[D]

Cotswold wool was being woven in Witney by the 12th century, and by the 17th century the town had come to enjoy a unique reputation for high-

98

quality blankets and coverings, such as capes and horse blankets. By the 18th century it was even exporting striped duffles to North American Indians. Several modern mills are still in production, and older traces of the industry can be found throughout and around the town.

The most obvious blanket buildings all belong to the 18th and 19th centuries, for until then the industry worked on a cottage basis. 16th- and 17th-century probate inventories show that weavers worked at home, their houses containing perhaps a wool store, a warping chamber and a weaving shop with up to three broad looms. As there is no mention of spinning or carding equipment, such work must have been done out of town, while fulling took place in mills on the fast-flowing Windrush.

Blanket Hall, in High Street, represents an early attempt to co-ordinate all these small-scale enterprises. Set high up under the pediment are the arms of the Company of Witney Blanket Makers, incorporated in 1711 as a result of growing concern about corruption and declining standards. The company aimed to control quality and terms of employment, and in effect set up a closed shop dominated by the Early, Marriott and Collier families. At first the company met at the Staple Hall Inn, but then built itself grand headquarters. Blanket Hall is dated 1721 and boasts a fine facade in amateur Baroque style. Inside, blankets were weighed and inspected, courts held for fining defaulters, and feasts consumed by company and workforce.

Industrialisation did not reach Witney until late in the 18th century. Weavers belatedly began to make use of the flying shuttle (invented 1733), and the Early family introduced water-powered spinning machinery at *New Mills*, a mile upstream from the town. When this burnt down in 1818 they made a special trip to Lancashire to buy the latest equipment. New Mills became a specialist spinning mill much resented by local hand-spinners. It was largely

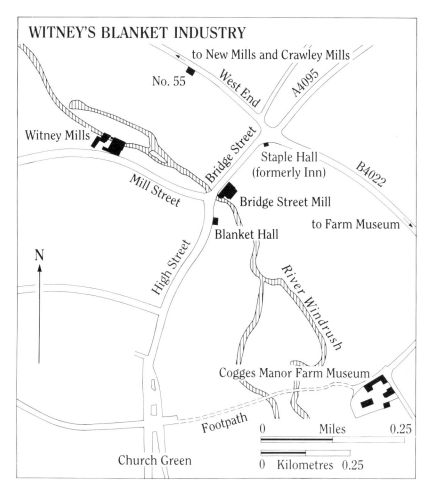

Witney's blanket industry. EH

rebuilt in 1883, after another fire, by the local architect William Cantwell.

The prominence of the Early family continued throughout the 19th century. One of their smaller concerns was the hand weaving of wide double blankets in a converted house with rear workshops and storerooms at *55 West End*. This survives as one of several small early 19th-century factories in the street. Later activities, however, were focused at *Witney Mills* in Mill Street, where the large four-storey block of c.1820 contained spinning and fulling machinery powered by the Windrush. Weaving continued to be done by hand until the 1860s. The chimney is evidence

of the later use of steam power, and was built in 1895 by Charles Early, along with new buildings fronting Mill Street. These are also by Cantwell, although much rebuilt after yet another fire in 1905.

The earliest manufacturer to use steam power in Witney was William Smith of *Bridge Street Mill* in the 1860s. Coal was then more readily available, via the new railway of 1861. This mill, now workshops, has a late 19th-century facade with Dutch gables, but retains some of the older factory buildings behind. It catered for spinning and weaving, while fulling took place up-river at nearby Crawley.

8

Travel and Transport

People have been trekking, riding, or boating through this area for centuries, often following the same well-worn paths. Prehistoric man trudged along the Ridgeway to get his flints all the way from Norfolk, and now we saunter along it for pleasure. The Romans marched along Watling Street (the A5) to control their territories, and now we hurtle along it at 70 m.p.h. to our business conferences in Birmingham. The major termini are beyond our bounds, but there is much to look at along the way. It may not be spectacular – there are no mountain passes or deep gorges to cross – but there is plenty to illustrate man's ingenuity and determination.

Whereas early man kept to the Chiltern and Jurassic ridges, the Romans decided where they wanted to go and went straight there, along fine, made-up roads. Not for them the ruts and ever-widening paths created by hundreds of feet picking through the chalky mire of the Ridgeway. The new roads were not only trade routes but also a means of maintaining Roman administration. They linked the main tribal capitals, and survive best where these remained important. Silchester disappeared with the Dark Ages, and its approach routes from London and Towcester (N) are now very fragmented. St Albans and Cirencester fared better. Akeman Street, which linked the two, is now the A41 as far as Bicester (O), and the Watling Street corridor northwards now serves the A5 and the M1, the London to Birmingham Railway and the Grand Union Canal.

Medieval roads were far cruder. They followed more natural routes and had no proper surface. Their only permanent structures were the bridges needed for river crossings, and even these have usually been swept away, rebuilt or repaired many times. The bridge at **Newbridge** (91, O), and the nearby one at Radcot, are fine survivals from the 13th century. Built to carry the wool trade, they helped to establish new

routes from the Cotswolds to London. They were a great investment, as was the bridge at Abingdon (7, O), which sealed the town's prosperity and led to the decline of its rival, Wallingford. Both Abingdon and Wallingford bridges have been spasmodically rebuilt, but their many arches, some medieval, are reminders of the long causeways necessary to cross marshy flood plains.

Inns testify to the volume of traffic along our roads from medieval times onwards. The **George Hotel, Dorchester** (84, O) is highlighted here on account of the rare survival of its late medieval hall and galleried lodgings. Similar lodgings can be glimpsed behind the former George Inn at Burford (12, O). Many other inns were updated in the prosperous coaching days of the 18th and early 19th centuries. Their smart brick or stone facades retain distinctive coach entries and hide rear courtyards with former stables and lodgings. There are numerous excellent examples, but a particularly good group can be seen along the old A5 at Stony Stratford (BU), where the Cock and Bull Inns became proverbial.

These new-look inns boomed with the introduction of turnpikes in the early 18th century. Parishes relinquished their duties of road maintenance to turnpike trusts, who improved surfaces to attract custom, and financed the work with tolls. A relic of the system is the Swinford toll bridge (cost 2p per car) near Eynsham (O). This handsome stone bridge over the Thames was opened in 1769 and still has its toll cottage. Elsewhere, toll houses are often marked by canted or bow fronts, as with the early 19th-century example at Dorchester, and some were quite exotic. The diminutive Gothick castle on the Bath Road at Halfway (BE) has sadly disappeared.

Early turnpike trusts were obliged to provide milestones. The A40 east of Oxford, turnpiked in 1718, still has a good set – two stones near

The Grand Union Canal near Grove, Buckinghamshire. ES

101

Newbridge. AFK

Stokenchurch (BU) have Roman numerals and are dated 1744. Such milestones usually conform to standard trust designs, but individual anomalies suggest a private patron. By the back gates to West Wycombe Park (39, BU), for instance, is a delightful column of 1752, with ball finial and inscriptions to 'The County Town', 'The City' and 'The University'. A rare early example is the guide post at Wroxton (O), set up by Francis White in 1686, with carved stone hands pointing the way to Banbury, London, Stratford and Chipping Norton.

Turnpike bridges could be very splendid affairs, symbolising the dignity of a town as well as bringing it more trade. Especially memorable are the later 18th-century stone bridges over the Thames – Magdalen Bridge at Oxford and the bridges at Henley-on-Thames (O) and Maidenhead (89, BE). Early 19th-century bridge builders looked for cheaper alternatives. The trustees at Newport Pagnell (BU) commissioned a study of the comparative costs of stone and iron, and accepted a cast-iron design based on the recent bridge at Sunderland. The result, Tickford Bridge, built in 1810, is extremely elegant. The suspension bridge at Marlow (90, BU) represents an even more daring choice.

Iron bridges bring us into the age of the canal and the railway. Canals came first, extending the already improved navigation routes of the major rivers. The Kennet and Avon, fully open in 1810, led west from Reading, while the Oxford Canal (1769–90) led north to link the Thames and the Midlands. This chapter focuses on the Grand Junction, now part of the **Grand Union Canal**

(85–7, N–BU), which was begun at Braunston (N) in 1793 to provide a wider, faster and more direct route down to London. The entries illustrate some of the major engineering problems faced by its surveyors, James Barnes and William Jessop, and the typically unpretentious style of canal building that now seems to go so well with the peaceful attractions of canal transport.

Railways have never been peaceful. Oxford regarded them as noisome and new-fangled, and initially refused to have a station anywhere near the city. There is also an apocryphal story that Northampton forced Robert Stephenson to re-route his London to Birmingham Railway away from the town through the tunnel at **Kilsby** (88, N). This tunnel is perhaps the greatest feat of engineering along the whole of that line, closely followed by the cavernous cutting near

The Grand Union Canal near Wolverton, crossing the Great Ouse in an iron trunk. CM

Blisworth (N) and the high embankment leading to the viaduct at Wolverton (BU). Wolverton itself became a railway town with works and terraced housing, but the earliest railway houses have only been preserved at nearby New Bradwell (20, BU). The Great Western Railway was built by the other great giant of the era, Isambard Kingdom Brunel, who dared to support his line on the exceptionally flat arches of the **Maidenhead Viaduct** (89, BE).

84

George Hotel, Dorchester, Oxfordshire
c.1500 and later

SU 578942. 8 miles (13 km) SE of Oxford, off A4074 (formerly A423), on W side of Dorchester High Street [C]

The historic village of Dorchester has always made a natural stopping place for travellers *en route* from London and Henley-on-Thames to Oxford and the Cotswolds, especially after the building of Abingdon bridge in 1416. The Oxford road, here the village High Street, was turnpiked as early as 1736, with a new bridge built over the Thame in 1815 and a toll house added shortly afterwards. Early hospitality would have been provided by the abbey (the guest house is now a museum), but after the Dissolution there was an increasing number of inns: at least eight by the late 17th century. The White Hart is 16th century, with brick infill dated 1691, but the George has the best early features, with a fine carriage entry and galleried lodgings in the rear yard.

The core of the building dates to c.1500 and may have been connected with the abbey. It has a splendid street frontage of jettied gables, a tall square carriage arch with hooks for doors, and heavy timbers with tension bracing and hollow chamfered mouldings. The left bays were remodelled in the late 16th century, acquiring carved jetty brackets, ovolo-mouldings and chimneys of narrow brick, and the whole facade was plastered and sashed in the late 18th–

early 19th centuries. Inside were three ground-floor parlours for drinking, dining and resting, and further parlours and chambers upstairs.

The restaurant behind the left bay formerly served as a hall-cum-kitchen. It is open to the roof and has a central truss with tiebeam and collar linked by a king strut. The heavy timbers and tension braces resemble those of the front range, but are rough and have been reused from an earlier building.

Beyond is the lodgings range, with chambers opening off a first-floor gallery. The modern kitchens below probably started life as stables. This part of the building is much restored externally, with recent weather-boarding and windows, but the main timbers are original, as are the two chamber doorways with shallow arches. The far end has been converted to a conference room, with king-strut trusses and curved windbraces displayed to advantage, but the other chambers remain. Now more luxurious, they would originally have been unheated and occupied by several guests in shared beds.

A later range added at right angles has been demolished, but at one time it would have formed a complete courtyard along with the buildings on the north side of the yard. These include a good mid-16th-century block with a timber-framed upper storey and the ground floor underbuilt in stone rubble.

85

Grand Union Canal, Northamptonshire– Buckinghamshire
1793 and later

The canal begins in Northamptonshire at Braunston (SP 532660), NW of Daventry. It leaves Buckinghamshire at Bulbourne (SP 933136), NE of Tring

[C]

The Grand Junction Canal (now part of the Grand Union Canal) was begun in 1793, to provide a fast new waterway between the Midlands and London. Instead of following a tortuous route along the earlier Oxford Canal and the difficult waters of the upper Thames, boats could turn off the Oxford Canal at Braunston and head down the Watling Street corridor to join the Thames at Brentford. The course of the canal was surveyed by James Barnes and William Jessop, and work began at both north and south ends, meeting at Cosgrove (86, N) in 1800. By 1805 the route was fully navigable.

Bulbourne Depot, on the Grand Union Canal. CM

Canal buildings give each half of the canal, north and south, its own style. At Braunston, for instance, you can see a toll house of 1796, with a canted end, and an informal variety of lock-keepers' cottages, all built of Northamptonshire red brick. The original hump-back bridges are of red brick too, although there are also some elegant cast-iron ones dating from 1829–34.

In Buckinghamshire, on the other hand, you tend to find later, standardised canal buildings, such as the maintenance depot at Bulbourne and the nearby toll house at Lock 45. These were mainly built in *c.*1848, of brown stock brick. Only the roofing slates, brought from Wales by barge, are the same as further north.

The canal itself is more consistent, as it faced similar problems along its whole length. For the sake of speed and efficiency it was built on as direct a course as possible, tunnelling under hills at Braunston and Blisworth (87, N), and crossing high above the Great Ouse near Cosgrove in an iron trunk. Lesser slopes were overcome with long series of locks, all built twice as wide as those on the Oxford Canal, so as to accommodate a wide barge or two narrow boats. This meant that boats went through more quickly, but so did the water.

Maintaining the water supply proved to be a major headache. One answer to the problem was to use a steam engine to pump water back up above the locks. A pumping station at Braunston, by Lock 1, goes back as early as 1805 (though the chimney bears the date of its rebuilding, 1897), and a further set of nine pumps were installed in Buckinghamshire, between Fenny

The George Hotel, Dorchester. CM

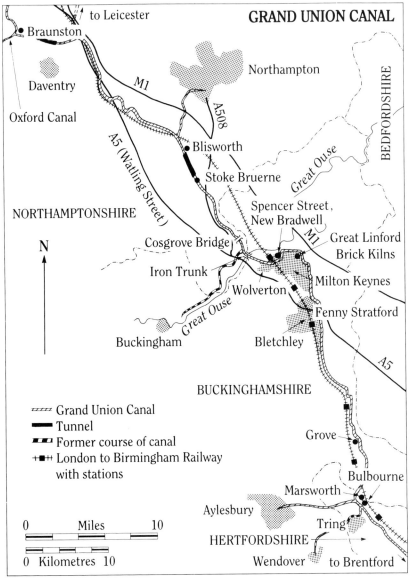

The Grand Union Canal. EH

Map legend:

GRAND UNION CANAL

to Leicester
Braunston
Daventry
Oxford Canal
M1
A508
Northampton
BEDFORDSHIRE
A5 (Watling Street)
Blisworth
Stoke Bruerne
Great Ouse
NORTHAMPTONSHIRE
N
Spencer Street, New Bradwell
Cosgrove Bridge
M1
Great Linford
Brick Kilns
Iron Trunk
Wolverton
Great Ouse
Milton Keynes
Buckingham
Fenny Stratford
Bletchley
BUCKINGHAMSHIRE
A5
Grove
Bulbourne
Marsworth
Aylesbury
Tring
HERTFORDSHIRE
Wendover   to Brentford

▨▨ Grand Union Canal
▬ Tunnel
▬■▬ Former course of canal
+■H London to Birmingham Railway
with stations

0   Miles   10
0   Kilometres   10

86

Grand Union Canal: Cosgrove Bridge and Wolverton Iron Trunk, Northamptonshire–Buckinghamshire
1800–11

SP 792427 and 800417. Bridge is at Cosgrove, 5 miles (8 km) NW of Milton Keynes, off A508. Iron Trunk ¾ mile (1 km) to SE can also be reached by walking NW along canal from Old Wolverton

[C]

In 1800 the north half of the Grand Junction Canal, begun at Braunston, met the south half that had started from Brentford, and the course of the whole was complete. The point of union is marked by a special bridge, very different from the standard hump-back type. Only where the canal passes through Cassiobury Park, Watford, is there anything of equal splendour, and there the style is classical. At Cosgrove the bridge is Gothick. It has a gracious wide four-centred arch, delicate blind tracery, and ogee turrets and niches. Unfortunately it was built of very soft limestone ashlar that has suffered serious erosion, and many of its delightful details are having to be renewed.

If you follow the towpath south-east, or walk north-west from Wolverton, you find that the Ouse Valley falls away below while the canal continues level, raised on an embankment. Almost a mile from the bridge the canal seems to launch itself into thin air as it passes over the river. In fact it is carried across by an iron trough, or trunk, which can be seen by leaving the towpath and venturing (bravely) through the narrow cattle creep. The aqueduct is not as dramatic as the nineteen arches of Telford's Pontcysyllte on the Llangollen Canal (1795–1805), but represents an extremely resourceful solution to a major engineering problem.

When the canal was first opened in 1800, it descended into the valley via a tedious series of locks. These were replaced by the embankment and a brick

Stratford and Marsworth, in 1838–41. Some of the small pumping houses still have their distinctive arched windows with cast-iron glazing bars.

Side ponds represent a later attempt to stem the loss of water through the locks, a problem that was exacerbated by the desperate measures taken to counter competition from the railways. In the 1830s the company built additional second locks alongside some of the original ones, so as to further increase the speed of traffic, and sometimes had to provide a second bridge arch as well. The scheme proved uneconomic, and most of the duplicate locks were filled in to minimise the drain on water. A few of them survive as dry docks (at Stoke Bruerne (87, N) and at Lock 45, Bulbourne), but often it is only the double bridge that tells the tale.

(The next two entries (86, N–BU and 87, N) explore some of the most interesting features of the canal in this area.)

104

Cosgrove Bridge. CM

aqueduct, which opened in 1805 only to collapse in 1808. The Iron Trunk, designed by Benjamin Bevan and cast by Reynolds and Co. at the Ketley Iron Works, opened in 1811. It is visually satisfying as well as practically successful. Its cast-iron sections are bolted together like voussoirs in a flat arch, and strengthened by bracing ribs that form elegant segments. Recent repainting emphasises the design. The centre is supported on a stone pier ennobled with cutwaters and cornice.

87

Grand Union Canal: Stoke Bruerne Wharf and Blisworth Tunnel, Northamptonshire
1793 and later

SP 744498 and 739502. 7 miles (11 km) S of Northampton, W of A508
[C]

The canal wharf at Stoke Bruerne is no quiet backwater, for tourism has taken the place of trade. However, the Waterways Museum, opened in 1963 in a former flour mill, is very well worth visiting. The adjoining terrace, formerly mill-workers' cottages, is little altered, and the Boat Inn opposite is still a public house. The stabling is less recognisable, but the wharfinger's office survives as a shop selling 'canalia'.

The canal itself presents fascinating evidence for the near-panic with which the canal company reacted to the coming of the railways (see Grand Union Canal (85, N–BU)). There are two parallel locks here: the original single

lock, now reconstructed as a dry dock, and a duplicate lock, now working, which was built in 1835, so as to speed up the flow of traffic. The original bridge, with its skew brick soffit, was extended at the same time, to cross the new channel with a second, flatter arch.

Beyond the museum the quieter towpath leads to Blisworth Tunnel. This, at 3,075 yards (2,810 m) long, is the longest canal tunnel still in use, and represents a remarkable achievement, both for the men who built it and the 'leggers' who propelled craft along it. The first attempts at tunnelling, in 1793–6, failed because of drainage problems, and freight had to be carried over Blisworth Hill by horse-drawn tramway. In 1802 the tunnel was re-started on a slightly different route, and was finished in 1805.

The tunnel has a section like a horseshoe arch and is completely lined with brick. Only the southern end retains its original brick facade. A line of brick ventilation shafts, surrounded by mounds of spoil, can be seen from the Blisworth–Stoke Bruerne road, with the tallest and most impressive shafts at the Blisworth end. Two more shafts were added after a particularly nasty tunnel accident in 1861.

Just as interesting as the structure are the methods of propulsion through the tunnel. There was no towpath and

Entrance to the Blisworth Tunnel, near Stoke Bruerne. CM

horses had to be led over the hill, along the former tramway. At first the boats were poled through. Then the precarious system of 'legging' was developed. The canal company provided registered 'leggers' who walked the boats through against the sides of the tunnel. As the tunnel was too wide for them to lie on deck, they lay on special boards that hung out either side over the water. Legging boards, and photographs illustrating the technique, can be seen in the museum. The effects of smoke inside the tunnel, when steam tugs were introduced in the 1850s, can only be imagined.

88

Kilsby Railway Tunnel, Northamptonshire
1834–8

SP 569708. 5 miles (8 km) SE of Rugby, off A5
[D]

As you drive along the A5 just to the east of Kilsby village, you suddenly come across a great brick tower standing in the middle of a field. It is not a displaced martello but a ventilation shaft for the London to Birmingham Railway, 136 ft (41 m) below ground level. There is another large shaft to the south-east, and a whole line of smaller ones. The north portal of the tunnel is visible from the A5 beyond Kilsby, the south portal from the small road to Ashby·St Ledgers.

The tunnel is one of those mammoth feats that characterise the heroic age of 19th-century engineering. It is 2,400 yds (2,194 m) long and lined with 30 million engineering bricks. The initial contractor, James Nowell, encountered terrible problems with quicksand and flooding at the south end, and handed the task back to Robert Stephenson, Chief Engineer and Surveyor of the line. After a secondary drainage tunnel failed, Stephenson resorted to a series of mighty steam pumps. Seven extra shafts were sunk and thirteen great engines pumped water out of the tunnel at a rate of 2,000 gallons a minute. By 1838, when the tunnel was completed, the cost

105

Kilsby Railway Tunnel, ventilation shaft. CM

had soared from an estimated £99,000 to the then enormous sum of £320,000.

Despite the practical problems, there was thought to spare for stylistic detail. The larger shafts, begun in 1836, have buttresses at the base, and castellated parapets with stone coping and corbels. Blue brick repairs do little to spoil the effect. The ashlar portals are even grander, with stepped corbels that pick up the castellated theme.

Stephenson was later to claim, in 1857, that tunnelling at Kilsby only became inevitable when his original route was diverted so as to avoid Northampton. Northampton, he said, 'distinguished itself by being rather more furious than other places in its opposition to railways'. The town would have had reason to be suspicious. In 1830, when the line became a serious proposition, railways were still very novel – the Stephensons' Manchester to Liverpool Railway had only just been completed, and the *Rocket*, designed by Robert's father, George, had only passed its trials in 1829. Historians loyal to Northampton, however, have shown that this claim has little basis, and that the present line was Robert Stephenson's own choice. Perhaps the problems he had encountered, and the cost of the work, had led him to present the matter in a different light.

89

Maidenhead Bridge and Railway Viaduct, Berkshire
1772–7 and 1837–9

SU 901813 and 901810. ⅔ mile (1 km) E of town centre

[C]

Both the Great West Road, now the A4, and the Great Western Railway cross the Thames at Maidenhead, providing us with a pair of splendid bridges. They may be the ones that appear in Turner's *Rain, Steam and Speed* of 1844. Although only 60 years and a small distance apart, they present a remarkable contrast in aesthetic ideal and technology.

The road bridge is a perfect piece of 18th-century classicism. It was built as a turnpike improvement, and replaced a late 13th-century wooden bridge. Robert Taylor designed an Italianate series of thirteen round arches in Portland stone, and John Townsend of Oxford was appointed as building contractor. Townsend also worked on other Thames bridges at Swinford (Eynsham) and Henley-on-Thames.

The bridge Townsend built at Maidenhead is extremely handsome. The seven arches that cross the river are the most impressive, as each arch has a fan of rusticated voussoirs. Above is a bracketed cornice and a stone balustrade. Modest cutwaters help to give a little vertical relief, but do not interrupt the basic horizontal sweep of the bridge. This descends gracefully on either side with three lesser arches, still with voussoirs but now set flush into the ashlar masonry.

There is no such ornate detail on Brunel's railway viaduct. This is built of brick, with plain pilasters and a simple stone cornice. The aesthetic impact of the bridge relies instead on the arches themselves. Semicircular land arches on either side suddenly give way to giant ellipses, which leap over the whole river in two great bounds. These arches are the widest ever built in brick, each spanning 128 ft (39 m), yet are also surprisingly shallow, avoiding any hump in the level tracks of the railway above.

The technological achievement made a virtue of necessity, since the Thames Commissioners only allowed one central pier, but the effect is one of immense elegance.

The present brick facades are copies of 1892, when the viaduct was widened to take two extra tracks. Brunel's original carried two of his speciality 7-ft gauge tracks, and is now sandwiched in the middle. Other viaducts on the line have been widened on one side only, and 1830s brickwork can still be seen. There is a good example at Reading, at the point where the railway crosses the Kennet near its junction with the Thames.

90

Marlow Suspension Bridge, Buckinghamshire
1829–32

SU 851860. Between High Wycombe and Maidenhead, off A404, at S end of Marlow High Street

[C]

The wonder of a suspension bridge has become almost commonplace in London, but this diminutive specimen at Marlow comes as a delightful surprise. It was built with the very latest cast-iron technology by William Tierney Clark, and was modelled on Clark's recent bridge at Hammersmith (1824–7). Whereas Hammersmith Bridge was completely remodelled by Sir Joseph Bazalgette in 1884–7, Marlow Bridge retains its original elegant form.

Marlow had previously been served by a wooden bridge slightly further downstream. This finally collapsed in 1830, and a stouter alternative was obviously required. It is surprising that stone was not used, as at nearby Henley-on-Thames and Maidenhead (89, BE). Suspension bridges were still very novel – Telford had only completed his great bridge over the Menai Straits as recently as 1824. The choice of this type at Marlow was therefore most adventurous, and was probably due to the persuasive powers of John Millington, self-styled Professor of Mechanics.

Marlow suspension bridge. AFK

Millington's designs, with cast-iron support towers, rapidly proved unworkable and he did a bunk to America. Clark was called in to the rescue. His reputation was much more sound – he had served his apprenticeship at Coalbrookdale, home of the very first cast-iron bridge (1777–9), and then worked with John Rennie at Blackfriars. He was later to bridge the Danube at Budapest. His work at Marlow survived until 1965, when all the cast iron was replaced with a steel copy.

The bridge consists of two stone towers, from each side of which hang two chains of long straight parallel links. From the bolting points are suspended slender rods which support the substructure of the road and footways. This substructure was originally timber, but was replaced with cambered iron 'I' girders, dated 1860 on the decorative round end plates.

This simplicity of structure contributes greatly to the beauty of the bridge. The white-painted ironwork is elegantly delicate and the chain links form a most graceful curve. Decorative detail is very restrained. The iron lattice balustrades have small daisy bosses and curious finials with petals arranged to form an open umbrella. The ashlar towers are modestly classical, with round arches and simple entablatures. Below the road deck, the masonry of the towers is channelled so as to look reassuringly sturdy, and the splay walls at each end of the bridge are treated in the same way. These walls have small piers capped with honeysuckle lunettes and handsome cast-iron lamp-posts.

91
Newbridge, Oxfordshire
13th century

SP 403013. 8 miles (12 km) W of Oxford, between Standlake and Kingston Bagpuize, on A415
[C]

The fine medieval bridge at Newbridge carried packhorses laden with Witney wool across the Thames, just after its confluence with the Windrush. At nearby Standlake, traders would have been beset by hermits exacting repair money for the bridge and alms for themselves. Nowadays the only hold-ups are the single flow of traffic across the narrow hump, and the temptations of two public houses.

Newbridge was only 'new' in comparison with Radcot Bridge, a smaller, three-arch bridge further upstream towards Lechlade. This was repaired and possibly rebuilt in 1208, and has much the same structural detail as Newbridge. Both have pointed arches built on broad stone ribs. At Newbridge these ribs have chamfered edges and can be seen under the second and fifth of the six arches. The ribs of the other arches have been cut away to allow more room for barges. At Radcot Bridge there are unchamfered ribs under the outer arches, but the central arch has been rebuilt, and has a smooth under-surface, constructed on wooden centering. This last technique became standard until ribs were revived by 19th-century architects. Sir George Gilbert Scott's bridge downstream at Clifton Hampden (O), opened in 1867, has splendid brick ribbing.

Another distinctly medieval feature at Newbridge are the pointed cutwaters on the upstream side, carried up through the parapet to form passing-places for pedestrians. The parapet itself has been completely rebuilt, but may originally have incorporated a shrine. At Radcot there is still the base of a niche that once held a statue of the Virgin.

Like all other structures in constant use, Newbridge has suffered over the centuries, most notably after the Civil War. Repairs can clearly be seen where the ashlar masonry has been patched with rubble stone, but the long causeways of stone arches at either end of the bridge, crossing the flood plain, have totally disappeared.

Despite these changes, Newbridge is remarkably complete, and the public houses at either end testify to its continued importance as a crossing place. One, now the Rose Revived, used its prominent position to hold twice-yearly fairs which became famous for the sale of cheese and horses.

9

Monuments

The design of most buildings is dictated by a practical function, but in some cases function is either non-existent or of secondary importance. Instead, the building sets out to commemorate an event, a person, an ideal, or a faith. These monuments are fascinating because they show not so much how people lived or worked, but how they thought. Northamptonshire has some particularly intriguing examples, but there are other gems dotted throughout the area.

The oldest and best known of these monuments are the **Eleanor Crosses at Geddington and Hardingstone** (92, N), put up in the 1290s by Edward I to commemorate his queen and invite prayers for her soul. They make impressive symbols of marital devotion, especially given the fact that the marriage was an arranged one, but you cannot rule out a sneaking suspicion that they commemorate Edward as well. They were also probably an attempt to keep up with the Royal House of France – the last journey of the saintly Louis IX had been marked with crosses too.

Whatever the motive behind them, Eleanor's crosses are beautiful pieces of medieval sculpture, and were duly admired by 19th-century Gothic Revivalists. Martyrs' Memorial in Oxford, designed by Sir George Gilbert Scott in 1840, was modelled on the similar but hexagonal cross at Waltham in Hertfordshire, but with necessary variation in the statues. The Oxford cross portrays the Protestant martyrs, Cranmer, Latimer and Ridley, burnt at the stake in 1555, and shows that not everyone was impressed by the glamorous Catholic flavour of the Oxford Movement.

Religion is also the starting point for two extraordinary buildings in Northamptonshire – **Lyveden New Bield** (93, N) and **Rushton Triangular Lodge** (97, N). Both were built for the eccentric Sir Thomas Tresham (1545–1605), who became a fervent Catholic in 1580. In an

age when the new Church of England was still fighting to achieve supremacy and outlaw dissent, this was not a very diplomatic decision. In Tresham's case it was to result in nearly 13 years of imprisonment or house arrest, over £7,000 paid out in recusancy fines (for refusal to attend Church of England services), and an acute awareness of the value of code. Both Tresham's buildings are coded expressions of his faith. The cruciform house at Lyveden pays homage to Christ's Passion, the Triangular Lodge at Rushton to the Holy Trinity and the Catholic Mass.

There are other themes in Tresham's work, however. The Triangular Lodge puns on his own name, and his **Market House at Rothwell** (95, N) is a secular monument to friendship and the local community. Tresham's mania for symbolism seems to have been influenced, at least in part, by the more general Elizabethan craze for devices and emblems. Similar inner meanings are often found in the literature, painting and decoration of the period, but examples in architecture – which, of course, is far more costly – are rare. Chantmarle, in Dorset, was planned on an 'E' for Emmanuel in 1612, and John Thorpe, the surveyor from Kings Cliffe (N), drew up a house planned on his own initials. He also credited triangular Longford Castle, in Wiltshire, with references to the Trinity. But none of these rival the ambition and complexity of the buildings included here.

Monuments commemorating great events usually have a less personalised flavour, and are mostly inspired by war. A somewhat incongruous example is the Round House that stands by the A510 north of Finedon (N). It was built with a roof balcony, for viewing a landscape that happened to remind the Duke of Wellington of the battlefield at Waterloo. Of truer local interest are the various Civil War monuments. The great battle of Naseby (N), in 1645, saw Charles I finally defeated by the Parliamentarians

Eleanor Cross at Hardingstone, Northampton. JB

under Cromwell and Fairfax. An obelisk commemorating the event was set up in 1823, in the wrong place, and the mistake was corrected with a new monument in 1936. Another obelisk at Chalgrove (O) marks the battlefield where John Hampden received his fatal injury. This great Parliamentary hero, famous for his refusal to pay Ship Money, is also honoured with a statue at Aylesbury.

The vast majority of monuments commemorate people. This chapter is far too small to do justice to the huge number of fine church monuments, and can only point to a choice few, such as the Hoby monuments at Bisham in Berkshire, or the 14th-century oak effigies at Sparsholt in Oxfordshire. Buckinghamshire boasts the early Renaissance monument to Sir Robert Dormer at Wing (46, BU), The Wrighte monument at Gayhurst (57, BU), and the grandiose Shelburne monument, by Scheemakers, at High Wycombe. In Northamptonshire there are the touching effigies of Sir Ralph Greene and his wife at Lowick (1415), the early 18th-century painted memorials by Mrs Creed at Titchmarsh, and the phenomenal creation above Sir Anthony Mildmay (c.1617) at Apethorpe. Oxford has its own special breed of monuments with academics holding books.

Many of these church monuments

belong to a family group or stand in a family chapel. (A particularly magnificent assemblage in the Bedford Chapel at Chenies (BU) is sadly inaccessible.) The Montagu Monuments at Warkton (94, N), however, represent a more concerted attempt at self-deification, and completely take over the chancel. This was rebuilt, to a design by Roubiliac, with special display alcoves and improved lighting. In effect the chancel became a family mausoleum.

When it comes to purpose-built mausoleums, the Royal Mausoleum at Frogmore (96, BE), constructed for Victoria and Albert, is undoubtedly the most spectacular in the area, if not in the country. It is not, however, typical of the English tradition, which stuck to church burial until the 18th century brought in its fashion for classicism. Two gentlemanly essays in the classical genre can be found in the Buckinghamshire Chilterns. One, in the churchyard at Fawley, is a modest octagonal building with a tall drum. It was put up in 1750 by John Freeman of Fawley Court, who based his design on the tomb of Cecilia Metella, on the Appian Way in Rome. The other, the vast open hexagon of flint that dominates the hill above West Wycombe (39, BU), was built in 1763–4 for the arch-dilettante and showman, Sir Francis Dashwood.

The Dashwood Mausoleum at West Wycombe, Buckinghamshire. CM

92

Eleanor Crosses at Geddington and Hardingstone, Northamptonshire
1291–4

Geddington cross SP 894830. Stands at centre of village, 3 miles (5 km) NE of Kettering to E of A43. Hardingstone Cross SP 754582. Stands beside A508 1¼ mile (2 km) S of Northampton, just N of junction with A43/A45 ring road. (See map of Northampton (16, N))

[A]

On 28 November 1290 Queen Eleanor, wife of Edward I, died at Harby near Lincoln. The king had her body embalmed and then conveyed south for burial at Westminster. To mark her resting places on the long journey, Edward commissioned twelve elaborate crosses, which would glorify the memory of the queen (and that of her devoted husband), and inspire passing travellers to pray for her soul. Louis IX of France had already been similarly honoured in 1271. Of Eleanor's crosses, only three survive. Two are in this area at Geddington and Hardingstone, the third is at Waltham in Hertfordshire. Of the others, those at Lincoln, Grantham, Stamford, Stony Stratford, Woburn, Dunstable, St Albans, and Cheapside have disappeared, and that at Charing is a 19th-century substitute.

Edward commissioned the crosses from his master mason, Richard Crundale, who was probably responsible for their basic design. They are shrine-like pinnacles, raised up on steps and built in three main tiers: a tall base displays shields with the queen's heraldry; a middle tier has canopied niches containing statues of Eleanor; and a tall shaft, now cross-less, rises out of the top. Within this framework, however, each cross delights in a different arrangement of geometrical shapes. The Hardingstone cross starts off as a sturdy octagon and then becomes a square, but with niches projecting to form a cross. The

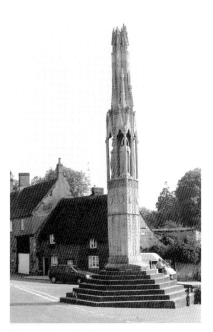

Eleanor Cross, Geddington. CM

Geddington cross is more of a slender needle, triangular at the base but rising as a six-pointed star. Its original elegance is only slightly marred by shafts added later to support the canopies.

There is also some variation in detail, for work was subcontracted to local masons, at Hardingstone to John Battle and Simon Pabenham. But for the most part the style is very consistent – early Decorated at its most up to date. Both crosses luxuriate in richly carved ornament. There are pinnacles galore, and lavishly crocketed gables full of naturalistic foliage. At Geddington the base is completely covered with carved diapers, and undulates in section towards a central ogee nib. The modish ogee reappears in the blind tracery at Hardingstone. These were no provincial works, but royal commissions of the highest calibre.

The statues were all carved by William of Ireland, and show Eleanor as a gently feminine figure, not personalised but ideally graceful in softly folding draperies. Her poses show variations on the elegant S-curve that was so much admired in the later 13th and 14th centuries.

93

Lyveden New Bield, Northamptonshire
1594–1605

SP 983853. 4 miles (6 km) SW of Oundle, signposted off minor road (Harley Way) to Brigstock. Last ½ mile (0.8 km) is on foot

[A] NT

Lyveden New Bield is one of three extraordinary buildings that express the faith and values of Sir Thomas Tresham of Rushton, prominent Northamptonshire landowner and Roman Catholic recusant (see the introduction to this chapter). Tresham's Market House at Rothwell (95, N) eulogises the bonds of friendship and community, his Triangular Lodge at Rushton (97, N) the glory of the Trinity and the Mass. This cross-shaped shell of a house at Lyveden celebrates the Passion of Christ and the blessedness of the Virgin Mary.

The design of the house was drawn up by Robert Stickells, later Clerk of the Royal Works, but the devout complexity of the religious message is pure Tresham. He ingeniously works it into the building on several levels. Firstly

there is the perfect cross-shaped plan, with each equal arm ending in a bay window. Then there are the details discreetly incorporated into the entablatures of the two main storeys: the upper entablature carries biblical texts; the lower Doric entablature has metopes carved with Passion symbols – the instruments of Christ's arrest, flagellation and crucifixion, his robe and PX monogram, and the purse of Judas. Lastly there is an obscure riddle of symbolic numbers – look out for features grouped in threes for the Trinity, fives for the Salvation, sevens for the Godhead, and nines for the Tresham trefoils. Each bay window, for instance, has five sides 5 ft long, while the inscriptions are carefully edited to exactly eighty-one (nine times nine) letters.

The symbolism is so pervasive that practical function is humbled into second place. In fact the New Bield was never intended as a serious residence. Tresham had it built in the grounds of his manor house at Lyveden as a 'Garden Lodge', a place of temporary retreat where architectural devices might stimulate the brain and pleasure gardens delight the senses. Its suitably modest accommodation is still recognisable, despite the removal of all the floors during the Civil War period, and the

Lyveden New Bield. JB

possibility that there never was any roof. The basement was, or was intended to be, a service area, and has a large kitchen fireplace, with rear ovens and copper, in the west wing. Above lay the hall and a room that was possibly the parlour, in range, while the south wing contained a staircase to chambers on the top floor – the doorways on the landings are grand ones, with architraves and keyblocks.

94

Montagu Monuments, Warkton Church, Northamptonshire
1749–1827

SP 893798. In Warkton village, 2 miles (3 km) NE of Kettering, to E of A43

[C]

Monument to Mary, 3rd Duchess of Montagu, at Warkton. CM

God has been outclassed at Warkton! You may just notice an altar at the east end of the chancel, but you are likely to be far more impressed by the magnificent monuments to the Montagu family of neighbouring Boughton. They had the chancel completely rebuilt in the mid-18th century as a family memorial and sculpture gallery. Two arched alcoves were built in either side, to take the monuments, and a large, untraceried east window was installed to give ample lighting. Initially there were even plans for a cupola. The new chancel was designed by the great sculptor Louis François Roubiliac, who also carved the first two monuments, to John, 2nd Duke of Montagu, and his Duchess, Mary.

Duke John died in 1749 and was commemorated in grand style by his wife (although she left the finer details of the commission to a Dr Martin Folkes). Roubiliac shows her leaning languidly against the tomb, gazing up at a profile medallion of her husband. Military trophies attest to the Duke's manly prowess, and Charity pays homage to his gentler virtues, but there is little hint of piety. Instead the allegorical seriousness is relieved by a charming small boy who sprawls precariously on the ledge above. He

clutches at the medallion and brings the winding composition to a close. With his chubby softness he also rounds off the sensual allure of the draperies that gently cling to the ladies' stretching limbs.

The Duchess's own monument, opposite, was made soon afterwards in 1753, and shows much the same appreciation for classical allegory and sensual beauty. It features the Three Fates, not as haggard crones but graceful maidens, disagreeing over the need to cut the thread of life. Above them, two voluptuously naked little boys drape the Duchess's urn with a luscious garland of flowers.

The later monument to Mary, the 3rd Duchess, who died in 1775, is more histrionic in tone. An exquisite marble alcove, designed by Robert Adam, provides a stage set for a dramatic scene carved by Peter Matthias Vangelder. The Duchess, depicted as Charity, wilts against her urn, and is directed heavenwards by an angel who bends consolingly down towards her. A stooping widow, baby and weeping child represent those who will feel her loss most keenly. The angel is the most

striking figure – in his concern he seems about to lose both his draperies and his balance – but the whole group has a wonderful sense of involvement and heightened emotion. Admirably lit from that large east window, it's a real eye-catcher!

By contrast, the last monument, carved by Thomas Campbell, is staidly Neoclassical and proper. It shows the Dowager Duchess Elizabeth, who died in 1827, as a worthy Roman matron, much more serious in her virtue but far less inspiring than her predecessors.

95

Rothwell Market House, Northamptonshire
1578–83

SP 816812. In centre of Rothwell, 4 miles (6 km) NW of Kettering, to E of A6

[D]

This is not just a market house but a monument to the local community. It was built by Sir Thomas Tresham, before his conversion to Catholicism in 1580, and before his obsession with symbolism turned daringly religious (see Lyveden New Bield (93, N) and Rushton Triangular Lodge (97, N)). Here at Rothwell, Tresham declares, in a Latin frieze, that he built 'in thanksgiving for his sweet country and town of Northampton, and especially for this neighbourhood', seeking 'nothing save the common good, nothing save the lasting esteem of his friends'.

To emphasise his theme, and pay homage to those friends, Tresham decorated the building with heraldic shields. He placed his own arms, with the Tresham trefoils, over the main south arch, and those of his neighbours in the Hundred of Rothwell in the spandrels. All round the top frieze are the arms of other county gentry. This symbolic bond of friendship and local unity was by no means unique – Sir Christopher Hatton, for instance, had shields of local gentry painted on three obelisks that stood like a shrine in his hall at Holdenby – but nowhere else is it given such architectural prominence.

In catering for the 'common good'

the building had a much more practical application. The arcades on the ground floor were originally open, giving access to a covered market area, while the top floor was intended to provide a community room. The form is a very common one (see the market buildings at Abingdon (7, O), Amersham (8, BU) and Burford (12, O)), but here the style is exceptionally polished. Projecting centre bays give a sophisticated cross-plan, limestone ashlar makes for an imposing finish, and architectural details aspire to classicism in a typically eccentric Elizabethan way. The two tiers of pilasters are indeed Doric and Ionic, but they are delightfully improved with small shaped panels and waist bands. On the round stair tower they even sport the familiar Tresham trefoils.

The plan of the market house was drawn up by William Grumbold, a mason who also worked for Tresham at Lyveden and Rushton. Sadly neither he nor his employer ever saw the building finished. It remained roofless until 1895, when the local architect J A Gotch restored it and completed the stair tower. It now serves the common good as council offices.

96

Royal Mausoleum, Frogmore, Berkshire
1861–71

SU 973759. In the grounds of Frogmore House, Home Park, Windsor. Entrance from The Long Walk

[A] Open 3 days in May

The Royal Mausoleum peeps out above the trees of Home Park like a Tardis from another planet. It is alien in conception, and foreign in style and craftsmanship, but inside lies Victoria, one of the greatest of British monarchs, together with Prince Albert, for whom it was built. The whole is a monument to majesty and marital devotion and has an awesome, if rather frigid, splendour.

In choosing such a monument, Victoria rejected the previous tradition of royal burial at Westminster or in St George's Chapel. Instead, she and Albert were influenced by the modest mausoleum to Princess Charlotte at Claremont in Surrey. Albert developed the idea on a grander scale at Coburg, with a mausoleum for his father, and then at Frogmore, with a domed rotunda for Victoria's mother, the Duchess of Kent. The latter was built 1859–61 by the architect A J Humbert to designs by Professor Ludwig Gruner of Dresden. When Albert died in December 1861, Victoria employed the same pair of designers.

The resulting Germanic character of the building is unmistakable. The style is not classical, in the manner favoured by the English aristocracy since the 18th century, but rather Early Christian-cum-Romanesque. This inspired a cruciform plan with a taller octagonal centre, a circular ambulatory to link the four arms, and an entrance portico. Externally the finish is plain, with arcading, groups of round-arched windows, and narrow dentil cornices. The walls are of severely smooth Portland stone with granite dressings, and the roofs are green copper.

After such pristine starkness outside, the loftily vaulted interior comes as a

Rothwell Market House. CM

blaze of colour. Every surface is painted, sculpted or inlaid with coloured marble. The marbles come from all over Europe, Africa and North America, the salmon-pink stone being a gift from a royal cousin, Luiz I of Portugal. The paintings are all in the style of Raphael, Albert's favourite artist, but were executed by the 19th-century Italian and German painters, Consoni, Frank and Pfaffer. They illustrate the three main themes of the Nativity, Crucifixion and Resurrection, show Evangelists standing in fields of gold mosaic, and then cover any remaining space with Renaissance grotesques. If only they had possessed Raphael's sensitivity!

Ice-like in the middle of all this lie the pure white effigies of Victoria and Albert, carved in Carrara marble by Carlo Marochetti. The Queen is still young, as she was carved in 1868, at the same time as her consort. Their sarcophagus, below, is a single vast slab of Aberdeen granite, enclosed by the outstretched feathery wings of four bronze angels who kneel in prayer. All is very still in death.

97

Rushton Triangular Lodge, Northamptonshire
1593–7

SP 830831. 4 miles (6 km) NW of Kettering, on minor road between Rushton and Desborough

[A] EH

Sir Thomas Tresham returned to Rushton in 1593 after paying for his Roman Catholic beliefs with a 12-year stint of imprisonment and house arrest.

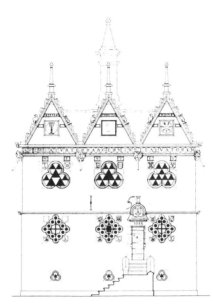

Rushton Triangular Lodge, the south-east front. After Samuel Buck's drawing of 1730.

Far from chastened, he immediately set about building the Triangular Lodge, an architectural emblem of his respect for the Holy Trinity and the Catholic Mass. Not only that, he built it on the very edge of his estate, blatant for all to see, in eye-catching stripes of pale limestone and brown iron-stained Lias. Inscriptions on the gables make it quite clear that he did not build it just for himself. Small wonder that his persecution continued!

The building does have a practical excuse, albeit a flimsy one. Tresham referred to it as the 'Warryners Lodge', but it is dubious whether it ever made much of a home for the rabbit keeper. The main hexagonal rooms are poorly lit, and only the top floor definitely had a

fireplace (though one was possibly intended for the floor below). Nor would the dank basement have made a satisfactory game larder. Instead, the building smacks more of a banqueting house, as Mark Girouard has suggested. Its interior is finely finished with ashlar panels and little corner closets, and upstairs there are window seats, inviting you to admire the view. It would have made an amusing place to take dessert, or simply to visit while strolling through the grounds of Rushton Hall.

Tresham's guests must have been amazed by the intricate symbolism of the lodge. The building is full of threes, alluding both to the Trinity and the 'Tres' in Tresham's name. There are three storeys and three sides, and each side has three gables and three windows on each floor. Even the windows are all different arrangements of trefoils (Tresham's family badge) and triangles. To make the allusions more specific, there are inscriptions and pictorial emblems that associate each side with a particular member of the Trinity – on the north side, for instance, the Pelican in her Piety symbolises the self-sacrifice of Christ the Son.

More obvious to modern eyes are the symbols of the Mass – the chalice, cross and nails, the Lamb of God and the IHS monogram. These appear on the triangular chimney, which rises as if by a miracle from the hollow centre of the building. The strange numbers in the gables, however, remain inscrutable, the extremes perhaps of a fanatical personality who had suffered years of enforced leisure and who had become obsessed with code. (See also Tresham's other symbolic buildings at Lyveden (93, N) and Rothwell (95, N).)

Interior of the Royal Mausoleum, Frogmore. EH

Select Bibliography

Of the weighty tomes that provide general reference for the area, the inventories of the Royal Commission on the Historical Monuments of England and the Victoria County Histories are now showing their age a little. Excellent exceptions include the RCHME volume on north Northamptonshire (1984), and the recent VCH volumes on north-west Oxfordshire. Other detailed information is often locked away in national and local journals: the *Archaeological Journal*, the *Journal of the British Archaeological Association*, the *Proceedings of the Prehistoric Society*, *Vernacular Architecture*, *Transactions of the Newbury and District Field Club*, the *Records of Buckinghamshire*, *Oxoniensia* and *Northamptonshire Past and Present*.

More accessible are the county guides. Three series shine out. Nikolaus Pevsner's Buildings of England (Penguin Books) covers all four counties: *Berkshire* (1966), *Buckinghamshire* (new edition by E Williamson forthcoming), *Northamptonshire* (revised by B Cherry, 1973) and *Oxfordshire* (J Sherwood and N Pevsner, 1974). The Making of the English Landscape, edited by W G Hoskins for Hodder and Stoughton, has volumes on *Buckinghamshire* (M Reed, 1979), *Northamptonshire* (J Steane, 1974) and *Oxfordshire* (F Emery, 1974). The beautifully illustrated Murray Guides to Berkshire and Buckinghamshire, by John Betjeman and John Piper, may be old (1949 and 1948) but still take top marks for sensitivity.

Many excellent guides, provided by English Heritage, the National Trust and others, are available on site. For other accounts of individual buildings and relevant themes, I recommend the following:

D Beckett, *Stephensons' Britain*, David & Charles, 1984.

J Buxton and P Williams, *New College, Oxford, 1379–1979*, New College, 1979.

J I Catto, *The History of the University of Oxford*, vol I, Clarendon Press, 1984.

A Clifton-Taylor, *The Pattern of English Building*, Faber & Faber, 1972.

H Colvin and J S G Simmons, *All Souls*, Oxford University Press, 1989.

J Cook and T Rowley, *Dorchester through the Ages*, Oxford University Department for External Studies, 1985.

J Dyer, *Penguin Guide to Prehistoric England and Wales*, 1981.

Celia Fiennes, *The Illustrated Journeys of Celia Fiennes 1685–c.1712*, ed. C Morris, Macdonald, 1982.

A H Faulkner, *The Grand Junction Canal*, David & Charles, 1972.

S Gillam, *The Divinity School and Duke Humphrey's Library at Oxford*, Clarendon Press, 1988.

M Girouard, *Robert Smythson and the English Country House*, Yale, 1983.

N Hammond, *The Book of Abingdon*, Barracuda Books, 1979.

D W Harding, *The Iron Age in the Upper Thames Basin*, Clarendon Press, 1972.

R Harris, *Discovering Timber-Framed Buildings*, Shire Publications, 1978.

W Horn and E Born, *The Barns of the Abbey of Beaulieu*, Cambridge University Press and University of California Press, 1965.

T Hughes, *The Scouring of the White Horse*, Macmillan 1859, new ed. published by Alan Sutton, 1989.

A F Kersting and J Ashdown, *The Buildings of Oxford*, Holmes and Meier, 1980.

J Lake, *Historic Farm Buildings*, Blandford Press, 1989.

G Lambrick, *The Rollright Stones*, English Heritage, 1988.

R and J Moody, *The Book of Burford*, Barracuda Books, 1983.

Oxfordshire Museums Publications: various leaflets, e.g., on turnpike roads, medieval bridges, the Oxford Canal; booklets on Oxfordshire brickmakers and the Oxfordshire brewer.

G Phillips, *Thames Crossings*, David & Charles, 1981.

M Reed, *A History of Buckinghamshire*, Phillimore, 1993.

J M Robinson, *Temples of Delight: Stowe Landscape Gardens*, the National Trust/ George Philip, 1990.

M Seabourne, *The English School 1370–1870*, Routledge & Kegan Paul, 1971.

J Swann, *Shoemaking*, Shire Publications, 1986.

R B Wood-Jones, *Traditional Domestic Architecture of the Banbury Region*, Manchester University Press, 1963, reprinted by Wykham Books, 1986.

Index

Note: gazetteer entries are listed in **bold**, by their *page* number

abbeys/priories   17, 30, 57, 62, 90, 92, 93, 102
Abingdon, Oxfordshire   7, 15, **17–18**, 34, 90, 101, 102
    almshouses, St Helen's churchyard   75, **86–7**
Acland, Sir Henry   24–5, 86, 90
Adam, Robert   44, 47, 53, 112
Adderbury   58
    Richard de   49
Addington, Buckinghamshire   90
Aelfgifu, Lady   63
Ahrends, Burton and Koralek   81
Akeman Street   9, 101
Albert, Prince   66, 110, 113–15
Alchester, Oxfordshire   9
Aldrich, Henry   30, 73, 80
Alfred, King   11
Alkerton, Oxfordshire   58
All Souls College, Oxford   73, 75, **79–80**, 84
almshouses/bedehouses   3, 17, 18, 59, 73, 75, 76–9, 86–7
Amersham, Buckinghamshire   5, 15, 35, 43, 75
    Museum   18, 33, 34, **35–6**
    Old Town   **18–19**
Anne, Queen   45
Apethorpe, Northamptonshire   110
Ascott, Buckinghamshire   43
Ascott-under-Wychwood, Oxfordshire   7
Ashby St Ledgers, Northamptonshire   17, 105
Ashdown, Oxfordshire
    Battle of   11
    House   41, 43, 55
Ashridge estate, Buckinghamshire/ Hertfordshire   98
Ashton, Northamptonshire   16
Avington, Berkshire   57
Aylesbury, Buckinghamshire   15, 42, 110
    Vale of   1, 16, 35, 43

Bampton, Oxfordshire   41, 74
Banbury, Oxfordshire   15, 58, 89, 90
Barbour, Geoffrey   86
Barnes, James   102, 103
barns, *see* farming
Barnwell St Andrew, Northamptonshire   79
    Castle   41
Baroque style   4, 18, 26, 42, 45, 46–7, 53, 55, 65, 70, 84, 99
barrows
    long   4, 7, 10, 12–13
    round   7, 10, 12

Basildon Park, Berkshire   42, **43–4**
Beaconsfield, Buckinghamshire   5
Bear Wood, Berkshire   43
Becket, Thomas à   71
Bede, the Venerable   60, 61
Bell, Henry   26, 58
Bell Inn, Waltham St Lawrence, Berkshire   34, **36–7**
Berkeley, William   66
Berkshire Downs   1, 3, 7, 12, 31, 43, 89
Bernwood, forest of, Oxfordshire/ Buckinghamshire   3
Betjeman, Sir John   15, 19
Bevan, Benjamin   105
Birinus, Bishop   57
Bisham, Berkshire   110
blankets, *see* industry
Bledlow, Buckinghamshire   9
Blenheim Palace, Oxfordshire   4, 42, **44–5**
Blewburton Hill, Oxfordshire   7–8, 11, 19
Blewbury, Oxfordshire   15, 16, **19–20**, 33, 34, 74
Bliss Tweed Mill, Chopping Norton, Oxfordshire   4, 90, **91–2**
Blisworth, Northamptonshire   1, 15, 16, **20–1**, 34, 102
    canal tunnel   21, 103, **105**
Blomfield, A   58
Bloxham, Oxfordshire   58
Boarstall Tower, Buckinghamshire   41
Bodleian Library, Oxford   5, 84, *see also* Oxford, University Buildings
Bodley, Sir Thomas   84
Borgnis, Giuseppe   53
Borra, G B   53
Boulton family   23–4
Bracknell, Berkshire   8, 15, 89
Bradford, William   94
Braunston, Northamptonshire   102, 103, 104
Bray, Berkshire
    Jesus Hospital   75, **77**
breweries   90, **94–5**
brick   16, 27, 30, 47, 55, 63, 77, 79, 82, 89, 90, 95, 97, 103, 105, 106
    High Victorian   59, 60, 66, 75, **80–1**
    infill   20, 34
    kilns/works   21, 90, 91, 94
    late medieval   1, 76, 77
    styles and patterns of   18, 19, 20, 21–2, 34, 87
Bridgeman, Charles   42, 52
bridges   17–18, 30, 86, 101, 102, 103, 104–5, 106–7
Brigstock, Northamptonshire   57, 79
Brill, Buckinghamshire   16, **21–2**, 34, 90, 98
British and Foreign School Society   75, 78
Brixworth, Northamptonshire
    All Saints Church   4, 57, **60–1**, 63
Bronze Age   7, 10, 12
Broughton Castle, Oxfordshire   41, **45–6**, 49, 63
Brown, 'Capability'   42, 45, 52, 55
Brudenell family   48–9, 51

Brunel, Isambard Kingdom   102, 106
Buckingham, Buckinghamshire   15
building materials   1–3, 4, 16, 20, 89, 90
    see also brick; chalk; clay; cob; flint; glass; limestone; paper; render/plaster; sarsen stones; slate; thatch; tiles; timber framing; wichert
Bulbourne, Buckinghamshire   103
Burford, Oxfordshire   1, 15, **22–3**, 34, 57, 90, 101
Burghley House, Cambridgeshire   49, 51
Burton Latimer, Northamptonshire   74
Buscot Park, Oxfordshire   42
Butterfield, William   58, 60, 66, 67, 73, 80
Byrd, William   82

Campbell, Thomas   112
canals   4, 94, 102, 103–5
Canons Ashby, Northamptonshire   41
Cantwell, William   99
Cardigan, 7th Earl of   48
car factories   30, 89
Carr, John   44
Castle Ashby, Northamptonshire   41
Castle Howard, North Yorkshire   44
castles   15, 30, 37, 41, 49–50, 53–5
Cecil, William, Lord Burghley   51
Chalgrove, Oxfordshire   110
chalk   1–3, 11, 12, 16, 20, 25, 31, 34, 43, 89
    figures   9, 11–12
Champneys, Basil   82
chantry provisions   5, 64, 66, 67, 67–8, 73–5, 76–7, 79, 81, 86, 87
charitable institutions   73–87
Charles I, King   43, 65, 66, 109
Charles II, King   55
Charlotte, Princess   66, 113
Chastleton House, Oxfordshire   41, **46**
Chaucer, Alice, Countess of Suffolk   76–7
Cheere, Sir Henry   53, 62
Chenies, Buckinghamshire   41, 110
Chester, Sir John   47
Chevynton, Richard   79
Chichele, Henry   75, 76, 79
    College, Bedehouse and School at Higham Ferrers   73, **75**, 76
Chicheley Hall, Buckinghamshire   42, **46–7**
Chiltern Hills   1, 7, 16, 18, 65, 90, 98, 101, 110
Chiltern Open Air Museum   89, 90
Chilton House, Buckinghamshire   55
Chipping Norton, Oxfordshire
    Bliss Tweed Mill   4, 90, **91–2**
churches and chapels   4, 17, 19–20, 22–3, 26, 27, 28, 30, 31, 53, 54, 57–71, 75, 77, 83, 112–13
    almshouse chapels   77, 79
    college chapels   75–6, 80, 81
Churchill family
    John, Duke of Marlborough   45
    Sir Winston   44

Cirencester, Gloucestershire   9, 10, 101
Cistercian Order   93
Civil War   50, 62, 107, 109, 111
Clark, William Tierney   106
Clarke, Dr George   73, 80
clay   1, 21, 90, 94
Claydon House, Buckinghamshire   42, 47–8
    estate housing   35
Clifton Hampden, Oxfordshire   107
Clipston, Northamptonshire   74
Cliveden, Buckinghamshire   41, 42
cob   16, 19, 20, 24, 35
Cogges Manor Farm Museum, Witney,
    Oxfordshire   89, **92–3**
Coleshill, Oxfordshire   43
colleges   54, 66, 67, 68, 73, 75, 76
    at Oxford   73, 79–82
Collyweston, Northamptonshire   1
Comper, Sir Ninian   58, 69
Connell and Ward   19
Corby, Northamptonshire   15
Cosgrove canal bridge,
    Northamptonshire   103, **104–5**
Cotswold Hills   1, 22, 101
Cottesbrooke, Northamptonshire   74
country houses   1, 4, 9, 41–55
Courteenhall, Northamptonshire   74
Cowper, William   27
Craven, William, 1st Earl   43
Creed, Mrs   110
Cripps, Sir Stafford   17
Crowmarsh Gifford, Oxfordshire
    Queen's Head   34, 38
Crundale, Richard   110
crusades, influence of   11, 26, 57
crypts   57, 61, 63
Culham, Oxfordshire   17–18

Danesfield, Buckinghamshire   25, 43
Dashwood, Sir Francis   25, 53, 110
    Mausoleum   53, 110
Daventry, Northamptonshire   8, 58, 89
Deanery Gardens, Sonning, Berkshire   43
Decorated style   58, 67, 71, 83, 111
Deddington, Oxfordshire   37
    Leadenporch House   33, 34, **37–8**
Deene Park, Northamptonshire   1, 4, 41,
    48–9, 51
Denton family   62
Dilettanti, Society of   53
Dingley Hall, Northamptonshire   49
Donnington Castle, Berkshire   41, **49–50**
Donowell, John   53
Dorchester, Oxfordshire   8, 9, 57, 58, 101,
    102
    George Hotel   101, **102–3**
Dorman, Charles   97
Dormer, Sir Robert   63, 110
Dorney Court, Buckinghamshire   41
dovecots   93, 96–7
Drapers' Company   78
Drayton House, Northamptonshire   41, 42
Durley, R   78

Earls Barton, Northamptonshire
    All Saints Church   57, **61–2**, 63, 65
    shoe industry   90
Early English style   58, 68
Early family, of Witney   99
Earp, Thomas   60
Easton Neston, Northamptonshire   42
Ecclesiologist/Ecclesiological Society   59,
    60, 75, 78, 80
Edlesborough, Buckinghamshire   90
education   73–5, 76, 78, 79, 80, 81, 83
Edward I, King   109, 110
Edward III, King   54, 66
Edward IV, King   66
Eleanor, Queen
    Crosses at Geddington and Hardingstone,
        Northamptonshire   109, **110–11**
Elizabeth, Queen of Bohemia   43
Emlyn, Henry   66
Eton College, Berkshire   4, 57, 58, 66, 73,
    75–6
Ewelme Almshouses, School and Church,
    Oxfordshire   3, 73, 75, **76–7**

farming   3, 15–16, 19, 89, 92–3
    barns   89, 90, 92, 93
    enclosure farms   16, 89
    farm buildings   10, 20, 21, 89, 97
    farming communities   21, 24, 38
    model farms   89, 98
Fawley, Buckinghamshire   110
    Court   42
Fawsley Hall, Northamptonshire   41
Fenny Stratford, Buckinghamshire   103–4
Ferrey, B   67, 68
Fiennes family   45
    Celia   15, 25
Filkins, Oxfordshire   17, 89
Fingest, Buckinghamshire
    St Bartholomew's Church   57, 61, **65**
Fishmongers, Company of   77
flint   3, 7, 18, 20, 49, 65, 66, 67, 89, 110
    axeheads and scrapers   12
forests   3
Fotheringhay, Northamptonshire
    St Mary and All Saints' Church   4, 58,
        67–8
Fox, George   63
Freeman, John   110
Friends' meeting houses   59, 63–4
Frogmore (Royal Mausoleum), *see* Windsor
Fulljames, Thomas   23
Fyfield, Oxfordshire
    White Hart Inn   33, 75, 86, **87**
Fyfield Manor barns, Benson,
    Oxfordshire   89

gardens/parks   42, 45, 52–3, 55, 82
Garter, Order of   54–5, 66
Gayhurst, Buckinghamshire
    St Peter's Church   4, 57, 58, **70–1**, 110
Geddington, Northamptonshire
    Eleanor Cross   109, **110–11**

geology   1–3, 20
George III, King   55, 66
George IV, King   54, 55
George Hotel, Dorchester, Oxfordshire   101,
    102–3
Gerbier, Sir Balthasar   43
Gerrards Cross, Buckinghamshire   8, 58
Gibbons, Grinling   45, 55
Gibbs, James   52, 84
Gifford, Thomas   71
glass   52, 86
Goddard, William   77
Godwin, Edward   26
Golafre, Sir John   86, 87
Goldsmith, Oliver   27
Gotch, J A   113
gothic revival
    18th-century Gothick   42, 48, 52, 58,
        79–80, 104
    19th-century Gothic   20, 55, 58, 60, 75,
        78, 82, 86, 109
Grafton Estate, Northamptonshire   89
Grand Union Canal, Northamptonshire/
    Buckinghamshire   21, 101, 102, 103,
    103–5
Great Billing, Northamptonshire   90
Great Coxwell Barn, Oxfordshire   34, 38, 90,
    93
Great Haseley, Oxfordshire   90
Great Linford Brick Kilns,
    Buckinghamshire   90, **94**
Great Tew, Oxfordshire   1, 16, **23–4**
Great Western Railway   102, 106
Green, John   89
Greene, Sir Ralph   110
Grenville, Sir Richard   55
Grim's Ditch, Oxfordshire/
    Buckinghamshire   8–9
Grumbold, William   113
Gruner, Ludwig   113
guilds and fraternities   17, 23, 86
Guilsborough, Northamptonshire   74

Haddenham, Buckinghamshire   16, 34
Halfway, Berkshire   101
hall houses   18, 23, 33, 34, 35–9, 87, 101,
    103
    aisled   34, 38
    Wealden   34, 36–7
Halton House, Buckinghamshire   43
Hambleden, Buckinghamshire   16, 90
Hampden, John   110
Hamstead Marshall, Berkshire   43
Hannan, William   53
Hanwell, Oxfordshire   58
Harcourt, Simon, 1st Earl   27
Hardingstone, Northamptonshire
    Eleanor Cross   109, **110–11**
Hardman and Co (stained glass)   60
Hare, H T   30
Harleyford Manor, Buckinghamshire   43
Harris, Daniel (of Oxford)   18
Harris, John (brewer)   94

Harris, Thomas (of Cublington)   78
Hartwell, Buckinghamshire   42, 58
Hatton, Sir Christopher   41, 51, 113
Hawksmoor, Nicholas   42, 45, 73, 79–80, 84
Hell-Fire Club   25, 53
Hengist and Horsa   11
Henley-on-Thames, Oxfordshire   90, 102, 106
Henry II, King   54, 73
Henry III, King   54, 66
Henry V, King   75, 79
Henry VI, King   66, 73, 75–6
Henry VIII, King   41, 46, 54, 66
High Wycombe, Buckinghamshire   90, 110
Higham Ferrers, Northamptonshire   4, 15, 90
   Chichele College, Bedehouse and
      School   73, **75**, 76
   St Mary's Church   58, 75
Hillesden, Buckinghamshire
   All Saints Church   57, 58, **62**
hillforts   7–8, 10–11, 19
Hoby family monuments   110
Holdenby, Northamptonshire   41, 51, 113
Holding, Matthew   26
Hook Norton Brewery, Oxfordshire   90, **94–5**
Hooke, Robert   58
Horwode, William   68
houses
   charity houses   16, 20, *see also*
      almshouses
   cottages   16, 19, 21, 24–5, 27, 35, 105
   council houses   17
   estate housing   16–17, 23–4, 24–5, 27
   railway housing   16, 30–1, 102
   shoemakers' terraces   97
   small houses   33–9
   squatter cottages   16, 24
   in towns and villages   18–23, 27–8, 30, 31
Hudson, Robert   25
Hughes, Thomas   11
Hulcot, Buckinghamshire   17
Humbert, A J   113
Humphrey, Duke of Gloucester   84
Hungerford, Berkshire   58
Hunsbury, Northamptonshire   8, 90
Hunt, Holman   81
hunting   43, 51, 53
Hylmer, John   66

Icknield Way, *see* Ridgeway path
Iffley, Oxfordshire   57, 69
Industrial Revolution   90
industry   4
   blankets   4, 90, 98–9
   brewing   90, 94–5
   food processing   89, 90, 95–6
   furniture   90
   high-technology light industry/
      computers   15, 89
   iron-working   90, 94
   lace   27, 28, 90
   shoes   15, 28, 90, 97–8

wool   3, 4, 22, 23, 38, 46, 90, 91–2, 98, 101, 107
   see also brick kilns; limestone quarries
Inkpen Hill, Berkshire   12
inns/coaching houses   22, 27, 30, 101, 102–3
Ipsden, Oxfordshire   89
Irchester, Northamptonshire   9
iron   15, 82, 86, 90, 92, 95, 102, 103, 104, 107
Iron Age   7–9, 10–12
Ivinghoe, Buckinghamshire   90
   Beacon   1, 7–8, 11

Jacobsen, Arne   82
Jenyngs, Henry   66
Jesus Hospital, Bray, Berkshire   75, **77**
Jessop, William   102, 103
John, King   93
Jones, Inigo   41
Jones, Walter   46
Jordans, Buckinghamshire
   Friends' Meeting House   59, **63–4**
Jurassic
   ridge   7, 33, 101
   Way   4, 7, 10, 38
   see also limestone

Keble, Revd John   80
Keble College, Oxford   58, 60, 66, 73, **80–1**
Kempster, Christopher   18, 90
Kennet
   River   106
   Valley   12
Kennet and Avon Canal   102
Kent, William   42, 52, 53
Kettering, Northamptonshire   15
Kilsby Railway Tunnel,
   Northamptonshire   102, **105–6**
King's Cliffe, Northamptonshire   1
Kingston Bagpuize, Oxfordshire   42
Kirby Hall, Northamptonshire   1, 4, 41, **50–1**

lace, *see* industry
Lacey Green, Buckinghamshire   90
Laguerre, Louis   45
Lambourn, Berkshire   7
Lamport Hall, Northamptonshire   41
Lancaster, Thomas of   71
landscape   1–3, 89
Langford, Oxfordshire   57
Langley Marish, Berkshire   58
Latham, Revd Nicholas   79
laundries   25
Leckhampstead, Berkshire
   St James' Church   58, **66–7**
Leadenporch House, Deddington,
   Oxfordshire   33, 34, **37–8**
Leoni, Giacomo   53
Leverton, Berkshire   16
Lightfoot, Luke   47–8
limestone   1, 17, 24, 30, 34, 46, 89, 90, 93, 96, 104, 107, 113
   Cornbrash   1

Lias/maristone/ironstone   1, 20, 23, 25, 27, 33, 37, 52, 68, 71, 90
oolitic   1, 20, 22, 23, 48, 51
Portland   106, 113
quarries/stone works   21, 90
roofing slates   1, 93, 96
stripes of (banded)   1, 16, 20–1, 26, 75, 115

lobby entries   24, 31, 34
London   4, 5, 15, 41, 42, 43, 58, 89, 96, 101, 102, 103, 106
London and North Western Railway
   Company   30
London to Birmingham Railway   30, 101, 102, 105–6
London, George   47, 55
Long Crendon, Buckinghamshire   33
Loudon, J C   24
Lovell, William Lord   97
Lovett, Robert   78
Lowick, Northamptonshire   58, 67, 110
Lucas, Henry   78
   Hospital, Wokingham, Berkshire   75, **78–9**
Luddington, Northamptonshire   79
Lupton, Provost of Eton   76
Lutyens, Sir Edwin   17, 43
Lyveden New Bield, Northamptonshire   109, **111–12**, 113

Maidenhead, Berkshire
   All Saints Church, Boyne Hill   58, **59–60**, 66, 75
   bridge and railway viaduct   102, **106**
Malthus, William   20
Mansart, François   43
Mapledurham, Oxfordshire   41, 95
   Watermill   90, **95–6**
Marcham, Oxfordshire   96
markets
   Covered Market, Oxford   30
   crosses   15, 86
   houses   15, 16, 18, 22, 109, 112–13
   places/squares   17, 25–6, 27
Marlow Suspension Bridge,
   Buckinghamshire   102, **106–7**
Marochetti, Carlo   115
Marsh Gibbon, Buckinghamshire   16, 19, 24–5, 34, 35, 86, 90
Marsworth, Buckinghamshire   104
Mary, Queen of Scots   67
mausoleums   53, 110, 113–15
May, Hugh   55
Madehamstede (Peterborough)   57, 60
Medmenham, Buckinghamshire   3, 16, **25**, 43, 74, 89
Mentmore Towers, Buckinghamshire   4, 16, 43, **51–2**
Middleton Park, Oxfordshire   43
Mildmay, Sir Anthony   110
milestones   101–2
Miller, Sanderson   45
Millington, John   106–7

Milton Keynes, Buckinghamshire   7, 15, 94
Milton Manor House, Oxfordshire   41
Minster Lovell Dovecot, Oxfordshire   96–7
Modern/International Modern style   19, 82
Montagu
    family   79, 112
    Hospital at Weekley,
        Northamptonshire   79
    monuments in Warkton Church,
        Northamptonshire   110, **112**
monuments   63, 66, 70, 109–15
    see also tombs
Moore, Henry   26
Morris, William   93
Morris, William (car manufacturer)   30, 89
mosaic pavements   9, 10

Naseby, Battle of   109–10
National Society   75, 78
National Trust   46, 52
Nene
    River   67, 90
    Valley   15, 90
Neoclassical style   44, 52, 53, 58, 112
Neolithic period   3, 7, 10, 12–13
Nettlebed, Oxfordshire   90, 94
New Bradwell, Buckinghamshire   90, 94,
    102
    Spencer Street   16, **30–1**
New College, Oxford   30, 58, 73, 79–80,
    81–2, 90
Newbridge, Oxfordshire   101, **107**
Newbury, Berkshire   15, 49, 90
Newport Pagnell, Buckinghamshire   102
Newton, Revd John   28
Nightingale, Florence   47
Nonconformism   59, 75
Nonsuch Palace, Surrey   41, 46
Norman period   57, 61–2, 65
Norreys family   64
North Leigh Roman Villa, Oxfordshire   **9–10**
Northampton   15, **25–6**, 41, 86, 89, 102,
    106, 113
    All Saints Church   26, 58
    boot and shoe industry   26, 90, **97–8**
    Holy Sepulchre Church   26, 57
    St Matthew's Church   26
    St Peter's Church   26, 57
Nowell, James   105
Nuneham Courtenay, Oxfordshire   16, **27**

Olney, Buckinghamshire   15, 27–8, 58, 90
Orchard, William   30, 83
O'Shea brothers   86
Ouse, River   27, 102, 103, 104
Oxford   5, 15, 41, 58, 90, 101, 102, 110
    Canal   102, 103
    Christ Church Cathedral   57
    city of   **28–30**
    colleges   5, 57, 58, 73, **79–82**
    Martyrs' Memorial   109
    Movement   58, 60, 75, 80–1

Plain   1, 21
University Buildings: Bodleian Library,
    Church of St Mary the Virgin, Divinity
    School, Radcliffe Camera, Schools
    Quadrangle, Sheldonian Theatre   5,
    58, 73, 80, 83–4
    University Museum   24, 26, 84–6
    University, origins of   73, 83
Oxfordshire County Museum, Woodstock   7

Pabenham, Simon   111
Palladio, Andrea/Palladianism   41, 42, 43–4,
    47, 52, 53
paper roofs (at Tew Lodge)   24
Papworth, J B   44
Paxton, Sir Joseph   51, 52
Penn, William   63
Perpendicular style   57, 58, 62, 65–6, 67,
    68–9, 71, 75, 77, 80, 81, 83
Pitstone Green, Buckinghamshire   89, 98
    Windmill   21, 90, **98**
Pitt, Thomas, Lord Camelford   53
Polebrook, Northamptonshire   58
portal dolmens   7, 10
Pratt, Sir Roger   43
prehistoric sites   1, 7–9, 10–13
Preston Crowmarsh, Oxfordshire   89
Princes Risborough, Buckinghamshire   41
public houses   36–7, 38, 87, 105, 107

Quainton, Buckinghamshire   90
Quakers   63–4
Quatremayne, Richard   64
Queen's Head, Crowmarsh Gifford,
    Oxfordshire   34, 38

Radcliffe Camera, Oxford   5, 80, *see also*
    Oxford, University Buildings
Radcliffe, Dr John   84
Radcot Bridge, Oxfordshire   101, 107
railways   4, 94, 99, 102, 104, 105–6
Rainsborough Camp, Northamptonshire   8
Rams Hill, Oxfordshire   7
Raunds, Northamptonshire   58
Reading, Berkshire   3, 15, 17, 89, 90, 102,
    106
Renaissance style   4, 41, 45–6, 49, 51, 63,
    69, 83, 110
render/plaster   17, 18, 25, 26, 27, 30, 41, 46,
    65
Rennie, John   107
Revett, Nicholas   53
Richardson, George   44
Rickman, Thomas   23–4
Ridgeway path   4, 7, 10, 11, 12, 19, 101
roads   101, *see also* turnpikes
Roberts, David   82
Robinson, Thomas (smith)   55, 82
Robinson, Sir Thomas (architect)   47
Rockingham, Northamptonshire
    Castle   41
    forest of   3

Rococo style   42, 47–8
Rollright Stones, Oxfordshire   4, 6–7, 9, **10**
Roman
    baths   7, 9, 10
    methods of construction   57, 60
    roads   101
    sites   7, 9–10, 11, 12
Romanesque style   62, 65, 69–70
Romantic style   54
Rose, Joseph   47–8
Rothschild family   4, 16, 43, 51–2
Rothwell Market House,
    Northamptonshire   15, 109, 111, **112–13**
Roubiliac, Louis François   70, 110, 112
Round House, Finedon,
    Northamptonshire   109
Rousham, Oxfordshire   42, 52, 96
royal influence   41, 58, 81
Royal Mausoleum, Frogmore, Berkshire   66,
    110, **113–15**
Royal Works   53–5, 75, 81
Rushden, Northamptonshire   15
Rushton Triangular Lodge,
    Northamptonshire   1, 20, 109, 111, 113,
    115
Ruskin, John   58, 66, 80, 86
Rycote Chapel, Oxfordshire   58, **64–5**
Rysbrack, Michael   45, 52

Salcey, forest of, Northamptonshire   3
St Catherine's College, Oxford   73, 82
Salter, Stephen   30
Salvin, Anthony   54
Sambee, Revd John   78
sarsen stones   11, 12, 13, 31
Saxon period   11–12, 13, 15, 28, 30, 57,
    60–2, 63
Scheemakers, Peter   52, 110
schools and schoolhouses   15, 20, 25, 27,
    31, 59, 73–9
Scott, Sir George Gilbert   55, 58, 62, 68, 81,
    82, 107, 109
Scott, George Gilbert   46, 81
Scott, Sir Giles Gilbert   84
Scott, John Oldrid   81
Segsbury Camp, Oxfordshire   7, 11
Shelburne monument   110
Sheldon, Gilbert   84
Shirburn Castle, Oxfordshire   76
shoes, *see* industry
shops   18, 22, 30, 37
Shottesbrookes, Berkshire
    St John the Baptist's Church   57, 58, **67**
Skidmore of Coventry   86
slate (Welsh)   4, 31, 93, 103
Slough, Berkshire   15, 89
Smith, Francis   46–7
Smythson, Robert   46, 51
Soane, Sir John   55
Somerset Protectorate   4, 41, 51
Soulbury, Buckinghamshire
    Lovett House and the Old School
        House   74, 75, 78

South Newington, Oxfordshire
  St Peter ad Vincula Church 57, **71**
Sparsholt, Oxfordshire 110
Spencer family, of Althorp 89
Stafford, Sir Humphrey 51
stained glass 60, 62, 76, 79, 81
Stephenson family 30
  George 106
  Robert 102, 105–6
Steventon, Oxfordshire 15, 38
  39 The Causeway 33, 34, 38–9
Stewkley, Buckinghamshire
  St Michael and All Angels' Church 57,
  69–70
Stickells, Robert 111
Stoke Bruerne, Northamptonshire 89
  canal wharf and museum **105**
  Stoke Park Pavillions 41
Stokenchurch, Buckinghamshire 102
Stokes, G H 51
stone circles 7, 10
Stone, Nicholas 51, 83
Stonesfield, Oxfordshire 1
Stonor Park, Oxfordshire 76
Stony Stratford, Buckinghamshire 58, 101,
  110
Stowe Landscape Gardens,
  Buckinghamshire 16, 42, 47, 52–3
Stratton, G F 24
Street family
  Arthur Edmund 59
  George Edmund 31, 58, 59–60, 66, 70,
  75, 78
Streeter, Robert 84
Strong family (masons) 90
Strong, Sampson 86
Stuart kings 41, 45
Sutherland, Graham 26
Swalcliffe, Oxfordshire 90
Swinford Bridge, Oxfordshire 101, 106
Sykes, Sir Francis 44

Talman, William 42, 80
Taylor, Sir Robert 43, 106
Taynton, Oxfordshire 23, 90
Telford, Thomas 104, 106
Temple family, of Stowe 15, 52–3
Teulon, Samuel Saunders 58, 66
Thame, Oxfordshire 64
Thames
  River 17, 25, 30, 42–3, 90, 95, 101, 102,
  103, 106, 107
  Valley 4, 54, 89, 90
thatch 1, 19, 20, 21, 23, 24, 31
  bundle 89, 93
Theale, Berkshire 58
Thompson, Flora 35
Thornhill, Sir James 45, 55
Thorpe, John 51, 109
tiles 20, 27
timber framing 1, 18–19, 20, 21, 22, 23, 24,
  27, 30, 35, 36–7, 38, 77, 86, 87, 89, 95, 103
  aisled construction 34, 38, 93

box-frames 4, 20, 33, 34, 38–9
cruck construction 4, 20, 33, 34, 37, 38,
  39, 93
Titchmarsh, Northamptonshire 110
Tite, Sir William 58
toll houses 101, 102, 103
tombs 62, 66, 67, 68, *see also* monuments
Tomkins family, of Abingdon 18, 75
Towcester, Northamptonshire 9, 101
Townesend, William 80
towns
  city of Oxford **28–30**
  country towns 15, 17–18, 25–6
  market towns 3, 15, 17, 18, 22–3, 27–8
  new towns 4, 15
Townsend, John 106
travel/transport 4, 17, 89, 101–7
Tresham family 49, 89
  Sir Thomas 109, 111, 112–13, 115
Trussell, Sir William 67
Turner, J M W 106
turnpikes 4, 23, 27, 101–2, 106
Turville, Buckinghamshire 16, 90
Twitty, Charles 87

Uffington, Oxfordshire 3, 16, 34, 89
  Castle (hillfort) 7, 8, **10–11**
  school 74
  village **31**
  Wayland's Smithy 3, 4, 7, 9, **12–13**
  White Horse 9, 10, **11–12**
Upton, Oxfordshire 18, 23, 91

Valdre, V 53
Vanbrugh, Sir John 45, 52, 53
Vangelder, Peter Matthias 112
Verney, Ralph, 2nd Earl 47
Verrio, Antonio 55
Versailles, influence of 45, 55
Vertue, William 66
vicarages 20, 28, 59
Victoria, Queen 66, 110, 113–15
villages 15–17, 19–22, 23–5, 31, 92
  estate villages 16–17, 23–4, 25, 27
villas, Roman 7, 9–10

Waddesdon Manor, Buckinghamshire 17,
  43
Wakefield Lodge, Northamptonshire 42
Walbury Camp, Berkshire 7, **12**
Walker, Romaine 25
wall paintings 18, 21, 24, 30, 57, 71, 76, 110
Wallingford, Oxfordshire 15, 18, 101
Waltham St Lawrence, Berkshire
  Bell Inn 34, **36–7**
Warkton, Northamptonshire 79
  Montagu monuments in church 110, **112**
Warmington, Northamptonshire
  St Mary's Church 58, **68**
watermills 90, 95–6
Watkins, Revd C F 61
Watling Street 9, 101, 103
Watlington, Oxfordshire 15

Wayland's Smithy, Oxfordshire 3, 4, 7, 9,
  12–13
Waynflete, Bishop 76
Webb, John 41
Weekley, Northamptonshire
  Montagu Hospital and the Free
  School 74, 75, **79**
Weldon, Northamptonshire 1, 51, 90
Wellingborough, Northamptonshire 15, 59, 90
  St Mary's Church 58, **68–9**
Wellington, Duke of 109
West Kennet, Wiltshire 7, 12
West Wycombe, Buckinghamshire 53, 90,
  102, 110
  Park 42, 43, **53**
White, Francis 102
White Hart Inn, Fyfield, Oxfordshire 33, 75,
  86, **87**
White Horse, Uffington, *see* Uffington
Whitehead, William 27
Whiteleaf Cross, Buckinghamshire 9
wichert 16
Wicken, Northamptonshire 58
Wilfrid, Bishop of York 57, 60
Willen, Buckinghamshire 58
William of Ireland 111
William the Conqueror 41, 53
Winde, William 41, 43, 55
windmills 21, 90, 98
Windrush, River 22, 99, 107
Windsor, Berkshire 78
  Castle 4, 41, **53–5**, 58, 75, 81
    Royal Mausoleum, Frogmore 66, 110,
    113–15
  St George's Chapel 54, 57, 58, **65–6**, 113
Wing, Buckinghamshire
  All Saints Church 57, 61, **63**, 110
Wingrave, Buckinghamshire 17
Winslow, Buckinghamshire
  Hall 41
  Keach's Meeting House 59
Wisdom, Simon 23
Wise, Henry 45
Witney, Oxfordshire 15, 74, 107
  blanket industry 4, 90, **98–9**
  Cogges Manor Farm Museum 89, **92–3**
Wittington, Buckinghamshire 43
Wokingham, Berkshire
  Lucas Hospital 75, **78–9**
Wollaton Hall, Nottinghamshire 51
Wolverton, Buckinghamshire
  iron trunk for canal 102, **104–5**
  railway works, housing and viaduct 30,
  94, 102
wood 24, 47–8, 68, 98
Wood, Robert 53
Woodhouse, George 92
Woodstock, Oxfordshire 90
Woodward, Benjamin 86
Woodyer, H 58
wool, *see* industry
Wotton House, Buckinghamshire 16, 41,
  42, 43, 47, **55**

Wren, Sir Christopher   18, 41, 84, 90
    style of   26, 58
Wrighte family   70, 110
Wroxton, Oxfordshire   102
Wyatt, Matthew   66
Wyatville, Sir Jeffry   54–5
Wychwood, forest of, Oxfordshire   3
Wykeham, William of   58, 73, 76, 81
Wynford, William   81

York, Royal House of   67–8

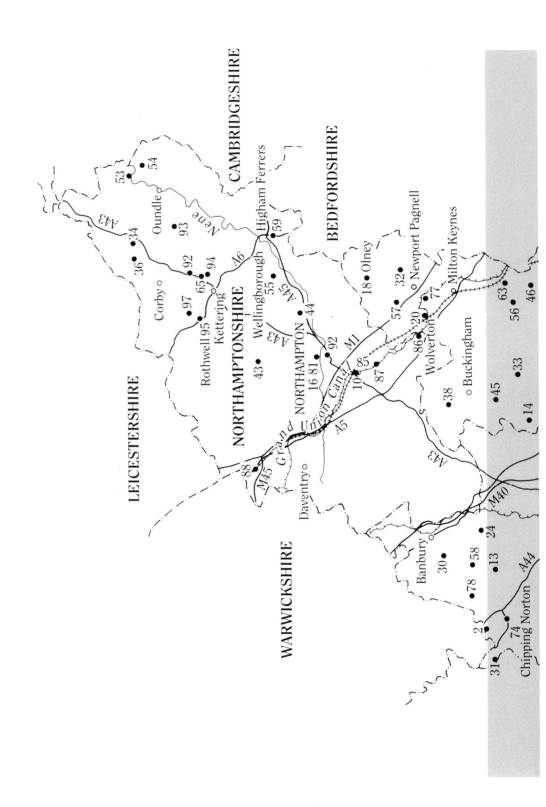

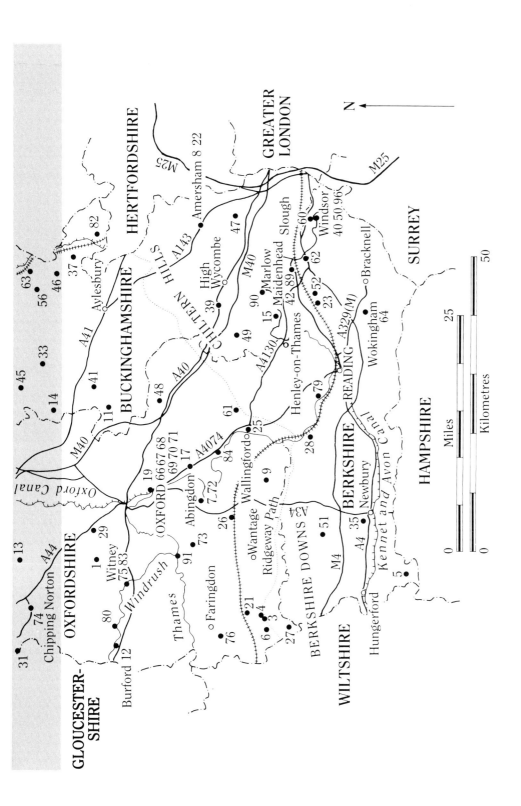

 **HMSO**

HMSO publications are available from:

HMSO Publications Centre
(Mail, fax and telephone orders only)
PO Box 276, London SW8 5DT
Telephone orders 071-873 9090
General enquiries 071-873 0011
(queuing system in operation for both
numbers)
Fax orders 071-873 8200

HMSO Bookshops
49 High Holborn, London WC1V 6HB
(counter service only)
071-873 0011   Fax 071-831 1326
258 Broad Street, Birmingham B1 2HE
021-643 3740   Fax 021-643 6510
33 Wine Street, Bristol BS1 2BQ
0272-264306   Fax 0272-294515
9–21 Princess Street, Manchester M60 8AS
061-834 7201   Fax 061-833 0634
16 Arthur Street, Belfast BT1 4GD
0232 238451   Fax 0232-235401
71 Lothian Road, Edinburgh EH3 9AZ
031-228 4181   Fax 031-229 2734

HMSO's Accredited Agents
(see Yellow Pages)

and through good booksellers

Printed in the UK for HMSO
Dd 294241   C60   9/94